THE CORRESPONDENCE BETWEEN HENRY STEPHENS RANDALL AND HUGH BLAIR GRIGSBY 1856-1861

A Da Capo Press Reprint Series

THE AMERICAN SCENE
Comments and Commentators

GENERAL EDITOR: WALLACE D. FARNHAM
University of Illinois

THE CORRESPONDENCE BETWEEN HENRY STEPHENS RANDALL AND HUGH BLAIR GRIGSBY 1856-1861

EDITED, WITH AN INTRODUCTION AND NOTES, BY

FRANK J. KLINGBERG AND FRANK W. KLINGBERG

DA CAPO PRESS • NEW YORK • 1972

Library of Congress Cataloging in Publication Data

Randall, Henry Stephens, 1811-1876.
The correspondence between Henry Stephens Randall and Hugh Blair Grigsby, 1856-1861.
(The American scene: comments and commentators)
Reprint of the 1952 ed., which was issued as v. 43 of the University of California publications in history series.
1. Jefferson, Thomas, Pres. U. S., 1743-1826. 2. Randall, Henry Stephens, 1811-1876. The life of Thomas Jefferson. I. Grigsby, Hugh Blair, 1806-1881. II. Series: California. University. University of California publications in history, v. 43.
E332.R178 1972 973.4'6'0924 [B] 73-37530
ISBN 0-306-70429-3

This Da Capo Press edition of *The Correspondence Between Henry Stephens Randall and Hugh Blair Grigsby, 1856-1861* is an unabridged republication of the first edition published in Berkeley and Los Angeles in 1952 as Volume XLIII in the *University of California Publications in History.*

Da Capo Press, Inc.
A Subsidiary of Plenum Publishing Corporation
227 West 17th Street, New York, N.Y. 10011

Manufactured in the United States of America

THE CORRESPONDENCE BETWEEN HENRY STEPHENS RANDALL AND HUGH BLAIR GRIGSBY 1856-1861

THE CORRESPONDENCE BETWEEN HENRY STEPHENS RANDALL AND HUGH BLAIR GRIGSBY 1856-1861

EDITED, WITH AN INTRODUCTION AND NOTES, BY

FRANK J. KLINGBERG AND FRANK W. KLINGBERG

UNIVERSITY OF CALIFORNIA PRESS
BERKELEY AND LOS ANGELES
1952

University of California Publications in History
Editors (Los Angeles): Theodore Saloutos, Brainerd Dyer, J. C. King
Volume 43, pp. xii + 1–196
Submitted by editors December 3, 1951
Issued October 20, 1952

University of California Press
Berkeley and Los Angeles
California

Cambridge University Press
London, England

PRINTED IN THE UNITED STATES OF AMERICA

To the memory of

ALBERT RAY NEWSOME

1894–1951

A TRUE JEFFERSONIAN

PREFACE

The Huntington Library Lists, Number 5, notes in its survey of American Manuscript Collections "An interesting supplement to the Jeffersoniana is the correspondence" between Henry S. Randall and Hugh Blair Grigsby, consisting of eighty-one letters written from 1856 to 1861. The means by which the letters were originally brought into a single collection is shrouded in the past. Presumably they were gathered in Virginia by Robert Alonzo Brock, the resourceful historian, collector, and antiquarian. He prepared a biographical sketch of Grigsby as an Introduction to *The History of the Virginia Federal Convention of 1788,* worked with him in the Virginia Historical Society, and was doubtless familiar with Grigsby's correspondence.

The migration of the Brock collection from Virginia to California is explained by Lester J. Cappon in "Two Decades of Historical Activity in Virginia," *The Journal of Southern History,* VI (1940), 190. The financial inability of either the State of Virginia or any of its institutional libraries to purchase the valuable Brock collection of Virginia manuscripts and imprints when they were offered for sale in the late 1920's resulted in their acquisition by the Huntington Library. The files of the Huntington do not indicate that these letters were part of the Brock collection.

Instances of supposedly lost or destroyed papers which are later discovered are almost a commonplace of history. In England, Parson James Woodforde's *Diary* was supposedly lost but reappeared as did the Boswell papers, recently acquired by Yale University. The two Americans of this collection, determined to restore the greatness of earlier generations of Virginians and to strengthen the democratic tradition of the country, classified their manuscripts in elaborate files to insure the preservation of the materials. Nevertheless, they designated various letters that were to be burned. Grigsby wrote, "You do well in classifying your manuscripts, and in arranging them in volumes. They may thus serve an important purpose in your hands or in those of your children hereafter; and must, at least, prove a becoming memorial of your industry and research." And again, he said, "by the way, in the event of my death, all your letters to me will be at your service. They are scattered according to their dates in my correspondence. All those which you desired to be destroyed, were instantly burned."

The Huntington Library Collection of Randall-Grigsby letters is presented here in its entirety and the editors have restricted this study to them. It is to be noted that occasional letters are missing and for the year 1858 only one side of the exchange is available. Grigsby's letters span the entire year and reveal that Randall wrote him although it was not until the early part of 1859 that Randall reappears. Recently the Virginia Historical Society acquired a rich store of Grigsby material, including, however, only a single Randall-Grigsby item. Randall's letters and papers at the New York State Library contain no Grigsby-Randall items. In his large collection of family papers, Hugh Blair Grigsby Galt of Norfolk discovered two Randall letters interestingly folded in Grigsby's personal copy of the *Life of Jefferson*. There are other instances of isolated unpublished letters as well as an occasional published one, but the items missing from this collection could not be found. For historical purposes, however, the Huntington holdings are sufficiently full and continuous to make a superb unit in the decade of the 1850's.

The notes are designed to clarify the letters and to relate the correspondence to the *Life of Jefferson* and the writings of Grigsby. Identifications are made as complete as possible. On occasion, despite generous aid from local historical societies, items and individuals could not be identified. Well-known persons are included when their contributions are of special interest to the correspondents.

Most particular thanks are due to the staff of the Huntington Library and especially to Godfrey Davies, Leslie E. Bliss, Norma B. Cuthbert, and Mary Isabel Fry. Dean Vern Knudsen and the Board of Research of the University of California have been generous in their support as have been Dean W. W. Pierson and the Institute for Research in Social Science at the University of North Carolina. Dr. Lawrence Powell, Librarian of the University of California, Los Angeles, and his able staff of the reference department, gave for this enterprise and many another, daily assistance over a long period. Thanks are due to Ruth M. Christensen, research assistant in history, for the final typescript and substantial assistance in the preparation of the notes and identifications. Professor Arthur P. McKinlay most kindly searched for and found, in Homer, Grigsby's passage and also checked the several Latin quotations. The librarians of the historical collections in Virginia, North Carolina, Pennsylvania, New York, and Massachusetts found many elusive items. Special thanks are due to John Melville Jennings, Virginia Historical Society; Edna Jacobsen, New York State Library; Herbert Ganter, William and Mary College Library; Francis L. Berkeley, University of Virginia Library; Paul North Rice, New York Public Library; Mary C. Brown, Norfolk Public Library; Milton C. Russell, Virginia State

Library; Norma B. Wilkinson, Pennsylvania Historical and Museum Commission; Lois Shoemaker, Boston Public Library; Jean Macalister Moore, formerly Associate Reference Librarian, Columbia University; and Page Ackerman and Ardis Lodge, University of California, Los Angeles, Library.

FRANK J. KLINGBERG

University of California
Los Angeles

FRANK W. KLINGBERG

University of North Carolina
Chapel Hill

July, 1951

CONTENTS

PAGE

Introduction 1

The Correspondence: 1856–1861

Of 1856 21

Of 1857 90

Of 1858 119

Of 1859 152

Of 1860 175

Of 1861 181

Appendix: Lord Macaulay on American Institutions 185

Index 187

INTRODUCTION

THE Golden Age of American ideas and ideals is not obscured by the mists of time nor dependent on legend and mythology. The beginning of our history as an independent nation is open to critical inspection in the voluminous records of the founders of the American Federal Republic: men of heroic stature. Under their guidance the Americanization of the European legacy and the adaptation of indigenous theories, such as the doctrine of dual citizenship, took place. Carl Becker has pointed out that it would be difficult to find in the history of any other land, or in the history of our country at any other time, within a single generation, as many statesmen, in proportion to the population, of equal distinction for learning, integrity, and political intelligence.[1] And of these men none exhibited the qualities peculiarly American to better advantage or more lasting effect than Thomas Jefferson. As a political philosopher, he formulated the American creed; as a statesman, he secured its embodiment into the laws and customs of the country.

The challenges to the American way of life in recent years have aroused renewed interest in the Jeffersonian legacy and its enduring content. The twentieth century, the age of uncertainty, with its frightening inhumanity, compression of events, and growing power of the Leviathan state searches for a restatement of the American faith in the dignity of the individual and the value of a limited, federal form of government. The essence of this creed can be found in Jefferson's analysis of the nature of human rights and the forms of government best suited to secure them. Current interest in Jefferson is reflected by numerous special studies, in a series of new biographies, and in the publication of *The Papers of Thomas Jefferson* in fifty volumes under the editorship of Julian P. Boyd by the Princeton University Press. This monumental work will cover the full range of Jefferson's interests. In the words of Henry Steele Commager:

> He was a man of sentiment; he was a man of reason. He was the perfect provincial, never happy but at Monticello; he was the complete cosmopolitan, at home in every society. He was the transcendentalist, guided in his search for truth by an inner light; he was the scientist, experimenting on his farm or in his laboratory. He was the shrewd politician, cunningly building a political party; he was the aloof philosopher, criticizing Plato and celebrating Locke. He was engineer and inventor, musician and architect, philologist and bookman, agronomist and horticulturist, scholar and educator, lawyer and statesman, administrator and diplomat.[2]

[1] Carl Becker, "What is Still Living in the Political Philosophy of Thomas Jefferson," *American Historical Review,* XLVIII (1943), 691–706.

[2] Quoted in the announcement of *The Papers of Thomas Jefferson* (Princeton, 1950).

Because of the universal character of his mind and genius his writings have a special freshness and direct value for the present day.

The devotion to Jefferson is obviously not new. On the eve of the Civil War statesmen, North and South, appealed to the Jeffersonian heritage for justification of their views on the nature of the Union and the character of American democracy. An important product of this heightened interest was the classic three volume *Life of Jefferson* by Henry Stephens Randall (1811–1876) published shortly before the outbreak of the war. The following Randall-Grigsby letters concern that biography. The editors feel that for a century the *Life* has served as the chief treasure chest for Jeffersoniana bridging the 1850's with the 1950's. Accordingly, they have stressed as the central theme in the Introduction the biography, its birth and public reception, and have left the reader free to follow the other threads as they appear in the narrative.

The correspondence between Randall, the New York biographer of Jefferson, and Hugh Blair Grigsby (1806–1881), the leading Virginia historian of his generation, began in January, 1856. Inevitably the two men, in the course of their respective scholarly interests, met on a wide intellectual front. Grigsby had written on the Virginia constitutional convention of 1776 and was currently engaged on his companion study of the constitutional convention of 1788. He knew important living Virginians and his research made him familiar with the records of Jefferson's contemporaries. Randall, in the throes of writing his monumental *Life,* was on the trail of all Jeffersoniana. In Grigsby he was to discover not only a key to Virginia circles and sources but a frank critic with a reservoir of information. The letters, initiated over the authenticity of the Mecklenburg Declaration of May 20, 1775, spanned four years and developed into a lively literary current. Fortunately many of them survived the major enemies of manuscripts: displacement, damage, desecration, and the injunction "destroy this." In surveying the sixty thousand words of the Huntington Library collection that are here presented, the reader soon senses that he is witnessing the formation of a friendship between two scholars and that he is a party to their behind-the-scenes discussions of biographical information and how to use it.

This correspondence and the vigorous biography belong to the great age of American historical writing of the Middle Period. Emerson, the correspondent of Carlyle, was active at this time. Prescott was finishing his life work with the history of *The Reign of Philip the Second.* Motley brought out his *Rise of the Dutch Republic* in this very year, 1856; and Parkman had published *The Oregon Trail* in 1849. The first of Parkman's series on the Anglo-French conflict, *The Conspiracy of Pontiac,* was published in two volumes in 1851. Jared Sparks was in the twilight of his remarkable career as a biographer, archivist, and collector. George Bancroft was concluding the sixth, seventh, and eighth volumes of his monumental study of the Colonial Period and The Revolution. The ninth and tenth were delayed until 1874 by the Civil War and his diplomatic services. John Gorham Palfrey and Richard Hildreth were blazing new trails respectively in regional history and in shading political narration with economic overtones. Appearing concurrently with these multi-volume histories were biographies of prominent Americans by James Parton. Thirty thousand copies of his *Life of Horace Greeley* (1856) were sold. *The Life and Times of Aaron Burr* (1857) and *The Life of Andrew Jackson* (3 vols.; 1859–1860) followed in rapid succession and revealed a great public interest in the careers of national figures. Parton, too, wrote *The Life of Thomas Jefferson* (1874). Randall had a grand design and he could hope to tap this ready-made market in an age when historians had not yet begun to write largely for one another.[3]

The writings of Hugh Blair Grigsby and Henry Stephens Randall fit into this renaissance of American letters. Yet their names are commonly absent from the standard works in American history. Both men were pioneers in methodology. Randall searched his voluminous treasure of sources with passionate zeal and pursued the most minute point with indefatigable energy. He neither edited nor suppressed documents. His *Life,* time tested, has not been condemned for inadequate documentation and extreme nationalism, faults that marred the writings of some of his better known contemporaries. Grigsby followed the same scholarly standards and his historical work is fundamental to any understanding of the constitutional development of Virginia. Within these limits, both scholars belong more to the twentieth century with its emphasis on the scientific documentary approach than to the mid-nineteenth with its open stress on nationalism and patriotism.

Randall and Grigsby had much else in common. Both men were ardent Democrats, heartily opposed to the Federalists, the Whigs, and the newly organized Republicans. Both were Unionists and regarded their opponents as Northern sectionalists from the days of Hamilton to the time of Fremont and Lincoln. Moreover, the two authors had a wide range of interests almost Jeffersonian in extent. After a distinguished aca-

[3] For an able discussion of the historiography of the Middle Period, see Michael Kraus, *History of American History* (New York, 1937). More extensive treatment of key individuals is available in John Spencer Bassett, *Middle Group of American Historians* (New York, 1917), and *The Marcus W. Jernegan Essays in American Historiography* (Chicago, 1937).

demic career at Union College, where he was a marked favorite of the celebrated President Eliphalet Nott, Randall turned to the study of law following his graduation in 1830. While in the offices of Henry Stephens, first judge of Cortland County, and William H. Shankland, subsequently a justice of the New York Supreme Court, he showed a bent for legal, constitutional, and political theory. In an intellectual conversion his studies made him an ardent Jeffersonian and an active member of the Democratic party. In a real sense his life was fashioned by the Jeffersonian creed.

Randall's political career began as a pamphleteer for the Democratic party, and this activity quickly gave him an influential role in party circles in state and national conventions. He was the youngest regular member of the National Democratic Convention of 1835, and a determined friend of the South at Charleston in 1860 in his relentless support of compromise candidates qualified to keep alive the Virginia–New York alliance. His success in seeking public office was limited by residence in a predominantly Whig and Republican community. He was twice the Democratic nominee for Secretary of State in New York. Defeated in 1849 with the rest of the ticket, he won in 1851. Unanimously nominated for State Senator in 1857, he ran substantially ahead of the general Democratic returns but lost. Selected as a candidate for Congress by his party in 1868, he refused to run. Against his wishes, he was nominated for Member of the New York Assembly in 1871 and elected as the first Democratic representative in many years from Cortland County. Keenly alive to party interests, he purchased and edited the Democratic paper of his county to prevent its discontinuance when it was threatened with bankruptcy.

It should be noted that Randall's interest in politics had two major objectives: at the national level, preservation of the Union, at the state level, promotion of public education. As early as 1839 he accepted the position of an unpaid visitor of schools, holding that post until the office of county superintendent of schools was legally established. In this new office he served from 1843 to 1847. His administrative work and his writings on education brought him offers to become superintendent of schools in several states. His strongest reason for serving as Secretary of State was that the post included the superintendency of public instruction. This steadfast interest in education led to his appointment as one of the examiners at West Point, and, when the State Normal School in Cortland Village was established, he was made one of the trustees and president of the board.

These educational activities did not prevent him from giving constant attention to another facet of the Jeffersonian program. Throughout his active life he called himself "a practical farmer." His special interest was sheep husbandry and an article in *The Cultivator* for March, 1838, heralded a period of remarkable productivity and influence. His *Sheep Husbandry in the South* (1848), a series of letters to R. F. W. Allston of South Carolina, was reprinted in 1852 under the title, *Sheep Husbandry,* and had five additional printings up to 1880. Numerous specialized articles on fine wool production became standard reference works available in governmental bulletins and through private editions. His summary volume, *The Practical Shepherd,* went through thirty printings, had an immense total circulation and greatly influenced the domestic wool-growing industry. Randall was corresponding secretary of the New York State Agricultural Society for years, and, as a member of its executive committee, proposed the New York State Fair, first among such exhibitions. From 1865 until his death in 1876, he was president of the National Wool Growers' Association and was responsible for the custom schedules of the Wool Tariff of 1867. In addition, from 1864 to 1867 he was editor of the sheep-husbandry department of *Moore's Rural New-Yorker.*[4]

A man so immersed in political theory and active in government, a ready writer, a farmer, and a champion of education was almost inevitably drawn to Jefferson. In the rich diversity of his achievements, Randall was especially qualified to present the many-sided Jefferson and the complex age of the founders. In 1853, he began the authorized *Life of Jefferson* which was completed in mid-year 1858.[5]

Hugh Blair Grigsby, like Randall, was a college man, a product of Yale, though not a graduate, a lawyer, a journalist, and a scholar of distinction. Deeply interested in legal and constitutional theory, British and American, he gave his major attention to the institutional development of Virginia. In order to trace the migration and growth of ideas and institutions, he collected a library of six thousand volumes, including English and American biography, history, and literature. In common with Randall and Jefferson, Grigsby never permitted the European heritage to overwhelm him, but kept his critical faculties sharp to select and to adapt for the American scene those features of British culture of value in the American environment.

[4] See sketch in the *Dictionary of American Biography,* XV (1946), 347–348, and [Paul K. Randall], *Genealogy of a Branch of the Randall Family 1666 to 1879* [Norwich, New York, 1879].

[5] Virginia honored Randall in 1858 when, by unanimous vote of the Legislature, he was invited with Washington Irving to be present as a guest of the state for the unveiling of a statue of Washington in Richmond. Paul K. Randall, *op. cit.,* pp. 61–62.

Grigsby early developed a network of friendships with like-minded people throughout the eastern part of the United States and became a member of the leading historical societies of the time. His list included the Massachusetts, the New York, and the Pennsylvania. He was an influential member of the Virginia Historical Society and its President from 1870 until his death in 1881. From youth he showed an aptitude for biography and his later writings or addresses were largely concerned with this phase of literature. He was thoroughly familiar with the history of nearly every native family within the borders of Virginia. Thus his volumes on the three Virginia Conventions (1776, 1788, 1829–1830), in addition to being the authoritative accounts of the proceedings, have incisive sketches of the men who sat in each body, significant for their pictures of the "second growth" of eminent Virginians as well as for their accurate summaries of the earlier nationally known figures. His skill in depicting key American figures is comparable to Clarendon's power of sketching the English leaders of the Civil Wars of Cromwell's time. His work has never been supplanted.

A delicate physique forced upon Grigsby a regimen of unflagging prudence from childhood, yet his life was one of incessant activity. Upon completion of his legal studies, he was admitted to the Norfolk bar but increasing deafness shortly ended his legal practice. He turned to journalism as owner and editor of the Norfolk *American Beacon* (1829–1836). Though ill health compelled him to abandon this venture, he managed his newspaper so successfully that he retired with a competency. In 1829–1830, he represented Norfolk in the House of Delegates and succeeded General Robert Taylor as a member of the Virginia Constitutional Convention for the same years. In 1840 he married Mary Venable Carrington and thereafter resided at his wife's patrimonial estate where he lived the life of an English squire. By precept and example, he sought to encourage higher education, taking a particular interest in William and Mary College. He served the College as a generous benefactor, as its most influential trustee, and became its chancellor in 1871. His wide range of activities included an unflagging interest in agricultural engineering, soil conservation, and crop diversification.[6]

Although Randall's manuscript was nearing completion by 1856, Grigsby left a distinct imprint on the finished *Life*. His suggestions

[6] *Dictionary of American Biography,* VIII (1946), 628–629. An excellent character sketch of Grigsby is in William Cabell Bruce, *John Randolph of Roanoke* (2 vols.; New York, 1922), II, 734–735.

enriched certain passages and modified the treatment of contested aspects of Jefferson's career. An examination of the letters reveals that these able historians found a broad common ground in their love for Jefferson and the American experiment. These sentiments are readily discerned in their letters and published works. National union, they wrote, could be preserved only by the protection of states' rights, not by a consolidation of the country into a central dictatorship, destructive of the individual states, autocratic, and inimical to various sections of the nation. For nationalism to these men was the Jeffersonian blending of state and federal power, more within the limits of Calhoun's compact theory than Webster's belief in greater centralization. Both men devoted their literary skills and political influence toward the unity of their country but neither was willing to purchase unity at the price of making one region a colonial dependency of the other. Their common hero, Jefferson, believed in a balanced division of power between the state and federal governments. Only the maintenance of his ideals could assure the future, they reasoned.

Moreover, Jefferson's two admirers shared the Jeffersonian philosophy of government. Like Jefferson they knew Europe and were determined that here there should be no state church; no caste society protected by primogeniture and entails; no bar to natural merit; no educational monopoly based on religious tests. In America, they did not wish to see the cleavage wrought by hereditary wealth and exclusiveness such as that fostered by the great English Latin grammar schools. Leaders in state and church arising from one educated class would perpetuate a stratified society.

Throughout the period of this correspondence bitter attacks against Jefferson and divers phases of his philosophy were being waged on various fronts. Francis Lister Hawks and others excoriated his supposed teachings while the protagonists in the slavery controversy distorted his philosophy.[7] The intensity of these attacks emphasize one frequently

[7] Nothing can illustrate the changed opinion during a century on Jefferson's place in history as effectively as a comparison between the severe judgment of the Reverend Francis Lister Hawks with that of Canon Anson Phelps Stokes in his recent monumental study of *Church and State in the United States* (3 vols.; New York, 1950). Hawks appears in this correspondence as a sharp critic of Jefferson; Stokes has high praise for Jefferson's leadership in the struggle for separation of church and state in Virginia, and he has chosen as the frontispiece of Volume II Mather Brown's portrait with the caption, "Jefferson shares with Madison the honor of being the most constructive statesman in the field of Church-State separation and religious freedom." Or again, ". . . to make some one branch of the Church the agent of the State in matters of education, religion, and moral instruction. . . . certainly shows that any extensive Church-State tieup tends towards tyranny, and that separation similarly tends toward freedom." *Ibid.*, I, lxix.

neglected aspect of Jefferson's place in history. He stood for moderation in the revolutionary era which subsequently left him open to criticism from the left and right extremes. As leader of his party and as president he prevented the violent reaction in the United States which cursed England from the beginning of the French Revolution to the Reform Bill of 1832. Burke's crusade against revolutionary doctrines triumphed in England and on the continent and in part of New England. But in the United States Joseph Priestly, Thomas Cooper, and Thomas Paine were Jefferson's friends though in effect outlawed from Great Britain. Dr. Dunglison, who grew to manhood in England and was Jefferson's physician, told Randall that Jefferson was never an enemy of Englishmen but only of their caste society. He cited in evidence the fact that the Virginian staffed the University of Virginia chiefly with professors from England.

Accordingly, the political and religious views of Jefferson come into full play as the correspondents discuss slavery, their deep desire to save the Union, their conviction that Jefferson must be restored to his full stature, and their opinion that no Virginian could make him a national figure as could Randall of New York. While the religious controversy was probably diminishing, but due to flare up again in 1859 with the publication of Darwin's *Origin of Species*, the slavery question had reached a fever pitch. Randall's outline to Grigsby of his chapter on Jefferson's consistency of view on slavery is presented under points readily summarized. Jefferson opposed heated discussion of slavery North or South, lest the Union be destroyed. He was baffled by the difficulties of the slavery issue; desired gradual abolition, accompanied by colonization with compensation to the owner; believed that the spread of slavery over the United States would lead to its extinction rather than its increase. Randall and Grigsby were in agreement with Jefferson that fanaticism on the slavery issue would break up the Union. Jefferson's moderation was distorted in the North as antislavery, as proslavery in the South.

Randall, too, was cautious in giving too precise an interpretation of Jefferson's religious views, not wishing to revive again the bitterness of the earlier controversy. Jefferson rightly prized authorship of the Statute of Religious Freedom in Virginia, stating that its passage was won after the most severe struggle of his life. For the remainder of his public career he was under constant suspicion of atheism and pagan philosophy. His religious views, Randall treated as a separate topic:

"I shall tell what Mr. J. *did* believe, & let others draw the inferences."[8] Today he is variously classified as a Deist or Unitarian, both terms of latitude.

The reader of Randall's volumes will find in a section on religion that Jefferson attended the Episcopal Church, contributed to parish support, and at no stage of his life was he an atheist. The charge of atheism was a political weapon and followed him beyond the grave, taking on regional manifestations. From the time of the disestablishment of the Episcopal Church in Virginia, the established Congregational Churches of Massachusetts and of Connecticut anticipated their own disestablishment, which came in the nineteenth century. Randall was anxious that the success of his book not be endangered by fresh controversy on this topic.

Instead Randall ardently desired to bring Jefferson by a meticulous examination of his record into a more national focus where he would stand side by side in historical literature as well as in fact with Washington as a founder of the Republic. Yet he wrote in the mid-nineteenth century when "slaveholders tended to deride his [Jefferson's] sayings about human equality and Unionists to deplore his emphasis on States rights."[9] The Federalists already had their definitive histories for the revolutionary decades and the national period. Moreover, Jefferson's career was inextricably entwined with the culture of an entire era. Randall surmounted these difficulties and made his biography a living document. In brief compass his evaluation of Professor George Tucker's work,[10] which he hoped to supersede, offers his analysis for the art of biography.

> Professor Tucker's work, usually accurate to the letter in facts—usually fair & liberal too—not without ability of Statement & dexterity in honest defence—yet after all, in my poor opinion, never goes below the *middle* of his subject.—He does not *skim*, but he does not go to the *bottom*. He did not understand the great ethnic features (if I may so term them) of his subject.—He did not understand the *inner* history of parties; the *spirit & soul of the times*.—His investigations were personal. He did not go vastly beyond official records. He did not enter into Jefferson's *feelings* any more than he occupied his stand point in the colder matter of opinion.—It was ice trying to represent fire! Not cowardly, he struck not one *unnecessary* blow; though the explanation or illustration of his Subject would have been oftentimes immensely cleared up by a *swinging blow*.[11]

Fortunately the literary exchange of these Americans was not interrupted until substantial agreement had been reached on the most con-

[8] Randall to Grigsby, May 25, 1856.
[9] Dumas Malone, *Jefferson the Virginian* (Boston, 1948), p. viii.
[10] George Tucker, *The Life of Thomas Jefferson* (2 vols.; Philadelphia, 1837).
[11] Randall to Grigsby, December 4, 1856.

tested aspects of Jefferson's career. But the sectional controversy became more and more violent and the disintegration of the Democratic party was foreshadowed by the overthrow of such national moderates as these by the extremists North and South. This national crisis appears in Randall's somber question on whether Virginians will prefer dissolution of the Union to the status quo, presumably demanding a further constitutional guarantee of states' rights. The argument of union versus disunion is ably presented by the Northerner. He is convinced that the North of its own free will and accord will not resort to sectionalism unless the South does so first, thereby trampling down its powerful friends in the tier of northern states. The South, he argues, has all the friends it needs in the North to prevent assaults upon it. If these friends lose their identity, "Then there is no barrier between you & the wild and furious spirit of Sectionalism, & disunion must come & with it, in all probability, civil war."[12] Nationalists in New York still outnumber the sectionalists and he warns that occasional division among the national men of the North may create the impression that abolitionism is much stronger than it really is. The northern nationalists will defend the Constitution in letter and in spirit and will protect the interests of the South. After further penetrating analysis of the situation he warns, in conclusion, that there can be no such thing as peaceable dissolution of the Union.

Between Randall's letter of December 14, 1859, and Grigsby's last letter in this collection, Union men, North and South, were overborne by events they were not able to control. The great body of public opinion could not find effective political expression of its desire for conciliation and arbitration within the American tradition of compromise. In this failure the dreams of Randall and Grigsby become lost causes. Grigsby's portrait was painted for William and Mary while secession was taking place and his description of the event is an eloquent passage on the American tragedy.

I sate for the portrait accordingly, and it was brought home; but my wife and my dear mother who left me for another world on the 31st of December last, could not abide it,—it was so sad. I looked, they said, as if I had lost every friend on earth. The portrait was sent back and painted anew. Now do you know the secret of that sadness? I sate when the southern troubles were in full blast, when South Carolina had seceded—and when I was sad unto death. Ought I not to have let the portrait remain as it was as a sign of a terrible epoch upon the heart of one who loved his whole country?[13]

[12] Randall to Grigsby, December 14, 1859. For a summary of the divided sentiment that persisted throughout the war in the North, see Wood Gray, *The Hidden Civil War* (New York, 1942), pp. 13–20.

[13] Grigsby to Randall, March 18, 1861.

The number of copies of the three-volume *Life* that were sold is now impossible to determine. J. B. Lippincott Company, which took over the publication from Derby and Jackson, reports that "a disastrous fire" in 1899 destroyed all records previous to that time.[14] The correspondence shows that the volumes were well received and immediately had a wide circulation. The most definite information comes from Grigsby's report on the sale in Norfolk. where "more than *one hundred* copies" were sold by the book agent by July 25, 1858, shortly after publication.[15] The sustained success of this initial acceptance is attested by the several printings found widely scattered throughout libraries and private collections.

As was to be expected in any life of Jefferson, judgments of Randall's work reflected regional preconceptions as well as dispassionate criticism. *The Atlantic Monthly,* under the editorship of James Russell Lowell, gave twenty-seven pages in November and December, 1858, to a review of the *Life* and its judgment might be accepted as that of New England.[16] William Dorsheimer in an essay of permanent value criticized the style, "The tropes and metaphors, the tawdry tinsel, the common tricks of feeble rhetoricians are reproduced here as if they were the highest results of rhetorical art."[17] But these strictures were made with reluctance for Randall was industrious, had a thorough appreciation of Jefferson's noblest characteristics, and an honest sympathy with his philosophy and "though we must dissent from some of his conclusions, he is entitled to the praise of being accurate, and is free from prejudice."[18]

The most serious criticisms were two; that Randall belabored the monarchical designs of the New England Federalists; and that his synthesis of the Jeffersonian philosophy was incomplete. Dorsheimer, as a political scientist, desired a fuller exposition of Jefferson's theories that all men are politically equal; that a representative government upon the basis of universal suffrage is one direct result of that equality, and the surest means of preserving it; and that the sphere of government must be sharply curtailed. Jefferson's major contribution was, in the judgment of the reviewer, the development of the limited power theory as an essential to human freedom in politics, in religion, and in

---

[14] J. B. Lippincott Company to Frank J. Klingberg, Philadelphia, Pennsylvania, September 12, 1949.

[15] Grigsby to Randall, July 25, 1858.

[16] William Edward Dorsheimer, "Thomas Jefferson," *The Atlantic Monthly,* II (1858), 706–717, 789–803.

[17] *Ibid.*, p. 706.

[18] *Ibid.*

public welfare. The *Life* served as a device for Dorsheimer to "make some poor amends for the wrongs which Jefferson suffered at the hands of New England."[19]

In the words of the reviewer:

He had none of the common qualifications for popularity. No glare of military glory surrounded him; he had not the admired gift of eloquence; he was opposed by wealth and fashion, by the Church and the press, by most of the famous men of his day,—by Jay, Marshall, the Pinckneys, Knox, King, and Adams; he had to encounter the vehement genius of Hamilton and the *prestige* of Washington; he was not in a position for direct action upon the people; he never went beyond the line of his duty, and, from 1776 to his inaugural address, he did not publish a word which was calculated to excite lively, popular interest;—yet, in spite of all and against all, he won. So complete was the victory, that, at his second election, Massachusetts stood beside Virginia, supporting him. He won because he was true to a principle. Thousands of men, whose untutored minds could not comprehend a proposition of his elaborate philosophy, remembered that in his youth he had proclaimed the equality of men, knew that in maturity he remained true to that declaration, and, believing that this great assurance of their liberties was in danger, they gathered around him, preferring the scholar to orators and soldiers. They had confidence in him because he had confidence in them.[20]

If the critics in England and New England made reservations, the writers of the South hailed the work. William F. Ritchie's fine review enabled Grigsby to affirm that this was a Southern book, a Virginia book, deserving to be supported by all Southern men. Grigsby, frequently forthright in condemnation as a reviewer, gave unqualified endorsement that echoed across the nation. His reviews of Volumes I and III for the Richmond *Enquirer*,[21] the most influential paper in the South, were recopied in full, at times with supplemental notes, by many of the nation's editors. The New York *Day Book* was typical in noting that the following "admirable review and synopsis of Randall's Life of Jefferson is understood to be from the able pen of Dr. Grigsby of Norfolk, Va., one of the most accomplished writers of the Old Dominion. An ardent friend of Jefferson, and devotedly attached to the fame of Virginia's noble sons, his testimony to Mr. Randall's work is one of the most flattering that could be given."[22]

Grigsby centered his fire on the fact that here, for the first time, was

[19] *Ibid.*, p. 803.

[20] *Ibid.*, p. 802.

[21] For an analysis of the influence of the Richmond *Enquirer* throughout the South with special reference to the war years, see Harrison A. Trexler, "The Davis Administration and the Richmond Press, 1861–1865," *The Journal of Southern History*, XVI (1950), 175–195.

[22] This and the following citations are to Grigsby's review of Volume I as reprinted from the Richmond *Enquirer* in the New York *Day Book*, February 2, 1858.

a counterthrust to the partisan Federalist distortions of Southern institutions and Republican leaders. "Indeed, we can safely declare that in none of the more important historical and biographical works which for the third of a century have emanated from the northern press, have we found a just appreciation for southern character and southern statesmen." From the biographies of Jay, Hamilton, John Adams, and of Governeur Morris, "we turn sometimes in disgust, sometimes in stern indignation." In this indictment Grigsby included the work of Marshall, for "pure, amiable and honorable as he was, [he] wrote under the excitement of a terrible political revolution . . . which had crushed the party to which he belonged, and of which he was a prominent chieftain. . . ." Even Sparks "flings a nettle most wantonly on the grave of Jefferson," and though Tucker "may be supposed to have regarded the republican leaders with the kindest of feelings . . . we find that in comparing Hamilton and Jefferson together, he awards the palm of genius to Hamilton. . . ." Nor do the works of Hildreth and George Bancroft escape his censure.

In the judgment of Grigsby, Jefferson was the chief author of half the opinions if not the institutions of America, the founder of the party that controlled the nation's destiny from the turn of the nineteenth century, and the most influential single individual in the shaping of the American mind. Yet of all Southern men "Jefferson was the most abused, and the most misrepresented . . . ," not only in the strongholds of Federalism, "but in the South and in our own Virginia." Grigsby was convinced that the difficulties of the theme, the innumerable complications of kindred, of affection, and of political and personal sensibilities made it impossible for a native Virginian, even of his generation, to write a full and free life of the author of the Declaration of Independence. "But what we could not do for ourselves has been done for us by another. Jefferson has not, indeed, been without a biographer." Tucker's *Life of Jefferson,* still valuable as a political treatment, "retains a claim to immortality," but those eager to have "the personal and political progress of Jefferson must contemplate the wide and admirable panorama which Randall has opened to our view."

The review, a synopsis of contents chapter by chapter, is analytical throughout and includes both praise and adverse criticism. Grigsby regarded the treatment of Richard Henry Lee on his failure to be invited to write the Declaration of Independence as unfair. The chapters on Jefferson as governor, however, were "the best history of that epoch ever written." The narrative reflected the highest honor on Jefferson, on Virginia, and, "we must add on the able and patriotic biographer." "Some one has said that Mr. Randall's book is a southern book; which is undoubtedly true; but it is true only in the sense that the Bible is a southern book and that every book is such that regards our country as a whole, and which, in estimating character and in weighing authorities, does not look to degrees of latitude but to truth and justice alone." The reviewer finds the style clear, bold, and if lacking exquisite polish, flowing, racy, and energetic. Randall emerges as a "master of rapid and thorough argumentation," and though he "loves Jefferson" he nevertheless holds "him to the standard of truth, and decides accordingly."

The appearance of the third and last volume enabled Grigsby to assess the full impact of the completed work for the columns of the *Enquirer.* Clearly it was, for him, the definitive study of Jefferson. With prophetic vision he wrote "It is as if it was written for posterity; for differences of place and nation, are very like a difference of time; and while we peruse the book, we feel as if we were reading the verdict of future times on the life and services of Thomas Jefferson."[23]

The three-volume *Life* that appeared in 1858 is in reality the only study of Jefferson of major importance prepared before the 1940's. Post Civil War history is often written as if for a cause rather than to discover causes. The "inevitable conflict" idea was traced back into the coming of the Civil War and undue emphasis placed on the divisive forces in American society at the expense of the cohesive forces. Randall, in the growing sectionalism of the 1850's, faced the problem of presenting Jefferson both as a national and a state figure. The triumph of American nationalism under the astute guidance of Washington, Hamilton, Marshall, John Adams, and Jay strengthened the powers of the federal government at the expense of the states', a process actively under way since the American Revolution and strengthened by the Civil War and the reconstruction period. The beginnings of large business enterprises were chronicled by partisan federalists, and that literature was primarily penned by the enemies of Jeffersonian ideals.

Randall restored Jefferson to his place in American history and gave him the stature of Washington. That his classic volumes are not widely known today and often overlooked in the sweep of Jeffersonian historiography does not in the least detract from this observation. His studies were partially lost to the reading public during the great crisis of the Civil War, but succeeding writers have leaned heavily on the work of the great biographer. Marie Kimball in her volume, *Jefferson: The Road*

[23] Grigsby's review of Volume III as reprinted from the Richmond *Enquirer* in the Norfolk *Daily Southern Argus,* June 30 and July 3, 1858.

to Glory, observes that "the majority of more recent biographies are little more than a paraphrase and condensation of Randall. Indeed, whole sentences, if not whole passages, may often be recognized. Again and again, particularly for the early years, the biographers have merely written with Randall open before them, without adding anything of their own."[24] Readers may feel there is nothing revolutionarily new in the *Life.* They thus pay tribute to the lasting qualities of the pioneer venture, which has been served forth in a succession of modern versions.

When Randall wrote, Jefferson's papers and accounts, shortly to be scattered, were still intact at Monticello in the hands of his descendants. Hence Randall worked not only with a sense of destiny and responsibility but with the panorama of the Jeffersonian literature spread before him. A contemporary visitor to his study noted that piles of books and manuscript materials lay stacked in every corner. "The library is a perfect magazine of personal mementos of Mr. Jefferson, manuscripts, pictures, views of Monticello, grand plans of its garden, and other surroundings in the days of its illustrious owner, personal relics and things not to be classed."[25] Among the papers observed was a neat drawing of Jefferson's plow of least resistance, a list of the pedigrees of his horses, tables of his annual and monthly expenses as a private man and as President, his receipts as a lawyer, his observations in various departments of science and natural history and on farming and gardening operations, his ledgers on the births, deaths, occupations of his slaves. This visitor also mentioned a tabulation of the horses and farm products carried off, butchered, or destroyed by Cornwallis. Material abounded on his nail making, manufactures of domestic woolens and linens, techniques of milling, estimates of distances established by a pedometer attached to his person or carriage wheel. Among the tables on natural history was one "giving the average earliest and latest appearance of all vegetables (perhaps thirty kinds) sold in the Washington market during the entire eight years of his Presidency!"

As an authorized biographer Randall had access to virtually all the existing family correspondence. Narratives, recollections, descriptions, explanations and letters, were freely furnished him by the grandchildren and he was given unrestricted use of them. The family, he informed a friend, started on the "profoundly sensible idea that their grandfather would 'pass muster' with posterity *exactly as he was;*—that exaggeration would both injure and discredit the whole picture."[26]

[24] Marie Kimball, *Jefferson: The Road to Glory* (New York, 1943), pp. 4–5. She has effectively placed Jefferson in his age not only in America but in Europe as well.

[25] New York *Commercial Advertiser,* March 24, 1858.

[26] *Ibid.*

Moreover, Randall wrote untroubled by a search for the influence of the frontier on Jeffersonian democracy, for the antecedents of the New Deal in the period from 1800 to 1808, or for the economic origins of the Jeffersonian movement. Deeply interested in agriculture and living in a basically physiocratic America, he could bring a refreshing candor and understanding to the task at hand. Perhaps it was because he and Grigsby were typical of the Jeffersonian standard of the gentleman statesman that the period comes to life in Randall's volumes in spite of a somewhat ponderous style and complex sentence constructions. Claude G. Bowers has done much to recapture and to present vividly and skillfully, the drama and fire of Jefferson and his decades.[27] Dumas Malone is constructing what promises to be the definitive study characterized by exhaustive research, rare understanding, and dramatic presentation.[28] Randall's biography may be placed in historical literature by a comparison with Carlyle's *Cromwell* published in 1845. This work changed the contemporary misrepresentations of the Protector and restored him to his proper niche in English history. Randall rendered a similar service to Jefferson.

The Randall-Grigsby letters describe the birth of the *Life*. Moreover, the correspondence is an intellectual bridge across the Mason and Dixon line, cemented by the loyalty of the two men to the ideal of Jefferson and the American democratic way of life. Two Americans of character and intelligence sought to make a wealth of documentary and personal knowledge of the American revolutionary decades a part of the American heritage by their study of the chief founder of American ideals. They lived in the decades of Seward, Toombs, and Andrew Johnson but belong to the age of Webster, Calhoun, and Clay.

Further, the correspondence itself is a commentary on the eventful 'fifties with sidelights on planting, printing, literature, and politics that have not been touched on here. Of the many subjects that might be singled out, the editors were especially impressed by the twentieth-century interpretations foreshadowed throughout these letters and published works of the two men. Their assumptions and comments reveal that slavery had reached its natural geographic limits; that Madison's work on the Constitution had been minimized; that the sectional complexities could not be reduced to terms of slavery alone; and that the

[27] Claude G. Bowers, *The Young Jefferson* (Boston, 1945); *idem, Jefferson and Hamilton* (Boston, 1925); *idem, Jefferson in Power* (Boston, 1936).

[28] Malone, *Jefferson the Virginian*, the first of four projected volumes. Malone notes (Introduction, p. viii) that "The massive three-volume *Life* by Henry S. Randall was issued shortly before the Civil War. Jefferson's reputation has grown enormously since then, especially in the years since the First World War. Much has been written about him lately, but no biography has yet matched Randall's in scope and impressiveness."

cavalier-poor-white theme in the South had been distorted. Virginia was not built by a few cavaliers of noble blood but on a broad base of Anglo-Saxon stock. "The chivalry of the Virginia character is not to be traced to the miserable offshoots of the British aristocracy, but to our manners, habits, and state of affairs. We were a *slaveholding, tobacco planting, Anglo-Saxon* people."[29] Grigsby further analyzed the economic conditions of Virginia during the Confederation period and concluded that the internal prosperity of the state did not justify the degree of sovereignty granted to the new central government because the critical period, was, after all, not so critical.[30] During the intervening century these arguments have been recaptured and developed into schools of interpretation by able historians.[31]

Randall and Grigsby understood Jefferson, as noted before, because they did their work only a quarter of a century after his death and under conditions similar to those of his age. Many of the tangible principles of his philosophy; laissez-faire in government, strict construction of the Constitution, belief in a basically agrarian economy, and political isolation from Europe, were still realities in the 1850's. If today the sinews of this message are sometimes distorted by the triumph of an industrial society and a centralized government, the intangibles of his philosophy still endure with the spirit of his memory. Freedom of religion, separation of church and state, universal public education, equality of opportunity, and faith in the perfectibility of man and the innate dignity of the individual remain the basic American creed. In the words of Grigsby, "His history is indeed the history of American liberty."[32]

[29] Grigsby's views on the cavalier myth in Virginia history are more fully developed in a letter to Thomas Ritchie, March 14, 1854, published in *The John P. Branch Historical Papers of Randolph-Macon College*, IV (1916), 415–418.

[30] Hugh Blair Grigsby, *The Virginia Federal Convention of 1788*, (2 vols.; Richmond, 1890–1891), I, 8–23. As to Madison's surrender of Virginia's commercial rights Grigsby notes, "Of all the men of his time, Mr. Madison possessed that caste of intellect best adapted for the discussions of commerce and political economy. But his sphere of personal observation was very limited. . . . He lived far beyond the scent of salt water in Orange. . . . The only breath of sea air he probably ever drew was in crossing the Jersey shore to New York to take his seat in Congress." *Ibid.*, I, 362.

[31] See particularly Charles W. Ramsdell, "The Natural Limits of Slavery Expansion," *Mississippi Valley Historical Review*, XVI (1929), 151–171; Max Farrand, *The Fathers of the Constitution* (New Haven, Conn., 1921); James G. Randall, "A Blundering Generation," *Mississippi Valley Historical Review*, XXVII (1940), 3–28; Avery Craven, *The Coming of the Civil War* (New York, 1942); Thomas J. Wertenbaker, *Patrician and Plebian in Virginia* (Charlottesville, Va., 1910); and Merrill Jensen, *The New Nation* (New York, 1950).

[32] Norfolk *Daily Southern Argus*, June 30 and June 31, 1858. For recent and penetrating analyses of the Jeffersonian legacy, see especially Charles Wiltsie, *The Jeffersonian Tradition in American Democracy* (Chapel Hill, North Carolina, 1935); Carl Becker, "What Is Still Living in the Political Philosophy of Thomas Jefferson," *American Historical Review*, XLVIII (1943), 691–706; Adrienne Koch, *Jefferson and Madison the Great Collaboration* (New York, 1950).

THE CORRESPONDENCE
1856–1861

1856

[Grigsby to Randall, January 30, 1856]

Philadelphia, January 30, 1856

Dear Sir,

The enclosed letter from Mr. Randolph[1] will constitute, I hope, a sufficient apology for intruding a few moments on your time, which, I know, is fully occupied in your noble work of putting the greatest statesman of his age in his proper light before the present and, I hope, all future generations. The subject of my business is this. In a recent discourse on the Virginia Convention of 1776, I endeavoured to prove the spuriousness of the Mecklenburg Declaration of the *twentieth of May* 1775; with what success you will be able to judge when Mr. Randolph forwards you my discourse, which, though published nearly a month ago in Richmond, has not reached this city yet on account of the ice.[2] I have been requested to prepare a separate discourse on the subject as an offset to Dr. Hawks' lecture before the N. Y. Historical Society a year or two ago.[3] When I prepared my review of the subject in my discourse, I had not seen the depositions taken by order of the legislature of North Carolina, which since my visit to this city, I have seen.[4] In my lecture before the Historical Society of this state, I will examine in detail these depositions, which I think I can overturn completely.

[1] George Wythe Randolph (1818–1867), a grandson of Thomas Jefferson, Secretary of War under Jefferson Davis.

[2] Hugh Blair Grigsby, *The Virginia Convention of 1776. A discourse Delivered before the Virginia Alpha of the Phi Beta Kappa Society, in the Chapel of William and Mary College, in the City of Williamsburg, on the Afternoon of July the 3rd, 1855* (Richmond, 1855), pp. 20–33.

[3] Grigsby, *The Virginia Convention of 1776*, p. 21, states: "The subject of the Mecklenburg Declaration has lately been discussed with great ability by the Rev. Dr. Hawks, in a lecture delivered before the Historical Society of New York. This lecture has been published in book form, with the discourses of Governor Swain and Mr. Graham on North Carolina history by Mr. Cooke of Raleigh, 1853." Hawks, *Revolutionary History of North Carolina, in Three Lectures, by Rev. Francis L. Hawks, Hon. David L. Swain, and Hon. William A. Graham. To which is prefixed a preliminary Sketch of the Battle of the Alamance* (Raleigh, 1853). Significantly Hawks (1798–1866), a native of North Carolina and a prominent Protestant Episcopal clergyman, edited *The Official and other Papers of the Late Major-General Alexander Hamilton* (New York, 1842), which strengthened his hostility to Jefferson primarily founded on religious grounds.

[4] Reports and resolutions adopted by the General Assembly of North Carolina at the 1830–1831 session are cited in Peter Force, comp., *American Archives*, 4th series (6 vols.; Washington, 1837–1853), II, 855.

This was the state of the case, when Col. Ellis of Richmond,[5] a member of our Va. Historical Society, visited this city some days ago, and informed me that Mr. Randolph had told him that you had discovered an original contemporaneous copy of the resolutions of the *twentieth of May*. If this be true, it is idle in me to undertake my task. Let me say to you, however, that I am inclined to think there is some mistake in the case, and that it is possible you may have said to Mr Randolph that you had found a copy of the resolutions differing from the generally received copy, and which do not contain the words "inherent and inalienable," which are found in the popular copy. The manifold discrepancies between the two copies, which I have pointed out in my speech, I have carefully attended to. The first or unadorned copy I call the "Martin" copy, because it was in possession of Gov. [*sic*] Martin of North Carolina and was published in his history;[6] and the other copy which is more elaborate, I have called the "Davie" copy, because it was found among the papers of the late Gen. Davie of N. C.[7]

Now if this statement does not include the extent of your discoveries in the premises, and if you have really discovered a contemporaneous copy of the resolutions of the *twentieth* of May, I should be delighted to know the fact. You are doubtless aware that the resolutions of the *thirtieth* of May are authentic, and may be found in two newspapers of the period.[8]

If you have been so fortunate as to make the discovery of those of the twentieth, you would greatly oblige me with the information. Such a discovery will necessarily supersede any new discourse from me. I need not say to you that your disclosures will be strictly confiden-

[5] Thomas H. Ellis (1814–1898), educated at the University of Virginia, Secretary of the Legation to Mexico 1853–1859, a Confederate officer, and for many years an influential member of the Virginia Historical Society as a contributor of rare books, documents, manuscripts, and paintings. See Thomas H. Ellis, *A Memorandum of the Ellis Family* (Richmond, 1906), p. 41.

[6] This version is discussed in Grigsby, *The Virginia Convention of 1776*, pp. 21–22, and the whole controversy in Henry Stephens Randall, *The Life of Thomas Jefferson* (3 vols.; New York, 1858), III, Appendix II, pp. 570–582. The Martin referred to by Grigsby was François-Xavier Martin (1762–1846), jurist, historian, and author of *The History of North Carolina from the Earliest Period* (2 vols.; New Orleans, 1829).

[7] The Davie copy is discussed in Grigsby, *The Virginia Convention of 1776*, pp. 21–22. William Richardson Davie (1756–1820), revolutionary soldier, distinguished public servant, "Father" of the University of North Carolina and governor of the state (1798–1799). Eliminated from politics by the Jefferson-Macon machine in 1803, he sought to minimize Jefferson's role in drafting the Declaration of Independence by stressing the earlier Mecklenburg version. See F. W. Hubbard, "Life of W. R. Davie," Jared Sparks, ed., *The Library of American Biography*, Series 2, XV (Boston, 1848).

[8] Grigsby's final view was that no resolutions were adopted on May 20, 1775.

tial should you desire it. I would say to you that in my discourse on the Virginia Convention of 1776 I have drawn a running sketch of Mr. Jefferson, which I hope may please you; and that I am devotedly attached to his memory.[9]

Perhaps I may say with propriety that I am a Virginia planter who resides on the Roanoke, and who takes an interest in Virginia history as an amusement only, contributing my time and labor to the good cause without fee or reward.[10]

I am at present in Philadelphia, where I will remain for one or two months longer, on account of the health of my wife.

It is a subject of regret to me that you cannot at once see my argument on the subject; but I hope it will reach you ere long. No copy of the book, except such as are brought on by travellers, has yet reached the city, nor do I possess one myself.

You will confer a great favor by responding to this note when it is convenient for you so to do.

With cordial wishes for the successful prosecution and completion of your great task, I am very respectfully,

Yours.

Hugh B. Grigsby

To/
Judge Randall
New York
My Address in Philadelphia is "at Mrs. Allen's, 309 Chestnut."
[Endorsed by Randall]
Hugh Blair Grigsby Esq.
Encloses letter of introduction from G. W. Randolph—
desires information in regard to Mecklenburg
Declaration of Independence
Reasons & Explanations
Jan. 30, 1856

[9] Grigsby, *The Virginia Convention of 1776*, pp. 168–188.

[10] Grigsby's principal publications include: *The Virginia Convention of 1829–30. A Discourse Delivered before the Virginia Historical Society, at Their Annual Meeting, Held in . . . Richmond, December 15th, 1853* (Richmond, 1854); *The Virginia Convention of 1776* (Richmond, 1855); *Discourse on the Life and Character of the Hon. Littleton Waller Tazewell, before the Bar of Norfolk, Virginia, and the Citizens Generally, on the 29th of June, 1860* (Norfolk, 1860); *The History of the Virginia Federal Convention of 1788 with some Account of the Eminent Virginians of that Era who Were Members of the Body,* (2 vols.; Richmond, 1890–1891).

[Randall to Grigsby, February 7, 1856]

Cortland Village: New York
Feb. 7. 1856.

My dear Sir,

I have delayed answering yours for several days,—for on the outgoing & incoming mail-bags of this goodly town, the lord has laid an Embargo, for the last five or six days, far more stringent than Mr. Jefferson's on our Commerce, in 1808. We are fairly snowed under! Not a car has passed on our Rail-Road (Syracuse & Binghamton) in about a week, unless one has burst through its Alpine barriers early this morning. At that period we heard Something that bore some resemblance to the locomotive whistle,—but it was an unearthly Squeak, like a whistle frozen near to death, or like one rendered almost inarticulate from grief & rage, rather than that full, ringing, startling *yell* with which the whistle in prosperity—the whistle "in the full tide of successful experiment," as St. Thomas of Monticello would say—is wont to assert its dignity & astonish the nat*ives*, as it goes tearing through a country village!—

Adventurous travellers, mounted the lord knows how, & skipping along super-incumbent drifts have reported trains of cars buried out of Sight in deep cuts—the passengers like ancient Pompeians flying from the burial which the skies poured down on them! Only to think of fifteen or twenty travellers of all ages & sexes crammed into every contiguous farmhouse, mustering on the average three bed rooms, & say four beds apiece! Then consider, (to say nothing of Short Commons), the short *wardrobes* of people who expected to be away from home only for a day!! I have half a dozen friends out in this dilemma, & among others a tremendous "Smart" youngerly married lady, accompanied by an equally "Smart" unmarried one. I'd match them against the State (& handicap them at that) as *talkers!* I have laughed an hour this morning (by Shrewsbury)[11] to think of their dilemma; & am laying wagers how much snow they would *blow off* & *thaw off* talking & fretting! The whole affair, Scant commons, dirty shirts, rumped & soiled looking women, peculiar sleeping accommodations &c, rises before my imagination so grotesquely that if I had all the dignity of Dominie Sampson[12] I could not withstand it—& you being the first person I write, on the prospect of the embargo being raised, I discharge Some of my feelings

[11] "By a Shrewsbury clock." W. J. Craig, edition, Shakespeare, *Henry IV*, Pt. I, Act III, scene i, line 158.

[12] A leading character and the tutor of Harry Bertram in Walter Scott's *Guy Mannering*.

of drollery on your unoffending head,—Stranger though you are. If you see Mr. Trist[13] & his family (he mentioned you to me) share the calamity among them, by reading them my letter. And I won't interdict you from letting Doctor Dunglison[14] know (if you are in the habit of meeting him) what *"whopping"* snow-storms we can, if we *try,* get up in the North. But, perhaps we have not *tried* so hard before in a century.

In reply to the enquiry of your letter I would say that I have no copy of the Mecklenburgh Dec. of Independence but the one you refer to, *printed* a week or ten days from the *date* of the copy which made so much talk, as establishing a plagiarism.[15] It was that which I spoke to Randolph[16] of as a Contemporaneous copy.—So! You have anticipated all "my thunder" on this subject? Well, I won't "begrudge" you *this;* but, my dear Sir, I shall be seriously alarmed, if you go to picking up *many* of my *"thunder"* points in advance! According to the old Federal theory (& Mr. Marshall's,)[17] the U. S. Supreme Court have a good deal more than monarchical (i.e. limited monarchy) powers, & rely upon it, I shall rummage its old armory for something to Stop you! Look out that you don't wake up some bright morning & find yourself called up in the straight jacket of an *injunction.* I won't give you leave to take another point! A vermillion edict! Tremble!

[13] Nicholas P. Trist (1800–1874), married Virginia Jefferson Randolph, a granddaughter of Jefferson, and resided at Monticello the last two or three years of Jefferson's life. He kept daily memoranda of his conversations with Jefferson and was present at Jefferson's death bed. Trist's recollections were put at the disposal of Randall during his visit to Philadelphia.

[14] Robley Dunglison (1798–1869), an Englishman, was educated at Edinburgh, Paris, London, and received the M.D. degree from Erlangen in 1823. His book on children's diseases attracted the attention of Jefferson and was responsible for his call as professor of medicine to the University of Virginia (1825–1833). Author of several treatises, he was professor of medicine at the University of Maryland (1833–1836), Jefferson Medical College, Philadelphia (1836–1868).

[15] Randall had the May 31 copy, recognized by all parties as genuine.

[16] G. W. Randolph.

[17] John Marshall (1755–1835), chief justice of United States Supreme Court (1801–1835), appears in this correspondence as a consolidator of the Union by judicial decision and as a proponent of Federalist ideas through his *Life of George Washington* (5 vols.; Philadelphia, 1804–1807). An advocate of evolutionary nationalism, Marshall was under constant fire from the political and literary leaders of the Jeffersonian party, but never lacked effective support. Hampton L. Carson observes: "The only work which approached, either in character or in dignity, the semblance of an American history in general was John Marshall's *Life of George Washington,* a work bitterly assailed upon its appearance by political antagonists, and too frequently regarded today as obsolete or insufficient." See Carson, *A History of the Historical Society of Pennsylvania* (2 vols.; Philadelphia, 1940), I, 29. The pertinent observation of J. Franklin Jameson, "Often, indeed, those earlier lives have for the student of today much more of the attraction of freshness and originality than the biographies written in our own time; the writers of these latter have frequently so full a sense of the American political history of which their subject forms a part that the individuality of the portrait is impaired by the attention paid to the background," is quoted in *ibid.*, p. 29.

Seriously, I shall be very glad to receive the promised copy of your production.[18] If in your researches you stumble on anything of interest in relation to Mr J. (outside your articles) I should be very glad to receive them of you—whether they pertain to large or small matters. Have you picked up no anecdotes this winter in Philadelphia, which would give zest to my volume? Pray, Sir, let us consider ourselves acquaintances,—& I would be glad always to hear from you on this or any other subject. I am, very respectfully

Henry S. Randall

Mr. Grigsby

[Grigsby to Randall, February 9, 1856]

Philadelphia, February 9, 1856.

Dear Sir,

Your esteemed letter of the 7th instant came promptly to hand, and while the subject of Mr. Jefferson is in my mind, I proceed to write to you at once. I thank you for your kind explanations in respect of the Mecklenburg Declaration. The discrepancies between the two copies I have noted at length, and argued against their authenticity on that score and on some others; but the main ground on which I rely to overturn most thoroughly the Declaration of the *20th of May* is that a series of resolutions was adopted on the *thirtieth* of May on the same spot and by the same men, which recognized the right of eminent domain in the British Crown; and the dilemma which I press upon the friends of the Mecklenburg Declaration is this: Either the declaration was not made at all, or it was made. If it was not made under the circumstances noted, it has of course no value; but if it was made, then was it recanted ten days after it was made, on the very spot where it was made, by the very men who made it, and amid the shouts of rejoicing of those who are supposed to have hailed the declaration ten days before with all the honors and is therefore without value. This dilemma, I think, is one not easily to be recovered from.[19]

I suppose you are now aware that Mr. Jefferson's ancestors came over before 1619, and one of them was a burgess, for Flowerdy hundred I believe, in the first house of Burgesses—being a meeting previous to the

[18] Grigsby, *The Virginia Convention of 1776.*
[19] Grigsby, *The Virginia Convention of 1776,* pp. 20–33.

full recess recorded in Hening's Statutes at Large. The Madisons also came over before 1624. Now neither Mr. Jefferson nor Mr. Madison knew these facts. You will find them stated in the last annual report of the Executive Committee of the Va. Historical Society, which has been published in the papers, but which will be republished in the annual pamphlet before very long.[20]

I will probably see this evening at the Wistar's party[21] of Dr. Pancoast,[22] Dr. Dunglison and probably Mr. Trist.

But my main purpose in writing you is to state a fact that came to my knowledge some years ago in conversation with my friend, Mr. F. N. Watkins of Farmville, Va.[23] He had just returned from a trip to the South whither he had gone to settle the affairs of a deceased relative. I enclose his letter received yesterday which will give you all the intelligence on the subject that I possess. You will oblige me by returning it when you have done with it, as it is the only memorandum which I possess of the facts.

My view of the case is this, that you can [not] obtain from these letters in possession of Mr. Michie[24] any thing *favorable* concerning Mr. Jeffer-

---

[20] "The Committee's Report. Report made to the Virginia Historical Society by its Executive Committee, at the Annual Meeting in January, 1856," *The Virginia Historical Reporter*, I, Pt. III (1856), p. 6, notes that a Jefferson was among those in the House of Burgesses that met in 1619 and that a "Capt. Isaac *Madison* and *Mrs. Mary Madison* were in the colony in 1623." Randall refers to the records seen by Conway Robinson of Virginia in the Public Record Office which contained the names of the burgesses attending a meeting on July 30, 1619. See *Life*, I, 6, n. 1. Dumas Malone, *Jefferson the Virginian*, p. 6, states: "The line can be traced with certainty . . . to an obscure man . . . a farmer . . . by the year 1679 . . . living in Henrico County . . . below the present location of Richmond." Julius W. Pratt "James Madison," *Dictionary of American Biography*, XII, p. 184, writes: "We can safely trace the family no further back than to John Madison who received considerable grants of Virginia land in 1653." Grigsby, *The Virginia Convention of 1776*, p. 84, has a memorandum on James Madison, corrected by Madison, which begins the family history in Virginia with the year 1623.

[21] Social gatherings in Philadelphia named after Caspar Wistar, a well known Philadelphia doctor of an earlier period.

[22] Dr. Joseph Pancoast (1805–1882), physician, professor of surgery and anatomy at Jefferson Medical College, author and editor of medical works.

[23] Francis Nathaniel Watkins (*ca.* 1813–1885), graduate of Hampden-Sidney College and a trustee of that institution (1844–1853, 1866–1885), treasurer of the Union Theological Seminary (1845–1885), a member of the Virginia House of Delegates. See *General Catalogue of the Officers and Students of Hampden-Sidney College, Virginia, 1776–1906* (Richmond, 1908), pp. 19–21.

[24] Probably David Michie is the man referred to. Jefferson brought suit against him in chancery in Albemarle County in 1814, and, on Michie's part at least, there was considerable animosity. The nature of this controversy is revealed in part in two letters in possession of the Massachusetts Historical Society: (1) David Michie to Jefferson, March 20, 1817, and (2) Jefferson to Michie, March 22, 1817. Edgar Woods, *Albemarle County* (Charlottesville, 1901), p. 275, calls Michie "a man of great enterprise and thrift."

son, or his old friends, Giles,[25] Wilson Cary Nicholas,[26] Abram Venable,[27] and others. I do not believe; but there is another aspect of the case that may appear not altogether unworthy of regard. *Sometime or other* these slanderous publications will appear, and it is worth knowing beforehand what charges they contain, so that it may be practicable to forestall their venom when they are made public. Of course, as Mr. Michie is a democrat, *he* will never allow them to be published with a view of injury [to] the memory of Mr. J.; but his executors may. That they will creep into print some day or other is almost certain.

I enclose the letter of introduction forwarded to me by Mr. Watkins (who is or was a Whig) that you may have all the knowledge of the subject which I possess myself. Let me observe that Mr. Watkins has fallen naturally enough into error when he says that I am preparing an edition of my discourse on the convention of 1776 for the press, and that I desired the manuscripts of Mr Michie with that view. I wrote to him wholly to ascertain the *nature* of the letters, and their whereabouts, that I might communicate them to you.

I have written in great haste; but if you can make out my scrawl so far as to infer that I wish you success in the noble cause in which you are engaged, I shall not be dissatisfied with the result.

Let me suggest to you that the information which you will have it in your power to obtain from Dr. Dunglison will be of the deepest interest, and will tend to illustrate not only the latter part of Mr. Jefferson's life but incidentally the earlier also. You should by all means see his intelligence before you model even your early chapters. I should say that you could not see him too soon; as he is advanced in life, though as hale as a man of forty. But his information oral and documental should be secured at all events promptly and thoroughly.

I have not yet got a copy of my discourse which was published in Richmond in December. The ice has stopped the Express company for the present.

---

[25] William Branch Giles (1762–1830), a powerful champion of Jefferson's political party in United States House of Representatives and Senate from 1790 to his retirement in 1815. Grigsby, *The Virginia Convention of 1829–30*, pp. 22–28. See also Dice R. Anderson, *William Branch Giles: A Study in the Politics of Virginia and the Nation from 1790 to 1830* (Menasha, Wisconsin, 1914).

[26] Wilson Cary Nicholas (1761–1820), Republican, helped frame anti-Federalist resolutions, collaborated with Jefferson in founding the University of Virginia. Grigsby, *The Virginia Federal Convention of 1788*, II, 299–360.

[27] Abraham Bedford Venable (1758–1811), resident of Prince Edward County, Virginia, member of the United States House of Representatives (1791–1793) and Senate (1803–1804). *Biographical Directory of the American Congress, 1774–1927* (Washington, 1928), p. 1648.

Should you visit Philadelphia between this time and the first of April, I will have the opportunity of seeing you.

In haste,
Very truly
Hugh B. Grigsby
(at Mrs. Allens, 309 Chestnut Street)

To/
Henry S. Randall esq.
[Endorsed by Randall]
Hugh B. Grigsby Esq.
The Mecklenburg Declaration
The Michie Paper
Dr. Dunglison
Feb. 8, 1856.

[Randall to Grigsby, February 15, 1856]

Cortland Village: New York
Feb 15th, 1856.

My dear Sir,

Yours & a long letter from Dr. Dunglison reached me by the same post—*both* giving me most gratifying evidence of the kindly interest which you take in my life of Mr. Jefferson.

I agree with you that the paper in the hands of Mr. Michie may be important for the reasons you mention considering the *locality* of the author, & the fact, which would be trumped up into importance, that he was a relative of Monroe. I thank you most sincerely for the steps you have already taken in reference to it, for the benefit of my work; & I think you can manage the future ones to obtain it (or a copy of it which would be just as well, unless Mr. Michie should be willing to have a foolish and untruthful paper destroyed) better than I can, for you have a link of *personal* connection with him, through Mr. Watkins, which I have not, & cannot obtain. If Mr. M. was asked it for *my* inspection, & a request coming from Mr. Trist or Mr. G. W. Randolph as representatives of Mr. Jefferson would add any weight to yours, they could be easily obtained. This might, if you thought best, be offered to Mr. M.—But, if you consent to trouble yourself further with the matter, pray take precisely the course *you* think best.—

New England slanders against Mr. J. I pay little attention to,—or those that dripped from the foul pen of Callender.[28] (By the by, the latter was helped by some of Mr. Jefferson's *neighbors;* & the author of the Michie manuscript may have very probably been one of them). These are old stories, & I have not thought it advisable to rake them up one by one, & then attempt to prove *negitious*—that they were not true. My statements in regard to Mr. Jefferson's character & morals have *generally* been *affirmative* ones, & it [is] rare that I have turned aside unless apparently accidentally to meet a specific personal charge. Still, I have written the whole biography with an eye steadily on those charges,—& taken the course which I thought would most effectually &, at the same time, most dignifiedly, refute them. If we should fail to get the Michie manuscript itself & could learn distinctly who the author was, & when he wrote, I think I could pick up traces enough of him to *wet his powder* effectually in advance.

The opinion which you expressed to Dr. Dunglison (as he writes me) that I ought to have at once, & at the outset, a coup d'oeil of my *whole* subject, is, in my judgment, *undoubtedly the correct one.* No painter or sculptor ever wrought a *great* work, without having a perfect & vivid ideal before him.

There can be no patching or dovetailing in high art.—There can be no growth in the *conception* after the execution is in part completed. It must come from the brain, as Minerva came from Jupiters—full-grown and armed! I pressed Dr. Dunglison, so far as propriety permitted, to let me take & use his work (his *"Ana"*) & I would have been glad to have stipulated to show him, before publication, every passage of his I had used, & every allusion to a passage, & then make him the final arbiter whether they should stand or be stricken out.—But, personally, he was a stranger to me,—& I could not & did not blame him for his disinclination to place his manuscript in my possession.—I had several reasons for not making an immediate journey to Philadelphia.—It was excessively inconvenient for me to leave home before Spring—& excessively disagreeable to do it, during the cold weather, I having been much out of health for a year or two (broken down by official labor)*

* As Secy of State, I was also a member of the Canal Board, A comm. of the Canal Fund, a Comm. of the Land Office, with a half a dozen trusteeships. I was also Supt. of Com. Schools, deciding *without appeal*

[28] James Thompson Callender (1758–1803), a political refugee from Scotland in 1793, was first a friend then an effective enemy of Jefferson as editor of the Richmond *Recorder.* He is the chief source of scandals about Jefferson. Randall, *Life,* III, 16–21; Worthington C. Ford, ed., *Thomas Jefferson and James Thompson Callendar, 1798–1802* (New York, 1897). See also "The Walker Affair," Malone, *Jefferson the Virginian,* pp. 447–451.

all the cases coming up before me (averaging 30 & frequently rising to 50 or 60 a week), & annually apportioning & disbursing about $1,100,000. For $800,000 of this I gave no security. I showed no vouchers of disbursement. The officers are now divided and *six* men do a *branch* of my labors that I accomplished with the aid of *one*. You see I had some excuse for breaking down!

---

until within the last few months. I wanted, when I did make the journey, to go on & complete some important matters at Washington, which were not then, & are not yet, ready for me.—I am not a very old man (forty-four) but owing to my exhaustion and ill health, I have contracted a morbid aversion to going abroad, unless driven by an absolute necessity.—Then I have found by experience, that breaking off the main thread of my story, to follow out very thoroughly incidental or side points, *puts me out,* as children say. I confuse dates, & jumble up incidents, forgetting whether I have referred to them before or not. The even, flowing, gradually widening & deepening current is broken.—The *spirit*—the confident decisive tone, is lost.—And then again, you cannot well tell how to take the facts, traits, allusions and the like, from the writings of another, before you have been over the ground and know how to apply them, unless you copy everything. This last I desired to do, through a Secretary, but Dr. Dunglison, has matter in his Ana, I suppose, which he does not choose to submit to a secretary—& indeed, he expects to be consulted in regard to all that is used. I could not, I feared, accomplish much *thus,* without first writing through my work, & then going back & *filling in* what he permitted me to use.—Dr. D's rule is one which he has every right to make;—but had he known me, & could he have relied on my discretion & my honor, with the *distinct understanding that I should show him every passage in any way referring to the contents of his Ana,* it would have been inexpressibly gratifying & *beneficial* to me. Then, unhurried, with attention undivided, with the *whole* subject calmly & clearly in my mind's eye, I could have completed my ideal down to the minutest particular & when its counterpart was given to the world it would have showed that perfect *unity* of expression, without which every effort of the mind or hand, is but secondary. It would be no substitute for *this,* for me to go to Philadelphia tomorrow, & spend two weeks in studying the Dr.'s Ana. I know my own ways, my own habits of composition, when & under what circumstances, the spell comes over me. I cannot mix the charm by rote & by rule, & hampered about by regulations, & broken in upon by clubs & dinners. Clubs to me are dullness, & dinners are literal abominations, when I have any engrossing object to accomplish.—No, as you say, I want the *whole* before me (not a part here & a part in Philadelphia). I want time—*my own time.* I want the deep, eloquent solitude of the country—& not the hot, hateful life-fever of the city about me. I want my own chair—my own table. I want to hear the winter wind moaning through ancestral trees, or the voices of countless birds pealing down from them in the fragrant & sparkling morning, or when the solemn twilight is deepening around. I want to look upon ancestral faces, & hear their mute lips whispering to me "up—onward—fear not—flag not!"—

It is most unfortunate to me that circumstances take just the Shape that they do. Dr Dunglison writes me very probably, most probably, he may leave Philadelphia by the first of April & that he will be gone so long that I cannot avail myself of his Ana at all, for my work must go to press this Summer. Yet it is almost madness in me to tempt another return of my long, dreary prostration by getting away from my own chimney corner during this terrific winter. The thought of it is *torture.* Tell me not of the benefit of changes of scene.—I have drank out all that is good in city life, to the bottom of the goblet. Until time & solitude bring restoration, I detest it. A new face is a dread to me. I am like the knocked hunter, knee-sprung, gravelled, backstrained & what not! A years run at grass (with shoes off) *may* recover me, for I naturally had the endurance of two common men.

And the worst of all this is that I cannot do half as well what ought to be done, by going to Philadelphia! Oh, that Dr. Dunglison fully knew me! What difference *can* there be, among men of Education & breeding & *experience* as to what it is delicate & proper & *expedient* to use, in a free journal, & what not?—I have no doubt I shall be more fastidious than the Dr. himself in committing *him* in any disagreeable way. I this day have the custody of an ancient & voluminous family correspondence deeply affecting the feelings & honor of the most distinguished family this state ever had, & that custody is continued by the wish of the present head of that family! Two days would bring the Dr.s papers *perfectly safely* here by express. They could all be sent back, with a citation of every line used or referred to, before his southern journey, & the citations be submitted to his decision. Is it not a pity that the thing stands as it does? I have gone into these details, on account of the great interest you have manifested in my work, & because Dr. D. in addition to speaking of you as a friend, himself mentioned that you & he had discussed the same topic.

Yours Cordially

Henry S. Randall

Confidential

My dear Sir,

I commenced going into great details in the enclosed letter to show *you* why I did not go promptly to Philadelphia to see Dr. D., because I desired to vindicate myself to you, who have so kindly enlisted yourself for me, from what *without* explanation, might seem a very strange omission.—I never have any *half* confidences. Before closing my letter (*just* as I was closing it) it occurred to me that if Dr. D. *knew precisely how things stood,* hc *might change his mind.* To write to him as I have to you, would have been a degree of importunity transcending the limits of good taste. Besides when he decided the point, we had arrived at none of our present freedom of correspondence.—A thought has occurred to me, & I submit for your consideration. Dr. D. spoke with *high respect* of you in his last letter to me. *He,* without any remark on my part, voluntarily reopened the subject of my having the use of his "Ana" in advance, by telling me *your* (perfectly correct) views on that subject, & then saying, that he thought the other course would do which "*I* suggested." (I *did* suggest it rather than not see the papers at all.) The Dr.'s tone, I *think,* is that of a man *shaken* in his opinion & who is looking round for a backer. I think he *felt* the force of your position. Now I shall very quietly tell him that I agree with you, but I shall enter into no argument, &, of course, shall not ask him to revoke what *he* has *settled.* I don't know him, nor what his texture is,—but it does seem to me that if he understood the whole, he would *send me his Ana.* You can judge what effect a full knowledge of the facts would have on him (I could, too, if I had had one look at him, & heard him speak three sentences.) If you make up your mind that he could be *carried*—& that reading to him what I have written *you* on the subject would be likely to have any effect on him, his re-introduction of the topic would be a full excuse for *my writing you,* & for you (as my letter to you *is not a confidential one*) disclosing to him what it contains. But entirely, I pray, you be governed by your own judgment & knowledge of parties in the matter.—The thing looks a little *stratagetic* at first blush. If I thought it savored a particle, in *spirit,* of trick or even of pious fraud, it might be d——d for all of me! The way it presents itself to my mind, at first view, is that of opening a convenient way for a gentleman who has put his foot down in an unfortunate place (for another) taking it up again gracefully, if the spirit moves him so to do.

Write me often—& pray don't wait for something to say. Your prompt, warm, *Virginian* friendship comes to me all blazè like a spring breeze over your own Blue Mountains. In my isolation (but for the barber shop, the street would not take the pattern of my boots once a month) I still live to hold converse with a few on paper—& talking little elsewhere, I pour out on those few a stream as continuous & long (though the waters are of different sort) as Macaulay pours on his little circle of listeners.—I shall send you some books, in a day or two, which may amuse an antiquarian hour. I shall write Dr. D. herewith—I will return your letters from Mr. Watkins in two or three days.

There are some passages in this which, disconnected from the surrounding facts, would have a disagreeable sort of sound,—so be good enough to burn it after perusal.—

I would like to come to P. to meet you. But that can come to pass hereafter. When my book is off the irons, my spirit will rise again. Then I'll see you, if I come to Va. for it. A meeting at the Va. Spring, or on a trip down our St. Lawrence or at Niagara, or Saratoga is always easy. By the by (for I may never think of it again) if you at any time want letters to any place in this State, I shall be happy to give them if acquainted—& there are few places in it where I am not acquainted.

Cordially yours,
H. S. Randall

[Endorsed by Grigsby]
Henry S. Randall
Cortland Village
Feb. 15, 1856.

[Grigsby to Randall, February 18, 1856]

Philadelphia, February 18, 1856

"At Mrs. Allen's 309 Chestnut."

Dear Sir,

Your letters of the 15th came safely to hand this morning, and, although I will take an early opportunity of seeing Dr. Dunglison, and conversing with him on the subject of the Ana, I have thought it best to chat with you at once, as I know more *now* about the Ana than I did when I wrote you. I have since seen the duodecimo pocket books which contain them, some four or six, and heard Dr. D. read passages from them. This is the nature of his Ana. He evidently prepared them as memoranda of his personal life for the eye of his wife now dead and of his children; and they contain a mass of matter which no other eye during his life save that of a descendant might be allowed to peruse.[29] So far as I could see and judge, there is no connected account of Mr. Jefferson, but simply here and there an allusion to him intermixed with his own private history. Much that he read me I, who am familiar with all that is printed about Mr. Jefferson and Mr. Madison, knew before; although for the purpose for which the memoranda here compiled the facts stated are of much interest. I remember a conversation of the Dr. with Mr. Jefferson, in which Mr. Jefferson expressed an utter disregard for posthumous fame—a mere flash of the moment evidently, as you remember in one of his more solemn letters to Mr. Madison he alludes to the fact that Mr. Madison was preparing a history of their joint administrations, and says: You have been to me a column of support through life—*take care of me when dead:* And in his last will he bequeathes "his daughter to his Country," which bequest could be justified only on the ground that his services would make a favorable lodgment in the bosoms of posterity.[30]

Since I have had a glimpse of the Ana of Dr. D., I do not think it so imperative as I did before that you should consult them at once—but I am free to say that the concluding chapters of Mr. Jefferson's life would be greatly enhanced by a free conversation with Dr. D. as well as by reference to his notes. Should you come on by the middle of March, I think it probable that you will meet with Dr. D., who, let me say, is a gentleman in every aspect of the term, eminently learned, liberal, courteous, and full of that chivalry of literature which leads him to think that the greater wealth he can bestow upon his literary compeers the richer he is himself. He was the confidential friend and physician of both Mr. Jefferson and Mr. Madison, and has a mind capable of comprehending the characters of the men. You and I may not embrace his conclusions, but we must highly value the facts which leads him to draw them. Could you get the Dr. to prepare an account of the last illness of Mr. J., I presume that, beside its authenticity as coming from the attending physician, himself a man of the greatest reputation, it would fill up the closing scene of Mr. J. with graphic effect, though,

[29] R. J. Dunglison, ed., *Memoir of Dr. Robley Dunglison* (1870), was published the year after Dunglison's death.

[30] Jefferson wrote Madison, February 17, 1826: "The friendship which has subsisted between us, now half a century, and the harmony of our political principles and pursuits, have been sources of constant happiness to me through that long period. And if I remove beyond the reach of attentions to the University, or beyond the bourne of life itself, it is a comfort to leave that institution under your care. . . . It has also been a great solace to me, to believe that you are engaged in vindicating to posterity the course we have pursued for preserving to them, in all their purity, the blessings of self-government. . . ." See Randall, *Life*, III, 532–533. Jefferson's will is printed in *ibid.*, III, Appendix XXXIII, pp. 665–667.

of course, you will prepare the account of his last illness with literal intelligence from other quarters.[31]

Gov. Coles,[32] my friend, knew both Mr. J. and Mr. Madison intimately. He told me the other day an amusing story of Mr. J. It should seem that Mr. J., on a return from some distant jaunt had a cutaneous eruption, which his physician Dr. D. pronounced to be the itch. Jefferson thought differently, but as his physician believed it to be the itch, he consented to use mercury which salivated him. This annoyed him excessively—and he complained to Gov. Coles of the unpleasant effects of the salivation. The Governor observed: Mr. Jefferson, you are the last man in the world, from your hatred of physic, whom I would have expected any excess in taking physic." Mr. J. added with warmth: Yes, but I would rather have *the devil* than the itch." So it seemed that, though he hated doctors, he hated the devil more.

Dr. Dunglison, by the way, read me a paragraph in which there was an allusion to the itch which Jefferson had caught on one of his jaunts.

My impression is that a few hours in Dr. D's study would enable you to get through his memoranda, and that you can obtain more from him orally than from his written words.

By the way, there is a fine portrait of Mr. Jefferson taken from life by Stuart for Mr. Madison, in the parlour of Gov. Coles. I mention this fact, that you may be able to give a list of the authentic existing portraits of Mr. Jefferson, which I deem a matter of no little importance.[33]

You are aware that the legislature of Virginia a year ago voted a full statue in Marble of Mr. J. for the Rotunda of the University of Virginia, to be executed by my friend Alexander Galt, a young man of great merit, a native Virginian. Galt has modelled the head in plaster, and the model was in my house for several months. Galt goes over to Italy in the spring to put it in marble. I have several exquisite pieces by Galt, such as his Bacchante, his Psyche, and his Columbus, all admirably done.[34]

---

[31] Randall, *Life*, III, 512–519, 547–549, 670–671, contains information obtained directly in conversation with Dr. Dunglison. Randall gives Dunglison's memoranda concerning Jefferson's last illness and his death. See *ibid.*, III, 547–549.

[32] Edward Coles (1786–1868), a Virginian, settled in Illinois in 1819, emancipated his slaves and served as second governor of Illinois (1822–1826). The leader of the effort to defeat the establishment of slavery in that state, he settled in Philadelphia in 1832.

[33] Randall, *Life*, Volumes I and II, reproduce two Stuart portraits. For a recently discovered likeness see *William and Mary Quarterly*, Third Series VI, No. 1 (January, 1949), 84–89.

[34] Alexander Galt (1827–1863), Virginian sculptor, trained in Florence, executed a statue of Thomas Jefferson for the State of Virginia, now at the University of Virginia.

I am obliged to you for your promise to forward me some documents relative to New York history.[35] I greatly need them in my researches, for all points of time, but especially from the Indian Wars and treaties of 1760 upwards. Such things cannot be obtained in Virginia. I have recently commemorated the name of Andrew Lewis, who negotiated on behalf of Virginia in your state the treaty of Stanwyx.[36]

Gov. Coles is a most graphic narrator, and even actor of the conversations of Mr. J., and may give most useful information in filling up your outline of the personnel and the morale of Mr. Jefferson.

I have written you as you desired *currente calamo;* and would only say that you will regard my letters as *suggestive* rather than as positive in any respect, or in any opinion.

Very truly,
Yours
Hugh B. Grigsby

Mr. Randall
Cortland Village N. Y.
Memo: I consider the testimony of Dr. D. as valuable, not only in itself, but as coming from an eminent foreigner. By the way, he quoted to me the remark of Von Raumer, I think, about coming to this country to see "the experiment of Jefferson;" showing that the fine minds of Europe regard republicanism and Jeffersonianism as convertible terms.[37]
[Endorsed by Randall]
Hugh B. Grigsby Esq.
Feb. 18, 1856.

[Randall to Grigsby, February 21, 1856]

Cortland Village
Feb. 21, 1856.

My dear Sir,

I today forward you a copy of the Documentary History of New York, compiled under the Supervision of an official predecessor.[38] It contains

[35] Edmund B. O'Callaghan (1797–1880), native of Ireland, physician and historian, devoted twenty-two years (1848–1870) to editing the old records of New York. Editor of *Documents Relative to the Colonial History of the State of New York* (11 vols.; Albany, 1853–1861); *Documentary History of the State of New York* (4 vols., octavo; Albany, 1849–1851); (4 vols., quarto; Albany, 1850–1851). It is not clear which volumes were sent Grigsby.

[36] Andrew Lewis (1720–1781), Virginia soldier, aided in framing the Indian Treaty of Fort Stanwix (1768).

[37] Friedrich Ludwig George von Raumer (1781–1873), noted German historian. See James Westfall Thompson, *A History of Historical Writing* (2 vols.; New York, 1942), II, 144–146.

[38] O'Callaghan, *The Documentary History of the State of New York.*

some curious old papers, but is not what it should have been with the materials which there were to choose from. I have put it in a package with sets sent to Dr. Dunglison, & one or two others, all directed to Dr. D. to save myself the trouble of making up separate packages, & the rest of you a considerable additional expense,—so I hope the Dr. will excuse me for the liberty I have taken.—Please accept the books as an evidence of my friendly regard.—We are under another snow embargo, so I am not at all certain when the books will reach you.

I remain, dear Sir

Very truly Yours
Henry S. Randall

H. B. Grigsby, Esq.
[Endorsed by Grigsby]
Henry S. Randall
Cortland Village N. Y.
February 21, 1856

[Grigsby to Randall, February 29, 1856]

Philadelphia, February 29, 1856—

Dear Sir,

Accept my cordial thanks for your most valuable and most welcome present of the Documentary history of New York. It is a noble work, and reflects honor on your state. It will be a mine of wealth to me some of these days. Dr. Dunglison and Professor Tucker[39] are much gratified with the possession of so valuable a work, and, I suppose, have made, or will soon make, their grateful acknowledgements.

I was with Professor Dunglison yesterday, and was sorry to learn from him that he had fallen on the icy pavement the day before, spraining his right wrist. He, however, shows a brave spirit, attends to his pressing duties at this season, without seeming inconvenience, and expects to hold his 'Wistar' tomorrow evening.

I took tea with Professor Tucker this evening, who said that he had recently written to you, or intended doing so; and observed that he had obtained some information from your volumes already that was of service to him.

On the subject of the manuscripts of Professor D., I have not pressed

[39] George Tucker (1775–1861), professor of moral philosophy, University of Virginia (1825–1845), author of *The Life of Thomas Jefferson* (2 vols.; Philadelphia, 1837), resident of Philadelphia after retirement. Tucker also published, *The History of the United States* (4 vols.; Philadelphia, 1856–1857). Both of his works appear repeatedly in this correspondence.

matters since I saw you, and I am inclined to think that you will agree with me that there is not that importance to be attached to an early perusal of them as I anticipated before I had a glance at them. They will be valuable indeed; but their value will be available as well, or nearly so, towards the close of your work as at an earlier period. To converse with him and with Gov. Coles will be most desirable for you; you will thus obtain information which neither of those gentlemen would put to paper, but not the less valuable on that account.

It would give me great pleasure to see you in this city. How long I shall remain it is difficult for me to say at present; but I presume until the first of April. My object here was the accouchement of Mrs. G., which has eventuated happily, though she is too weak to form plans for the future.[40] Lest I might forget to do so at another time, I would state that my address is Norfolk, Va., until June 1st, and from that time until Nov. 1, at Charlotte C. H., Va.

Gov. Coles told me anecdotes of Mr. Jefferson and Mr. Madison for two successive hours Sunday evening last. One was to this effect. When Mr. Jefferson was returning to Washington from his plantation in Albemarle, he had proceeded as far as Alexandria, when, finding the roads excessively bad for wheels, he mounted his horse, and set off alone, leaving his carriage to follow. He soon overtook a plain substantial Kentuckian, who was on horseback on his way to Baltimore and Philadelphia to purchase Goods. They chatted freely with each other, the Kentuckian being, as he said, exceedingly anxious to get a sight of Mr. Jefferson. Mr. Jefferson promised to gratify him, and told him that he must call at the President's House the next day at eleven, when he would take care that he should be well received by the President. But, said the Kentuckian, you don't know *me,* and I don't know *you;* I am afraid my visit would be an intrusion on the President. Finally, however, they fixed an hour for calling on the President the next day. In the mean time the Kentuckian, who saw that his fellow traveller was intelligent and versed in politics, inquired of him about the tales told of Mr. Jefferson—his wearing red breeches—his intercourse with Black Sal—and fifty other equally vacuous charges made by the federalists against Jefferson. Mr. Jefferson answered all these charges in detail, as Gov. Coles did, giving the dialogues of the parties with exquisite humour. At last when they approached the President's house, Mr. Jefferson turned aside, and having tied his horse, ascended the steps of the building. The Kentuckian who was evidently struck with the intelligence of

[40] Hugh Carrington Grigsby was born on February 13, 1856.

his companion, thought that he would inquire of a passer-by who he was, and was told that he was the President, which, however, he stoutly denied. At last when he could resist the truth no longer, he was overcome with confusion. But he was a gentleman, as Mr. Jefferson had evidently seen from the beginning, and as he afterwards found out to be the case. "What must he do," he said to himself? "One thing is clear—" he said—he must apologize to the President—he must assure him that he did not dream of his real character." The upshot was that he called next day, was heartily received, laughed with Mr. J. about the chat of the previous day—dined with him &c. This story told by Gov. C. is most amusing.

He also mentioned another. As Mr. Jefferson was returning from Charlottesville to Monticello on one occasion, he met a man with a saddle and bridle over his shoulders, and unable to cross the creek, which was much swollen. Stranger, said Mr. Jefferson, what is the matter? "Why, sir," said the man, "I am anxious to cross this creek, but I can find no crossing place." "Well," said Mr. J., "suppose you mount behind me—my horse will carry double, and I will assure you a safe passage." The man got to a fence and jumped behind Mr. J. and was landed on the other side in safety. He was very grateful; and on some gentlemen riding up who were going to dine with Mr. Jefferson, he asked them who that kind gentleman was that put him over the creek. Why, said the gentlemen, that was President Jefferson. You don't say so, said the man. Well then, gentlemen, don't say any thing more about the matter; for if it were to reach Kentucky that I mounted with my saddle and bridle behind Mr. Jefferson, I shall never hear the last of it as long as I live.

Such amusing incidents as these the Governor tells remarkably well, while he knows more important matters touching the rise and fall of politicians both during Mr. J's and Mr. Madison's terms.

I have not seen Mr. Trist lately, as I have been indisposed with a bilious attack which confined me to the house for several days.

I have just received a few copies of my discourse on the Convention of 1776, and send you one. You will at once perceive from the nature of my subject that I am compelled to deal in general touches rather than in detail.

Very truly,
Yours
Hugh B. Grigsby
(309 Chestnut)

Mr. Randall
[not endorsed]

[Randall to Grigsby. March 3, 1856]

Cortland Village, March 3d, 1856

My dear Sir,

I enclose back the letters of Mr. Watkins, with thanks for their perusal.—On reflection I do not care a great deal about getting *possession* of the Michie manuscript—at least, not enough to have you put yourself to any particular trouble, on my behalf, on the subject. I do, however, think it very desirable to get a general knowledge of the *nature* of its contents, & who and what the author of it was, & what was his quarrel with Mr. Jefferson.—

On the whole you are probably right about the expediency of my coming to Phila.—I must rouse myself & take off this morbid disinclination to move. I sit here musing & writing—not stirring—& taking on a *load* of unhealthy flesh.—Dr. D. writes me that it is very doubtful whether he gets away from Phila. by the first of April; but I must come before that for the purpose of making your acquaintance. Unless something unforeseen prevents, I will start for there about the 17th inst.

Are you "posted up" enough in regard to Phila. to tell me where I can find a quiet hotel convenient to Dr. D. I know about as much of Philadelphia (as is generally the Case with New Yorkers) as I do of Pekin. The last time I stopped there I stopped at a very quiet House, kept by Glass or Grasse I think.[41] It was a plain house, but a fashionable one I suppose in the City of Brotherly love, for Mr. Dickinson[42] took me there & he said it was the house Mr. Webster &c. stopped at. I prefer such a place to either a private boarding house, or a great babel like the N. Y. St. Nicholas. If you cannot answer my enquiries without the trouble of an enquiry, drop this paragraph.

I have received your Discourse before the Va. Hist. Socy.[43] I perused it with deep interest. It contains a good many things which I want to converse with you about, but I will leave them until we meet.—Your discourse must have created a good deal of sensation in Va. bringing their ancestors So vividly before them.—I *may* have one or two small

[41] Possibly Graff or Graaf, keeper of a lodging house in Philadelphia where Jefferson resided on occasion and where he drafted the Declaration of Independence. Malone, *Jefferson the Virginian*, p. 216.

[42] Daniel Stevens Dickinson (1800–1866), friend of Randall, a Democrat, United States Senator from New York, active in securing the Compromise of 1850, held the North responsible for secession and worked for a compromise until the attack on Fort Sumter.

[43] Grigsby, *The Virginia Convention of 1776.*

bones to pick with you about it! Nous ouvrons, as Mr. Ritchie[44] used to say!*—

I write you worried & wearied because it suddenly occurred to me I was keeping Mr. Watkins letters altogether too long.

I am, dear Sir, very truly,
Henry S. Randall

H. G. Grigsby, Esq.

* I shall read it again before I visit Phila. & then I shall be all "charged & primed."

[Endorsed by Grigsby]
Henry S. Randall
March 3, 1856
(Cortland Village)

[Grigsby to Randall, March 9, 1856]

Philadelphia, March 9, 1856

Dear Sir,

Your letter of the third was received yesterday. I am gratified that you contemplate an early visit to this city. "The St. Lawrence Hotel" is the very house for you. It is new, quiet, elegant, and distant fifty yards from my residence and one hundred and fifty from Dr. Dunglison's. It is on Chestnut between 10th and 11th.

I am pleased that you have looked over the discourse on the Convention of 1776 not without interest. It certainly did produce something like a sensation. When the scantiness of my materials is considered, and the fact that no successor of the body existed, and that other fact that even the names of many of the leading men had been forgotten, I think the candid reader will give me some credit for my trouble.[45]

As I wrote you a few days ago, I have only in view the telling you of a good public house in writing this note.

Respectfully
Yours,
Hugh B. Grigsby
"at Mrs. Allen's, 309 Chestnut"

Henry S. Randall, Esq.
Cortland Village
New York
[not endorsed]

[44] Thomas Ritchie (1778–1854), Virginia educator, journalist, and politician, editor of the Richmond *Enquirer* (1804–1854) and member of the Richmond "Junta."

[45] Grigsby, *The Virginia Convention of 1776*, p. 194.

[Randall to Grigsby, March 20, 1856]

Cortland Village: N. Y.
March 20, 1856.

My dear Mr. Grigsby,

On Monday next if health permits & as the Connecticut folks say "the Lord is willing," I shall start for Phila. Tuesday (railroad & ferry disasters excepted) I hope to reach the City of Brotherly love,—& I devoutly hope you will not be off before that time.—I should have been there this week, but I had a wicked attack of old fashioned Cholic—which made me sing all sorts of unpleasant melody for 24 hours. How I *did* ache? Now, for conscience sake, don't get your eye fixed to meet an *interesting* looking *invalid!* I am as stout & *poddy* as Mr. Jehosaphat.

"There was a King Sennacherib
Who said that he could crack a rib
Of any but Jehosaphat
He couldn't his, he was so fat!"

I jumped on a pair of *pork* scales last week, & *they said* I made 204½ lbs weight kick the beam! A confounded pretty fellow that to talk of being ill!

I used to be a broth of a boy for High Jinks, but I'm the dullest fellow now you ever met! They say (the ladies say) that I am the dullest man in this town but one—& *he* sleeps in his chair *all* day long. A flash of the old merriment sometimes sweeps across me *on paper;* & should I chance to thoroughly *cotton* to you & the Dr., & the old Govr. &c. why, I shall wake up in part.—Heigho! Heigho!—

May your shadow never be less,

Truly Yours
Henry S. Randall

Hugh Blair Grigsby, Esquire
[Endorsed by Grigsby]
March 20, 1856

[Randall to Grigsby, March, 1856]

Saturday Morning

My dear Mr. Grigsby

I breakfast this morning with Govr. Coles. I have his pictures to look at, & having made memoranda for that purpose I intend to draw him out very fully—i.e. his recollections of Jefferson.[46] Should he appear to

[46] Randall used Cole's recollections for John Adams' high opinion of Jefferson. Randall, *Life,* III, 366, 639–640.

have nothing to do, & to be in the humor, I may talk with him until after the period we talked of going to the Phil. Soc. rooms together, in which case I presume it will be no disappointment to you.

I learned you caught a fall. I trust you were not injured. Cordial salutations.

Yours truly
Henry S. Randall

[Endorsed by Grigsby]
Henry S. Randall
March, 1856
Note

[Randall to Grigsby, April, 1856]

My dear Mr. Grigsby

You voluntarily & deliberately offered to be a "Slave of the lamp," as long as I staid in Philadelphia. *Didn't* you? Well, now resolve me of a difficulty. Yesterday you told me that Professor Tucker (no, today) told you that he had been to my hotel to call on me & that he should invite me to dine with him tomorrow—to meet Dr. Dunglison, yourself, etc. I found his card, & by & by a letter came from him. I opened it & there was a folded billet-sheet & *not one word of any kind* written on it! There it opened in its virgin purity! Not a word! Not a mark! Not a Speck! All white—all virgin white! I trust, my dear Mr. Grigsby, you catch my meaning. I mean to be understood that there was not a ——— of a word on that *white* sheet!

The superscription on the envelope was in Professor George Tucker's (late professor of morality in the Va. University) hand writing. But further that deponent said not. I hope, dear Grigsby, you, as Mr. Weller[47] would say, *twig* me,—that is to say, that you clearly embrace the idea.—I will take that for granted & proceed.

I was tremendously mystified at the reception of such a billet—or rather such a capital piece of paper to convert into a billet. Seeing nothing, I set my ingenuity to work. I divided the paper first into three & then into nine imaginary sections.

—Thrice the brindled cat hath mewed—& examined each one separately. Not an ink mark did I discover! Grigsby, weren't such things profane, I would *Swear* to you that I hunted over that paper *diligently,*

[47] Samuel Weller, a character in Charles Dickens, *Pickwick Papers.*

& found nothing! Suddenly a panic seized me. There might be witchcraft in that mysterious piece of white paper. Didn't the Professor come from the vexed Rev. Moothes? I thought of dire transformations. I expected I would suddenly turn into a bottle-imp. Then it occurred to me how I would look as a plethoric rat, with a wiry, Scotch terrier hard after him, his clear sharp yell of fury mingling with the cadence of the Bermudan Enchantors Sharp humorous laugh.—

Finally, getting over my agitation & fright, it occurred to me that there might not be any diabelrie about it after all—but that the Professor might have tucked the wrong piece of paper into the envelope, as I did once when I sent a description of a turnip crop to the President of a College & claimed *a premium;* & by some fatality, the same day, I sent a learned discourse to a fat old farmer, the Prest. of an agricultural Society, & asked him how it cöincided with his notions? (The fat old J—k—ss informed me that he had *no notions* on the Subject!)

Nextly—admitting this solution, it struck me that it would be an exquisite piece of tom-foolery to let an accident of this kind interrupt an arrangement made, I take it, with some reference to myself. And yet it would be crowding the mourners *a little* to formally *accept* an invitation *never made!!!*—Hang me, if I should know how to word it, unless I should begin with the old saying "blessed be nothing, &c" If I knew T. well enough, I would write him a quizzing letter acknowleding the receipt of his very *laconic* billet-doux. He *curtailed* it as short, & shorter, than the butcher cut off the Frenchman's *curs-tail*—just back of the ears! (Quere? Grigsby is *that* the etymology of cur-tail—the habit of docking so very short the caudal appendage of base blooded canine quadrupeds? What's your "theory" on that subject?) I rub the lamp. I command you to put things "rectus in tuckerdumia!"

Yours in a quandary
Henry Stephens Randall
quite late Thursday night

Hugh Blair Grigsby, L.L.D.
&c&c&c&c
&c&c&c
[Endorsed by Grigsby]
Henry S. Randall
Phil. April–1856

[Randall to Grigsby, April, 1856]

Monday 9. P.M.

My dear Sir,

I have waited to show you the papers till now, but I presume you have been engaged—I have to spend the remainder of the evening at Mr. Trists.[48]

I hope, Sir, we shall meet hereafter. It would be a painful thought to me to think otherwise. Write me before long & tell me how you get along with your lameness & how you are in all particulars—mind and body!

Cordially & truly Yours
Henry S. Randall

H. B. Grigsby E.
[Endorsed by Grigsby]
Henry S. Randall
Philadelphia April–1856
(parting note)

[Randall to Grigsby, May 2, 1856]

Cortland Village, N. Y.

May 2d, 1856.

My dear Sir.

How fare you? Have you recovered of your lameness? Are your wife & little one doing well? Are you in Phila. or Norfolk? (I will enclose this to Dr. Dunglison to make sure of hitting you.) Are you rejoicing in the opening Spring?—feeling like a lark?

Oh, my friend, I have *paid,* if not *dearly,* yet *paid* for my flow of health & spirits in Phila—drawn out by the noble genial men I met there. Dr. Dunglison, Mr. Gilpin,[49] yourself, Judge Woodward,[50] good old Govr. Coles, &c. &c.—How I wish I could colonise some fine Poly-

[48] Nicholas P. Trist's recollections of Jefferson's death appear in Randall, *Life,* III, 546–547.

[49] Henry Dilworth Gilpin (1801–1860), attorney general under Van Buren (1840–1844), a Philadelphia lawyer, author, and editor. Also a prominent member of the Pennsylvania Historical Society, which inherited his fine library, and a trustee of the University of Pennsylvania. He published a second edition of John Sanderson, *Biography of the Signers of the Declaration of Independence* (Philadelphia, 1829) which contains Gilpin's sketch of Thomas Jefferson. *The Papers of James Madison* (3 vols.; Washington, 1840), and *Opinions of the Attorneys General of the United States* (Washington, 1841) appeared under his editorship.

[50] George Washington Woodward (1809–1875), superior court judge in Pennsylvania (1852–1867), mentioned with other Philadelphians in Randall's "Preface."

nesian isle with the persons of my choice (ladies *of course* included) carry there the Bodleian, Rome, the Florentine gallery (& a few tough old *Anglo-Saxons* to keep my friend G —— s —— by good natured)[51] & wouldn't we have a perpetual time of it?

But Heigho! Castles in Spain rise but dim & unbrilliant before a sick mans fancy! I'm just out of bed—dressed the first time for a week. I have been drenched like a horse—calomel, opium & the lord knows what all—pronounced severely ill—& partly convinced of it by intolerable pain. But the Dr. thinks it, I believe, a sort of clearing up shower, & that I am to be better according to the goodby promise held forth at Phila.

Grigsby, come now & go to work like a good Samaritan. Write me an everlasting long letter, cheerful. I had like to have said as the song of a bird, but what's a birds song to charm away pain & weariness? During my illness there never has been a moment except the few central hours of the night when the song of innumerable birds has not been in my ear. And at matins & vespers tens of thousands join in the concert.

Yours cordially

Henry S. Randall

H. B. Grigsby, Esquire

[Endorsed by Grigsby]
H. S. Randall
Cortland, N. Y.
May 2, 1856
Re'd May 8, 1856

[Grigsby to Randall, May 12, 1856]

Edgehill, May 12, 1856

Dear Sir,

Your kind note addressed to Philadelphia and forwarded to Norfolk reached me at the latter place a day or two before my departure for Charlotte on a hurried visit; and here from my country home I respond

[51] Grigsby in his *Virginia Convention of 1776*, pp. 38–45, takes the view, widely held by the Cromwellians in England, that the virtues of the British came from the Anglo-Saxon heritage which the Parliamentarians were restoring against usurpation by the Normans. He includes the Scotch-Irish as "'coming, of course, from the great Anglo-Saxon stock. . . . It was the spirit of Anglo-Saxon liberty, inculcated for generations by the peculiar circumstances of the Colony in their race, that made the names of Washington, George Mason and the Lees a bulwark in the cause of independence." For a more extensive statement of Grigsby's ideas on the development of free institutions in Virginia, see Grigsby to Thomas Ritchie, Norfolk, Virginia, March 14, 1854, in *The John P. Branch Papers of Randolph-Macon College*, IV (1915), 415–418.

to your kind greetings. Like yourself I have been indisposed; that is, within the last four days I have been confined by a slight fever to the house, but I was out today in our genial atmosphere and in our magnificent woods.

Our trip to Norfolk was safe and pleasant to Mrs. G. and her infant; though since then the boy has suffered from a dreadful breaking out supposed to have originated from vaccination. When I left home some days ago, he was doing well.

I trust you have recovered from your attack, and that you are prosecuting your great work with becoming energy. Truly do I wish that we could carry with us the delightful society of Philadelphia. Yet all great works must be wrought out in solitude. Mix with the bustling crowd occasionally, but when we are to fix the outlines of a literary work, country or a retired home is the place. Should all things turn out well, I've next to write my history of the Va. Convention of 1788 this summer, and when away from my library.[52] I am daily expecting to hear that the first pages of Jefferson's Life have been put to the press. When I was in Philadelphia, Mr. Hazard,[53] the publisher and bookseller, said that he would like to publish it, and requested me to mention the fact to you; but I told him that your intimate acquaintance with men and things in New York would probably induce you to select your office of publication in that city.

One word about your health. You have probably heard that dead men tell no tales; I may add, nor do they write books. Now to be able to write books, they must be active and vigorous certainly in mind, and, to a certain extent, in body. Hence the body must be cared for. You have a colossal constitution. Wounded as you now are, you are capable of more labor in a single day than I ever could accomplish in my prime in six; and all that is necessary in your case is care. Bathe every morning with a free use of coarse towels. Keep the chest erect under all circumstances. In your diet follow the excellent rules laid down by Mr Jefferson, especially as relates to animal food, using it rather as a condiment than as a substantial article of food.[54]

Now that we are in our respective homes, and as neither of us is a traveller by choice, may we not felicitate ourselves that it was our

[52] Grigsby, *The History of the Virginia Federal Convention of 1788.* This work was not published until ten years after Grigsby's death by the Virginia Historical Society.

[53] Samuel Hazard (1784–1870), ed., *Pennsylvania Archives* (12 vols.; Philadelphia, 1852–1856).

[54] Jefferson's letter to Doctor Vine Utley, March 21, 1819, contains his health rules. Randall, *Life,* III, 450–451.

fortune to meet and know one another? How much more satisfactory will be our future correspondence? Had you not known me, you might have regarded my recommendation to you to wash every day as a reflection on your habits of personal cleanliness; but when you know my Anglo-Saxon tendencies, and remember that an Anglo-Saxon never took a bath unless when caught in the rain, or when he was driven through a river by a Norman, you see at once how the case stands.

Whenever I can in any way subserve your historical purposes, I need not, I hope, say to you how cheerfully I am at your service.

In the meantime I am very truly

Yours,

Hugh B. Grigsby

Henry S. Randall Esq.
Cortland Village
N. Y.

P. S. My sprain still continues and is at times as bad as ever—but I think the summer will finish it.
[not endorsed]

[Randall to Grigsby, May 25, 1856]

Cortland Village: New York
May 25th, 1856

My dear Sir,

I am glad to hear that your family are so safely restored to your country home. But it is very annoying that your lameness should hold on to you so pertinaciously. I did not dream of such a thing. How our comfort, our health, & sometimes our success or our failure turn on the blowing off of a hat! What have you named the little boy? Is it Cedric, or Ethelwulf, or Ivanhoe, or Thor, or Balder? By the way, I never asked you—is this your only Son? Pray tell me how many shoots have sprung up round you. I have four. I married very young, & I was 45 years old the 3d day of this month. My oldest Son is nearly 21—my Second a Son & my third a daughter follow at about 2 years intervals, & the fourth a daughter after twice that interval, one having been lost out of the string by death. My oldest son is as tall as I am—my youngest only a hair behind.—So you see I feel *patriarchal* when I count up my flock!—My sons neither of them incline to follow the life of Scholars. It is perhaps fortunate, for stripped of my earlier expectations, they must carve out their own fortunes. They have already begun this, & are widely Separated from me, one in New York & one in Buffalo.[55] I am situated like a thousand Virginians, except that I do not, as too many of them are said to, surrender to supineness & despair.—But it is a dreary thought to think these old ties, that Stately family pile, must in a few years go into the hands of Strangers—I hope, my friend, you have been a fortunate business man, & that *this ghost* does not haunt your waking or sleeping hours.—

I am well again, though the boyish elasticity of my spirits at Philadelphia has subsided. I am making a Stout effort not to fall clean back into the old rut again. A resolution that rarely flinches in contending with the stern outward pressure. Nous ouvrons. My joy, my Solace, my antedote to thick coming fancies, is *work*. And I love it for its own sake.—

You say truly that Solitude is the place for the minds labors. There it leans on itself. Its individuality is not rounded off by the contact of other minds. But you want books of reference. You want one or two trusted & appreciated friends. Occasionally the boldest confidence shrinks!—occasionally the best balanced mind gets so warmed with its Subject that it grows controversial in manner & partial in matter.—You want a clear headed friend who has intelligence, taste, candor, judgment, in short, whom you can rely upon, to encourage you when you falter, to pull you back where you are going wrong. If he had a crochet, a "theory" or two, (Anglo-Saxon or other,) which you can suck diversion out of, all the better, provided you feel that you can rely on him in the Serious!

Since I am on my feet again, I am going like a ship before the wind with my biography. I think I had brought it down about to 1815 or 1816 when I went to Phila. I am now in 1822. I think eight days will suffice for the four remaining years—ten certainly will.—Then I have got a tough chapter before me on the subject of Mr. J's *religious* beliefs. I have preferred for several reasons to handle this topic by itself. I mean to do it discreetly but manfully. I shall tell what Mr. J. *did* believe, & let others draw the inferences.—[56]

By the by, do you know where in John Quincy Adams writings he espouses the idea that there was at any time (after the Revolution) a

[55] Randall's five children were: (1) Roswell Stephens Randall, born in 1834; (2) Henry Polhemus Randall (1836–1872); (3) Jane Polhemus Randall, born in 1837; (4) Francis Rotch Randall (1842–1844); (5) Harriet Stephens Randall, born in 1845. [Paul K. Randall], *Genealogy of a Branch of the Randall Family 1666 to 1879*, p. 61.

[56] Jefferson's religious beliefs are given in Randall, *Life*, III, 553–567.

monarchical party in the United States? Do you know of any such expressions on the part of his father John Adams?—[57]

I am trying your suggestion about eating meat. I eat it now but once a day, & rather sparingly. I shall be able to report progress on this regimen when I write you again.—

I have carefully read your description of Mr J.[58] It is done with *great* discrimination & ability; though in *features,* of course (as no two pair of eyes will see any man or thing just alike) your ideal of him differs from mine—

I have found one fine chance to quote your work in mine—I shall find more I doubt not as I review—What was that coincidence about the age of one of the Mecklenburg witnesses you mentioned to me?[59] This was new to me & of course I shall give you the credit.

Sincerely yours,
Henry S. Randall.

H. B. Grigsby E.
[Endorsed by Grigsby]
Henry S. Randall Esq.
Cortland Village N. Y. May 25, 1856
Answered June 11, 1856

[Grigsby to Randall, June 11, 1856]

Norfolk, June 11, 1856.

My dear sir,

Your letter of the 25th reached me today, having been forwarded from Charlotte C. H. When I wrote you, I was merely on a visit to my plantation, my family having been left in Norfolk. My little boy is named Hugh Carrington Grigsby, thus bearing his mother's and father's names. He is my only child, and the only one I ever had, and born fifteen years after my marriage. He was vaccinated in Philadelphia, and with that disease, or from the milk of his Irish nurse, he took a complaint which has made the little fellow a martyr to intense pain nearly ever since. The disease is a scablike breaking out over his entire body. I wish

[57] John Quincy Adams in a review of *The Works of Fisher Ames. Compiled by a Number of his Friends* ... (Boston, 1809), charged that the ultra Federalist leaders of New England were a monarchical party merely waiting for a favorable time to declare themselves. He cites evidence that the first seven presidents were all convinced that such a party existed. See Randall, *Life,* I, 589–593.

[58] Grigsby's sketch of Jefferson in *The Virginia Convention of 1776,* pp. 168–188.

[59] See Grigsby to Randall, June 11, 1856.

I had your number of children and in their advanced condition. As I was born during Mr. Jefferson's administration (1806), I have nearly reached my half century, and will have reached the three score years and ten of the Psalmist ere my boy will attain his legal age. You in the vigor of manhood have your children nearly grown and likely to sustain and comfort you for years before you own decline shall take place. Thus are you more fortunate than I have been; and when a moody fit comes upon you, do you cheer up under the fullness of the blessings which Providence has allotted you.

It is a superficial view of human affairs that saddens us in the prospect of a separation from our children. It is for their good and for our good that such a separation should occur. Among the many *private* considerations that follow from such a course is the greater certainty of the perpetuation of our race, which degenerates and becomes extinct when confined to a specific locality for ages; and in a public view it tends to strengthen the ties of country and the perpetuity of the Union—a political blessing beyond all others as all reflecting men must consider it at that solemn moment when they are about to commit their offspring to the future.

I have never been in a strict sense a business man, having only edited a paper for six years, a commercial paper in Norfolk; but derived from my labors during that interval a competent fortune.[60] My wife has a fine estate and plenty of hands to work it; but tobacco estates are rarely profitable to those who are unable to reside upon them. This estate is large, and will be inherited by her son, should he survive the mother; if not, the estate reverts to my wife's relations in pursuance of the will of her father. Should our son survive to one & twenty, he will be rich in lands and negroes on his mother's side alone, to say nothing of my property.

I have thus answered your kind enquiries. I ought to say that I began life, at one and twenty, as a politician with every prospect of success, but my deafness induced me to withdraw from public employments. From what has since transpired, I have every reason to believe that I would have attained all that I desired; but I do not regret that I was so early withdrawn from the turmoil of a public career.

I cannot recall the particulars about John Quincy Adams's declaration about a monarchical party with any minuteness; but I remember something of the kind. You must write to Boston where authentic information can be readily obtained.

---

[60] Owner and editor of the Norfolk *American Beacon* (1834–1840). Lester J. Cappon, *Virginia Newspapers, 1821–1935* (New York, 1936), p. 134.

I approve your design of confining the religious character of Mr. J. to a single chapter, and of making him speak for himself. You could not have adopted a wiser course. If your last chapter shall contain a summary of his character, it must be written with great care *politically* and in a literary view. Nor must you be content with your own supervision. You must consult friends not so much politically as *critically*. Be sure and let Dr. Dunglison see it, and let it receive his critical emendations. To draw such a character in its due proportions is one of the most difficult achievements in literature.

On the subject of the Mecklenburg Declaration, if its falsity can be demonstrated fairly and conclusively, a great point is gained in favor of Mr. Jefferson. That [it] is a forgery I have not the slightest doubt. I don't think that my argument, which seeks to demonstrate its falsity by showing that the same men, who are supposed to have made the declaration of independence on the *twentieth* of May, did ten days after adopt a series of resolutions which distinctly and unequivocally acknowledge the right of eminent domain in the British Crown, has made the impression upon you which its importance demands. It is conclusive and overwhelming; for it reduces the friends of the Mecklenburg Declaration to this dilemma, either horn of which is fatal to them, viz: Either the declaration was *not* made at the time and under the circumstances stated, or it was so made. If it was *not* so made, it is worthless and a forgery; but if it was made, then was it recanted by the men who made it ten days after it was made, and it is therefore without value in a court of honor. But, as the men who adopted the resolutions of the *thirtieth* were perfectly acquainted with progress of the controversy from the beginning, it is impossible that they could have been guilty of such an inconsistency.

The answer to the question about the *age* of one of the deponents in favor of the Mecklenburg declaration requires a cursory review of the depositions taken in the case. There are fourteen witnesses in all. Of these *seven* testify that the Mecklenburg meeting was held "in the month of May, 1775," "towards the end of May," and one of them that "it was certainly *before* the fourth of July 1776." The testimony of these *Seven* are more in favor of the last of May, the *thirtieth*—than the *19th or 20th,* which was but four or five days beyond the middle of the month.

The remaining *Seven* declare as follows: Four of the Seven, George Graham, William Hutchinson, James Clark, and Robert Robinson, unite in a single deposition. This deposition was evidently drawn at a time when it became important to discriminate between the twentieth and the thirtieth of May, and was penned by some individual who was determined to group all that was known on the subject—and a good deal more—in a single deposition.

Now a joint deposition containing a variety of details is usually a suspicious thing; but when it contains not only many minute details, but those details of the remote date of near half a century gone, and which were passed over by or unknown to the other deponents who are said to have been active participants in the scene, it is well calculated to awaken distrust. This consideration led me to examine as minutely as I could the history of the document, and I think you will agree with me that a simple statement of its pretensions is fatal to its worth. It is the joint deposition of four persons who depose with the freshness of yesterday and with minute particulars concerning incidents which occurred more than forty years before, and who were, according to the statement of their ages added to their names by themselves, two of them but boys of *fifteen* at the time, and two of them but *twenty two*—their ages averaging eighteen; and who address their statement to Col. Polk, who was a son of the Col. Polk who is said to have read the Declaration from the Court House steps, who might be supposed to have heard the details of the scene again and again from his father's lips, but who, tho' a boy of eighteen at the time of the Declaration and present at the Meeting as alledged, and now very anxious to get the deposition of others, does not venture to give to the public any deposition of his own! When it is farther added that many of the facts stated in this deposition were unknown to the earlier deponents who were active persons on the occasion, and some of them, such as the description of a regular signing match in evident imitation of scene attendant upon declaration of the fourth of July 1776, and so unusual at public meetings, we may very reasonably conclude that the document is not worth the paper on which it is written.

The deposition of Humphrey Hunter, another of the seven, written after it became important to get additional testimony, with a vew of identifying the *twentieth* of May, takes for granted that the *twentieth* of May was the date of the meeting. In order to confirm the exact date of the meeting, however, he tells us: "On that memorable day I was twenty years and fourteen days of age." Now in a note accompanying the deposition the exact date of the birth of Mr Hunter is given: viz. "that fourteenth day of May, 1755,"—a date that may be said to settle conclusively the question: for if we make the calculation it will appear that on the nineteenth of May (the meeting holding over to the twentieth) instead of being "twenty years and fourteen days old," he was only twenty years and *five* days old, a mistake of nine days in fourteen, but when we look to the *thirtieth* of May the "twenty years and fourteen days" are within *two* days of that date,—a mistake he might readily make if he trusted to memory alone, which it is evident from the face of the mistake he did. Mr. Hunter then is an unconscious and on that account not the less valuable witness in favor of the thirtieth of May. The depositions of the sixth and seventh witnesses, written like the preceding, after the interest in behalf of the *twentieth* of May was evinced, I cannot examine in detail, and will merely add that they evidently take date as something not called in question and strive to call up other topics.

What strikes us forcibly in examining these depositions is the manifest caution of the deponents who were the reputed responsible actors in the scene, when contrasted with the full, elaborate, and graphic descriptions of those witnesses who were either children at the time, or too young to have taken any part on such an occasion.

On the whole subject my conclusion may be something like this: That it is not impossible that the officers present at Charlotte on the twentieth of May might have met and called a general meeting for the thirtieth; that the meeting of the twentieth, if held at all, was private and informal; and that on the thirtieth of May *the* meeting was held (such as is described by the deponents as the meeting of the twentieth) when the resolutions which were published at the time far and wide were adopted. The fact that some of the deponents affirm that numerous bye-laws were adopted on the twentieth, when according to the supposed true account of the meeting of that date no voluminous byelaws were adopted, or, if adopted, were ever heard of, shows that it was the *thirtieth* (and not the twentieth) when a long series of bye laws in the shape of resolutions was adopted.

You will find the depositions in the American Archives, Fourth Series, Vol. II.[61]

I rejoice that your work begins "to appropinque an end;" for I am most anxious to see it. It will be most grateful to me to appear in your pages, and if I thought that in any respect I have contributed to extend the fame of Jefferson, I would desire no other reward for my historical labors.

---

[61] Force, *American Archives*, 4th series, II, 855, contains "The Declaration of Independence by the Citizens of Mecklenburg County of North-Carolina on the Twentieth Day of May, 1775, with the Accompanying Documents, Published by the Governor." Force (1790–1868), is credited with discovering that there was something wrong with the May 20 version.

My lameness begins to show signs of relenting; but I am yet unable to place my foot securely in descending a step;—the left foot always takes the lead. It is only within the last six days that I have ventured without a cane, and now every morning and night I pour cold water from a height upon my ancle. The shin bone was evidently scaled. I fear a year or more must elapse before I can use my foot freely.

I have thus written you a long letter. Mr. Tucker will publish his first volume in July.[62] Of our excellent friend Dr. Dunglison I have not heard directly since I left the quaker city. I never think of his goodness and his rich stores of learning without regretting my destinies have removed me so far from him. Until the fourth of July I shall remain in Norfolk; after that address me at "Charlotte C. H. Va."

With cordial salutations, I am

Yours

Hugh B. Grigsby

Mr. Randall:
Cortland Village
New York

P. S. Excuse any errors in this letter, as I have not been able to read it over before closing.

Your fine folios of Documentary History of New York are in my cases directly in front of me as I write this sheet.

[Randall to Grigsby, June 18, 1856]

Cortland Village June 18, '56

My dear Sir,

I have read yours with great interest, & am most gratified to learn that, in most particulars, your lives have fallen in so pleasant places.— All you seem to lack is that number of Children which is sufficient to give strong reasonable prospect of succession;—& more would be desirable to you in the way of company, particularly daughters. A boy is company for his mother,—but you cannot, not having experienced it, know how much daughters can fill up of a fathers heart & time. Sidney Smith wished his daughter had been born with but one eye & that in the middle of her forehead so that nobody could marry her away from

[62] Tucker, *The History of the United States.*

him![63] One of my neighbors lived as long as you, without children. After the first, he had four or five born along at the usual intervals—& has now a grown up family while he is still enjoying a fresh & green old age. I trust this may happen in your case. So far as having Children is concerned it, I should say, would be a more probable result than the contrary.—

You entirely mistake, my dear Sir, about my underrating any part of the Mecklenburg argument. I have taken substantially the *same* ground with yourself; &, I think, carried out the arguments still more in extenso. I spent a great deal of time on it—*tried* not to leave a nail undriven—& I do not recollect a point of yours which I do not make, excepting the one in regard to the man's age.—Don't you remember in one of my first letters to you I accused you of *using up* my thunder in advance?[64] There may *possibly* be points where you have gone further than myself for having tied up & put away my deputation on the topic (for an Appendix Article)[65] I never have looked at since reading yours or since you first wrote me; but I feel very confident that such is not the fact.—Perhaps I have discussed the matter less with you for that very reason. And I confess to another mental habit which *always* belonged to me.—I have seen few men who entered an investigation with such zeal as myself. I find myself often (unnecessarily) tracking a fact which I might as well, or about as well, omit, through twenty octavo volumes. I think I have blood hound staunchness in *running down* game. To write a half a dozen letters to settle a date, is nothing for me.—I will wager that for every page I have written of Jefferson I have Consulted *ten* authorities. But the moment the hunt is *up*—the moment I have passed over, &, as far as practicable, *exhausted* my topic, then I have not a particle of interest more in discussing it, or even in mentioning it. And, moreover, I never was fond of colloquial or epistolary disquisition.—When I work, I work so fiercely that talking & letter writing is only a rest—an amusement—an unbending to me. I rarely write a letter, at home, except after a hard days work of ten steady hours at least.

For example, I worked *eight* hours today on Jefferson. Since then I have written say 25 pages of letters, half of them of the size of these, before taking this up. On casting my eye on my letter book, I see that I have written *seven* letters—& you may guess the subject in part by the

[63] Sydney Smith (1771–1845), English divine, essayist, and humorist. Contributor to the *Edinburgh Review* and a bitter critic of the United States.

[64] See above, Randall to Grigsby, February 7, 1856.

[65] Randall, *Life*, III, Appendix II, pp. 570–582, deals with the Mecklenburg Declaration.

names & the list of occupations—Richd. Randolph of Washington;[66] Hon. Wm. H. Shankland of our Sup. Court:[67] Gen O. F. Marshall, one of our most eminent farmers; Amos Dean, Professor of law &c;[68] Governor Coles; Hon. W. L. Marcy;[69] & a Mr. Marshall of Va. about sheep!—When I was Sec'y of State, I have written 60, 70, & even 100 letters in a day. The *two* swiftest clerks in my department could not *copy* letters as fast as I could write them.—

You see then, that I do not, I cannot make *work* of letters. In fact I have no taste for it. Let this, my dear Sir, be a solution to you *of many things.*

Now I want your opinion on a very important question—& one which you from your locality, ought to be well qualified to judge *at least one side of.* It is how am I to handle the *Slavery* question?—There is an intense sensibility in the public mind in regard to it—Both *extremes* have (meo arbitrio) swung away from the moorings of common sense, and certainly of common coolness, and discretion in their way of talking on the Subject.—It would be the easiest thing in the world for me to put myself under the ban of one Extreme or the other—or even of both;—& the last is, with my present ideas of what is proper in the Case, perhaps the most *probable result.* In my own views & feelings I am decidedly *national,* i.e. opposed to sectionality. I stand (though I once thought differently on one of the questions) on the Cincinnati Platform, & shall cordially support its nominees.[70]—I want to take a fair, manly course in my book, neither quixotic nor cowardly. I would

[66] A document copied by "Mr. Richard Randolph, of Washington (of the Tuckahoe family of Randolphs)" is mentioned in Randall, *Life,* I, 131, n. 1. Bishop William Meade, *Old Churches, Ministers and Families of Virginia* (2 vols.; Philadelphia, 1857), I, 110, speaks of a visit to Jamestown with a group including Richard Randolph: "Mr. Randolph, our Virginia antiquary, was also quite at home as to all that belonged to the scene." A "Letter from Richard Randolph to Hugh Blair Grigsby, February 12, 1856," *William and Mary Quarterly,* 2d series, III (1923), 155–156, makes some corrections of Grigsby's *The Virginia Convention of 1776* and speaks of Randolph's memories of associations with prominent men of the revolutionary era in both Virginia and Massachusetts.

[67] William Henry Shankland (1804–1883), Cortland lawyer, district attorney (1832–1842), justice of State Supreme Court (1847–1849), formed part of Court of Appeals bench. H. P. Smith, ed., *History of Cortland County* (Syracuse, 1885), pp. 140–141.

[68] Amos Dean (1803–1868), professor of medical jurisprudence at Albany Medical College (1838–*ca.* 1858), later chancellor of the University of Iowa.

[69] William L. Marcy (1786–1857), United States Senator, Governor of New York (1833–1839), United States Secretary of War (1845–1849), United States Secretary of State (1853–1857).

[70] Randall here endorses popular sovereignty as the solution of the slavery question in the territories. For a discussion of this convention and its platform, see Allan Nevins, *Ordeal of the Union* (2 vols.; New York, 1947), II, 456–459. The nominees were James Buchanan and John C. Breckinridge.

neither crouch to, nor unnecessarily defy, either extreme. On the other hand after spending years of labor on my work, I don't want to sit between two stools & strike the ground, if I can *decently* help it!

I had thought of this course:

1. To give Mr. Jeffersons *views in his own words.* I would not propose to give *all* his expressions—for that would give particular prominence to this topic & I desire it to occupy just its proportionate share & no more.—

2. To give a just expression of his views, it would be necessary to give some of those passages from his Notes on Va.[71] & his correspondence where his denunciations of Slavery are Strongest & most vehement. And you remember his language on some occasions is *very Severe.* Govr. Coles gave me a copy of Mr. J's *very strong* letter to him on the subject.[72] This *ought seemingly,* to go in, because it shows that his *later* corresponded with his *earlier* enmity to slavery.— Suppose then a half a dozen quotation to be given from him of these kinds.

3. To give *all* his expressions (they being brief) where he so bitterly denounces the *Missouri Compromise*—and the motion of the northern agitators—and where he asserts the danger & impropriety of such agitation—and his deep hostility to sectionalism in any shape.[73]

4. To connectedly sum up, or give the heads of Mr. Jefferson's opinions, showing—

   1. His deep individual hostility to slavery & desire for its abolition.
   2. That he was only for gradual abolition accompanied by deportation.
   3. That he thought no one had the right of taking Slaves from their masters without paying for them.
   4. That he believed the extension of the area of Slavery *not objectionable*—that it would lead rather to its extinction than its increase.
   5. That he was fully opposed to geographical lines for slavery, or to the excitement to prevent its extension into new States &c &c.

[71] *Notes on the State of Virginia* (1784), appeared in many editions. Its text may be found in Paul Leicester Ford, ed., *The Writings of Thomas Jefferson* (10 vols.; New York, 1892–1899), III, 68–295.

[72] Jefferson to Edward Coles, Monticello, August 25, 1814, printed in Randall, *Life,* III, Appendix XXVII, pp. 643–645.

[73] For Jefferson's statements on the Missouri Compromise, see Randall, *Life,* III, 434–460.

5. Lastly to express no opinion of my own on the Subject.—

Now the principal fact I want to obtain from you *as a Virginian* is this: would the *Southern people be satisfied with such a handling of the Subject*—or would they take fire & taboo the book because it contained the Coles Letter & some of the *Strong* anti slavery expressions in the Notes on Va?—

I want an *exact chart* of all the locks & quicksands before I put to sea on this question—whether I can hope to avoid all of them or not.— Pray be *very* explicit in your reply.

The course I propose would offend all the northern *fanatics*. They would say I have ruined Jeffrns character as the great Apostle of Anti Slavery*—that I ought not to have put in such a *summing up*. Will it, on the other hand, offend your ultras? Would they demand I tell one side & but one side?—or give the play of Hamlet with Hamlets part left out?—

Pray think maturely on this. Talk (if you feel like so doing) with friends, especially those who are most heated against abolitionism. Then tell your & their views. Give your opinion on the course I propose. Propose, if you feel inclined, some other one to me.[74]

Your friend
Henry S. Randall

Mr Grigsby.
[Endorsed by Grigsby]
H. S. Randall
Cortland Village, N. Y.
July 6, 1856
Ans. Aug. 18, 1856

[Grigsby to Randall, July 11, 1856]

Norfolk, July 11th, 56

Dear Sir,

I would have answered your late letter immediately but for an accident which has befallen the fourth finger of my right hand.

A felon has taken possession of that part of my body & has prevented entirely the use of my right hand. It has given me great pain which is

* My business ought to be tell truth. Mr J. character will take care of itself.—

[74] Jefferson's views on slavery are summarized in Randall, *Life,* III, Appendix XXXIV, 667–669.

now disappearing, & I hope in a week or ten days to be able to use my pen once more—

(The subject to which you allude—the religious opinions of Mr Jefferson—will then receive full attention. In the mean time with kindest regards I remain

Very sincerely Yours
Hugh B. Grigsby

Henry S. Randall Esq.
P. S. (I use the hand of a young friend)

[Grigsby to Randall, August 18, 1856]
My post office until November is now Charlotte C. H. Va.

Charlotte C. H. Va. August 18, 1856.

My dear Sir,

Today for the first time I am able to write for two months with an unbandaged hand, and I proceed at once to reply to your letter of the 18th of June. Three fingers of the right hand have been afflicted with whitlows, and, for the first time in my life, I have been troubled with boils, the *forty second* now ready to burst upon my left temple. But, above my afflictions, I have lost the friend and guide of my youth and maturer years, my stepfather indeed, but the only father I have ever known, my own having died in my third year. Dr N. C. Whitehead (of Norfolk) is his name.[75] He died instantaneously, after chatting pleasantly with his children until within ten minutes of his death, when he passed in an instant and almost with a smile upon his face from his home on earth to his home in heaven. My heart has almost been broken by this blow, for our relations were those rather of intimate and lifelong friends than of mere affinity.

I have, my dear sir, the greatest confidence in your judgment in the handling of any topic which you will undertake to discuss in Mr. Jefferson's history. The five points which you make in your letter show that you fully comprehend the importance of your topic, and that you are fully competent to manage it in a way which, while full justice is done to Mr. Jefferson's views, will not needlessly offend the great body of the

[75] Dr. Nathan Colgate Whitehead (1792–1856) married Grigsby's mother when Hugh Blair was ten years old. John B. Whitehead was an issue of this marriage. Dr. Whitehead, a physician, was president of the Farmers Bank of Virginia in Norfolk for twenty-seven years.

Southern people. Have those five points in mind, and all will be well.

Your capacity for labor exceeds all that I had any idea of before. Eight hours per diem at the desk would kill me in a fortnight. I could argue for that time *viva voce,* and could exert my mind to its utmost, but I could not write at the desk three hours without severe suffering. It is the physical labor of writing, and bending head and body that kills me; for I am compelled to put my face within three or four inches of the paper.

But how comes on the Magnum Opus? Do write me word, and let that word be that it will be put to press on the first day of October next, and that both volumes will appear on the fourth of next March.

I am now reading the first volume of our friend Professor Tucker's history.[76] It stretches from the first settlement of the Colonies to the close of Washington's administration. It must, therefore, be synoptical in a great degree. The style is plain, sometimes exceedingly careless, and even ungrammatical; but I think the work will succeed. He shows no indisposition to grapple with any topic, and is strong when finance and population are concerned. But, perhaps ere this you have read it for yourself.

My family have now been here at my country home several weeks, and the health of my little boy improves daily. I wish you could have seen and known my wife; but this may be yet I hope.

The corn crop is utterly ruined here, or nearly so. By the way, I have been putting up a barn of logs 25 by 30 (and as thick as your body,) all day, and have been in my tobacco fields; and not a line of my speech have I written yet. O! for that constitution of yours, which, though shamefully abused by overwork in past times, still exceeds all that we Southern people can do at our best!

Did I tell you that I received a letter from Mr. Bancroft in which he states that the man who would deny that the Mecklenburg declaration was a forgery, would deny that the sun at midday was shining in the heaven?[77] This is good. Professor Tucker in his history admits that my

[76] Tucker, *The History of the United States.*

[77] George Bancroft (1800–1891), American historian, statesman, and intense Jeffersonian nationalist. His place in American historiography is assessed by John Spencer Bassett, *The Middle Group of American Historians* (New York, 1917), pp. 138–210. Randall in his discussion of the Mecklenburg Declaration states: "We have been favored by Mr. Bancroft with an inspection of the proofsheets of his forthcoming volume of the History of the United States, where allusion is made to the Mecklenburg Declaration of Independence. It is known that he has carefully and specially investigated the subject. He makes no allusion to any other meeting or declaration than that of 31st of May." *Life,* III, 581–582. See Bancroft, *The History of the United States* (6 vols.; New York, 1886), IV, 196–198.

arguments are "facille, and he may say, conclusive,"[78] and your thunder added to that of the duo will certainly kill the joint object of our attacks.

I still write with an unnatural hand, and with a sense of numbness in my fingers.

Do let me know the progress of your work, and believe me

Very truly Yours
Hugh B. Grigsby

To Henry S. Randall Esq.
Cortland Village
N. Y.

P. S. I heard from Gov. Coles on the 8th of July at Saratoga, suffering from diarrhea. I fear much that our venerated friend will hardly survive to have another collogue with us in Philadelphia next winter. When we lose him, we will lose one of the purest men of our times. If you have heard from him since the 8th ult., do let me know. The letter of Mr. Jefferson to Mr. Coles ought certainly to appear in your book, in the Appendix if no where else.[79]

H. B. G.

P. S. My sprained ankle is just getting strong enough to enable me to walk without a cane. I dare not, however, put my right foot foremost in stepping across a gutter or in coming down stairs. But when it particularly incommodes me, I think of our dinner at Professor Tucker's, of Dr. D., of yourself, and of our Philadelphia Jefferson friends,[80] and regard my poor ancle in the light of a gentle remembrancer of pleasing hours with friends whom I love and whom I hope to meet again.

I have perfect confidence in your arguments about the Mecklenburg Declaration. What I was ticklish about was this single argument, which I claimed, as I thought, as my own thunder: that the people of Mecklenburg did not declare independence of the British Crown on the *20th May because* on the *thirtieth,* or ten days after, they distinctly and in express words, acknowledge the right of eminent domain in the British

[78] "While I admit the force, I may almost say, the conclusiveness of Mr. Grigsby's views as to the 'Mecklenburg Declaration of Independence,' I do not agree with him respecting the resolution of North Carolina of twelfth of April, 1776. That resolution, in indicating not only the wish for independence, but the readiness to declare it, went further than any other colony had previously gone. It is true that the Virginia resolution, a month later, in giving positive instructions to its deputies to declare independence, was still greatly in advance of North Carolina; but as the resolution of the latter had the advantage of priority, the merit of first proposing a separation from Great Britain may be regarded as an honor divided between the two States." Tucker, *History,* I, 163–164, n. 3.

[79] See Randall, *Life,* III, Appendix XXVII, pp. 643–645.

[80] Nicholas Trist, Edward Coles, George Woodward, and Henry D. Gilpin joined in Grigsby's and Randall's sessions.

Crown. This argument, with its necessary results, I thought I had alone hit upon.[81]

The volumes of Documentary History of New York, which you gave me, have afforded me great pleasure and instruction, and I never open them without thinking of the source whence I obtained them.

[Randall to Grigsby, November 14, 1856]

Cortland Village, N. Y., Nov. 14, '56

My dear Sir,

Excuse this *big* sheet, taken for the facility of swift writing.—

The election is over & happily over.[82] At one time I was seriously alarmed. I foresaw what was coming in *this State* far better than most of our leading friends. There is a sort of an instinct in me (as in certain *frogs* in regard to *weather!*) which a few weeks before an election, where any great issue is up, tells me with a strange certainty what is to be the result. I make no figures, having nothing to do with past statistics, or present estimates based on tangible & declared data. I open my mouth like a Scotch seer & speak,—& be the presage for weal or woe, I have often been startled at its definite accuracy.—I ran for Secy of State in 1849. We appeared to have carried the State. I was congratulated on my election (The Sec'yship then was not a nominal & clerical office. The Sec'y was ex officio Supt. of Com. Schools with more than a million of dollars to appropriate among schools—& he was the Court of last resort on all school questions appealed to him, with a broad & indefinite margin of power, more resembling a Court martial than a Civil Court)—Well, as I have said, being considered a youngerly man to hold *that* office, I was Congratulated.—But the seer like prescience told me that I, after running a little ahead in a multitude of counties, & losing no where (yet heard from) should be *just beaten* in the Anti-rent district! I wrote a number of letters, giving the majority against me. I came within 500 of it!* When I ran two years after, the general impression was that I was beaten. Condolements came. I then wrote, that I was certainly elected. So it proved. Again I was within a thousand of the figure! This thing has happened over & over again. I count it an instinctive feeling of the prevailing current of—the lord knows what! I dare swear it is as good an *instinct* as that by which Falstaff knew the *true Prince!*—

* When not far from 500,000 votes were given.

[81] Grigsby, *The Virginia Convention of 1776*, p. 27.

[82] Buchanan and Breckinridge were elected.

Two or three weeks before the Pa. *State* election,[83] the Vision was on me in regard to *this* State. I wrote several of the most eminent men of Pa. I wrote our friends in Washington. I wrote our leaders in New York City. I cried woe—woe—woe! I told them *this State* would be swept down by a perfectly overwhelming tide of fanaticism, excitement, unconstitutionalism. I told them that we were gone by tens of thousands & that if the *rock of Pennsylvania* was overtopped by the surging tide, all was lost. I warned them that into Northern & central Pa. this tide was pouring from New York.—Letters from Pa. satisfied me that I was *one* of the causes (though perhaps but a small drop in the bucket) of the late-taken alarm there.—But our friends here thought I was wild. One candidate for Govr. (Parker)[84] told me & *wrote* me, he thought we should carry this State. Ex-Governor Seymour[85] told me the same thing (or that he was *inclined* to the same belief) within a week of election! You see the result! But if the new Administration is *allowed to act & does act wisely,* the storm is over.

I started merely to tell you I had been *busy,* & that among usual literary labors I had *packed in* some political ones—to fill up those gaps oftimes which a man after doing a full day's work, finds in his—his—his—*proper* hours of Sleep!! You understand me.

Well, Now for St. Thomas. I wrote you I am revising *for publication.* But it goes slower than I expected. I am like stout De Vaux walking the hall of fear—whose furious lions ramp on each side.—I *aim* not to be *too* controversial, but I have thrown all milk & water non Commitallism to the winds! It is no more painful to die pierced by a thousand lances than by one! The martyr wants to feel that he dies *for something!* I shall seek the naked *truth,* I *aim* to tell it as if I were a naked soul before the judgment bar of God. I care not any longer for

[83] Pennsylvania was a pivotal state in the election of 1856 because "it was apparent that if the Republicans should gain the State of Pennsylvania in the State election of October, there was a very strong probability . . . that the electoral votes of all the free States in the Presidential election would be obtained by that party, while there was no probability that it would prevail in a single slave-holding state." George Ticknor Curtis, *Life of James Buchanan* (2 vols.; New York, 1883), II, 175. The Democratic victory averted the sectional division of the free and slave states which occurred in 1860. For a discussion of the local issues, see Alexander K. McClure, *Old Time Notes of Pennsylvania* (Philadelphia, 1905), I, *passim.*

[84] Amasa Junius Parker (1807–1890), lawyer and educator. In 1856, when the New York Democrats were weakened by a division, he was defeated for the governorship. His constitutional views made him conciliatory to the South until the attack on Fort Sumter.

[85] Horatio Seymour (1810–1886), governor of New York (1853–1855), regarded the election of Lincoln as a political disaster. Although a war Democrat, he thought the military conquest of the South unwise. See Stewart Mitchell, *Horatio Seymour of New York* (Cambridge, Mass., 1938), *passim.*

the consequences. I scorn consequences. I will not bow neck or knee to that spirit which now sweeps the north like a whirlwind. I will not bow neck or knee to those literary judges & dictators who in the north (where books *sell*) control public opinion. But I will strike a blow for the truth which will *live*. The thinking men of after times shall say, 'there fell a *true* man!—

I hope to get to press in a couple of months at furthest—but I do not feel safe in my accuracy without a good deal of reëxamination. I have just been casting my eye over my remarks on the Mecklenburg Declaration; & then over yours.—There are a good many resemblances (as could not be otherwise with the same facts to work upon) and there are also points of entire difference in our method of *handling* the argument (as would also be expected). I had already engrafted a notice of your paper, *& of its anticipating me in several of my propositions;*[86] also a quotation from your letter in regard to Rev. Humpy. Hunters testimony—showing that *he* really testified in favor of the 30th instead of the 20th—this being a wholly new point to me.—[87]

I think you asked me, if I had thought of the point that admitting both of the Declarations, that of the 30th was substantially a *retraction* of that of the 20th. I *had;* & pressed it pointedly in my original draft.

I ought not, of course, to regret your priority, in handling this subject—but as it pertained to *my saint,* and as my thunder was all *new, quo ad hoc,*—I gave up the *first handling,* if the truth must be told, not without a sigh!!! (Such Children we are!!)

I have quoted you in two or three other places—once saying "my *friend* Mr. Grigsby."[88] Shall I strike out that word? As I turn like Dr. Argentine [?], on a thousand pursuers, shouting my battle-cry, but only to fall covered with wounds,—do you want me to confer on you the *dubious* compliment of calling you "my friend?" Ha ha ha!!

But now about this Mecklenburg Declaration aforesaid.

1. Have you noticed that in Forces American Archives, 4th Ser. Vol. 2. 855. that he dates the *Second set* of resolutions May 31st (instead of

[86] Randall discusses the Mecklenburg Declaration at length and ends with the following statement: "Those who wish a fuller and much more convincing exposition of this subject than has here been given, will receive it when a recent lecture, delivered by Dr. Grigsby, at Richmond, shall be published." *Life,* III, Appendix II, pp. 570–582.

[87] See above, Grigsby to Randall, June 11, 1856.

[88] In quoting from Grigsby, *The Virginia Convention of 1776,* Randall describes his correspondent as an "able and candid Virginia writer, critically versed in both the written and unwritten history of his State." Randall, *Life,* III, 429–430. Grigsby's January 15, 1858, letter, in which he corrects some statements made by Randall in Volume I as to Patrick Henry's lukewarmness on independence in the Virginia Convention of May, 1776, is printed in *ibid.,* III, Appendix XXXVIII, pp. 679–680.

30th)?—What does Force *mean* by this? Do you understand there is any dispute or question as between 30th & 31st, or any discrepancy between the preserved Copies?

2. Have you Gov [*sic*] Martin's History of North Carolina? I have not the work (& can't get it without some trouble.) I would much like *his* Copy of Dec. compared & attested by *yourself* (so I shall know it authentic, *sub.* [?] *et lit.*) Or if you have not Martin, the next best thing would be what you have every reason to suppose a copy of it.—I want to publish *Martin's copy, as such,* in my Appendix (Please let a Sec'y copy it *very legibly* writing but on one side of paper.)[89]

3. What *authority* is there for saying the Davie copy can be traced back to 1793? (see yr Address p. 22.) Be good enough to put me clearly & fully on the track of that authority.—If this is *really so,* it will be a new fact to me.—[90]

4. What *authority* have you for saying (Address p. 24) that Mr. Sparks saw a printed cop. of the Martin set, in "State Department," in England?[91]

5. (On entirely a different Subject) What *specific authority* have you for saying (address p. 176) that Madison "affirmed that it would take more than one Hamilton to make a Jefferson"[92]

I put the preceding questions on a separate paper for greater convenience of reference.—If you will take the trouble of answering them

[89] Randall quotes from a writer in the *University of North Carolina Magazine:* "Although inquiry was made of Judge Martin [François-Xavier Martin], it is not known whence he obtained this paper ... His copy is evidently a polished edition of the Davie copy—polished, because its guardians knew that this was not an extract from original records, and therefore felt no particular reverence for it." Randall, *Life,* Appendix II, pp. 574–575.

[90] "It is urged by the friends of the resolutions that the Davie copy was in existence as early as 1793." Grigsby, *The Virginia Convention of 1776,* p. 22. Randall states: "Hon. Montfort Stokes, Governor of North Carolina, declared (in 1831) that he saw a copy in Hugh Williamson's possession in 1793." Randall, *Life,* III, Appendix II, p. 574.

[91] "The proceedings of the same committee which is said to have framed them [the Mecklenburg Declaration of May 31, 1775] ... were duly emblazoned through the northern and southern press, and a printed copy of them, by the way, was enclosed by the royal governor [Josiah Martin (1737–1786)] in a letter, which Mr. Sparks recently saw, to the state department in England." Grigsby, *The Virginia Convention of 1776,* p. 24. Randall, *Life,* III, Appendix II, p. 576.

[92] In discussing the respective abilities of Hamilton and Jefferson, Grigsby drew upon some remarks of James Madison who was perhaps the person best qualified to decide on the relative merits of the two men. "In the decline of life, when the fires of party, ... had burned out, he [Madison] affirmed that it would take more than one Hamilton to make a Jefferson." Grigsby, *The Virginia Convention of 1776,* p. 176. Randall quotes Madison's remark, and in a note says that upon applying to Grigsby for authority, Grigsby gave "the Hon. George Loyall, for a long time an honored Member of the Congress from Virginia, who was very intimate with Mr. Madison. Loyall repeatedly heard the latter make the declaration contained in the text, when comparing the intellectual capacities of the two men." Randall, *Life,* II, 248, n. 1.

in forms which you will have no objection to my *quoting* (should it become desirable) I will be very greatly indebted to you, & where practicable, make the proper acknowledgements.—

And I will be still more indebted to you, if you will (health permitting) send your answer *soon* after the receipt of this. I do not count to put my remarks on the Mecklenburg Declaration back on the shelf until they are *finished* to the last *note.*—

If Martin's Hist. of N. C. is not conveniently accessible to you do not put yourself out of the way to send me the Copy asked,—for I can get it elsewhere. I preferred your attestation as a literary & critical man.—

I trust your wife becomes more & more confirmed in her recovery; & that that sturdy little *Anglo Saxon,* Hugh II, waxes like a young oak! God bless you & yours.

Cordially & respectfully Yours

Henry S. Randall

Hugh Blair Grigsby E.
[Endorsed by Grigsby in pencil]
H. S. Randall
Nov. 14, 1856

[Randall to Grigsby, November 26, 1856]

Cortland Village
Nov. 26, 1856.

My dear Sir,

I have little to say now, & would not write you just yet, did not justice to Mr. Tucker require it. On receiving my letter which you have seen, he sent me an explicit retraction of & apology for all offensive expressions. I immediately wrote back meeting him half way. So "All is well that Ends well." I am glad of it, for I really respect & like the old gentleman though he *has* a crochetty & rather presuming temper.

My veneration for age is strong & it increases on me. Naturally my temper was very fiery. I have learned generally to govern it, & had rather be a thousand times insulted than be betrayed by partial provocation or by passion into the attitude of an *aggressor.*

Winter has set in here—the snow is nearly a foot deep. Sleigh bells jingle incessantly past my window. Ask Hugh why he dont come up here, & *ride down hill on a hand sled!* Tell him that is "fun alive" for young gentlemen of his years.

With cordial regards to Mrs. Grigsby, Hugh & yourself I am truly

Your friend

H. B. Grigsby. H. S. Randall

[Endorsed by Grigsby]
Henry S. Randall
Nov. 26, 1856

[Randall to Grigsby, December 4, 1856]

Cortland Village, N. Y.
Dec. 4, 1856

My dear Sir

I have sprung out of bed at 3 o'clock in the morning; for the fierce gale without which soaks my house & drives the snow in huge wreaths against the window panes, is not borne outward by more irresistible impulses than those which now drive thoughts & feelings through my mind!—Yesterday I had two or three most painful tasks. One of them was to do *justice* to Chas. Francis Adams. He, by innuendo, charges Mr. Jefferson with a *falsehood,* in the *Notes* to his grand father's Writings I took severe notice of this in passing, pronouncing it *indecorous* in any one & *indecent* in the g. son of John Adams! I averred that on the same style of reasoning, *all* the great men of the Revolution could be proved falsifiers, & John Adams *fifty times* where Mr. J. could once. I afterwards doubted the good taste of this stern retort, & probably should have greatly modified it, but I have just got C. F. A.'s *Life* of his grandfather (to be prefixed to the Works) & there in *summing up* Mr. Jefferson's character, he deliberately lugs in his twopenny story again in proof that Mr. J. would if necessary to his interest—*lie!!!* I then instantly made up my mind—*not* to follow up all of C. F. A.'s vulnerabilities—but to clasp him in one *hug*—that *intense* hug which is closer than that of lovers—that hug which *crushes* (quo ad hoc) *one* of the parties. Yesterday, amidst two or three other disagreeable feats, I assayed this.—Hence the elemental jar within, as well as without!! Pah! Ugh! how I scorn the little twopenny *Boston* cliquist![93]

[93] Randall has reference to the statement that Jefferson was "More ardent in his imagination than his affections, he did not always speak exactly as he felt towards either friends or enemies. As a consequence, he has left hanging over a part of his public life a vapor of duplicity, or, to say the least, of indirection, the presence of which is generally felt more than it is seen ... it can scarcely be denied that the publication of Mr. Jefferson's letters since his death, has fixed rather than relieved this shade of his character." Because John Adams considered Jefferson "a false and dangerous man," Adams withdrew his confidence from Jefferson at the close of his administration, going so far as to fill all places open under the revised judicial system. See Charles Francis Adams (1807–1886), ed., *The Works of John Adams* (10 vols.; Boston, 1850–1856), I, 616–622.

I will answer your letter recd. last evening at random,[94] so far as order is concerned, for it will be two hours before my library will be warmed up to get at my papers. *Answer me so as to show my question for I cannot well have this copd.*

1. Thank you for Martin's Copy. *Does he state where he got it?* What *year* was his work *published?* What *date* does *he* give.[95]
2. Please send me Hawks. I had not supposed it necessary to see his remarks, & have taken no steps to look them up. You are undoubtedly right that I had better see them—[96]
3. Obliged for the Intelligencer article, & will see it returned.—
4. I should be very glad of your hints to Bancroft. Make sure of every assertion & date, as I shall rely on any thing new I find in them, without further examination.—[97]
5. You *did* send me your criticism in regard to Hunters mistake (concerning his age) & I have quoted it *entire* in your words & crediting it to you. I have not even attempted to test yr. accuracy, assuming that as of course.—[98]
6. I shall quote your remark of Madison (about Hamilton) saying in a note, that *you* recd. it *from Loyall,* in the absence of any objection from you.[99]
7. *Cram* me with any [and] all the new thoughts that occur to you.
8. I *do* think I grasped all the larger points in the question originally; but every new *brace* put in a new *prop.* In reviewing I gave you credit in general (without specification) of anticipating me in several points & I specified the main ones (all) I think I recd. from you as I separately reached them. I will again rewrite the article shd. it be necessary after Rec'g Your papers & Hawks's, following the same course as to credits,—(I think I have on four separate occasions referred to you.)

And now a word which to one whose judgment & proper feelings I less trusted in, I would not write. You admire Tucker's Jefferson. So,

---

[94] This letter is not in this collection.

[95] François-Xavier Martin, *The History of North Carolina.* See this correspondence and the notes, *passim,* for references to this book.

[96] Hawks's lecture defending the Mecklenburg Declaration of May 20, 1775, was published as part of a *Revolutionary History of North Carolina.* See above, Grigsby to Randall, January 30, 1856, n. 3.

[97] Bancroft does not mention May 20; gives only the date of May 31. See above, Grigsby to Randall, August 18, 1856, n. 77.

[98] See above, Grigsby to Randall, June 11, 1856.

[99] See above, Randall to Grigsby, November 14, 1856, n. 92. George Loyall (1798–1868), member of the Virginia House of Delegates (1817–1827), of the Virginia Constitutional Convention of 1829–1830, and of the House of Representatives (1831–1837).

in many respects, do I—Since Dr. Dunglison's & your friendly intervention at Phila. I have placed T. on the footing of a *friend;* & when I eat salt with a man, I am true comrade in life & death. I have once or twice written him since I left P. *asking his authorities &c.* You will judge I would not do this if I did not feel friendly. I have alluded in most respectful terms to his work in *various instances,* & have actually gone back & *quoted from him & referred to him,* when his authority was of no more real use to me than is a fifth wheel to a carriage; & all this to do credit to the "older soldier"—(& somewhat to his excellent *intermediating friends!* In short, I have been *marked & pointed* in my quasi *juniorial* deference—There has been no *hypocrisy* in this. I *do* respect him. I consider him a remarkably *clear, accurate, candid* man of a good deal more than the average of what may be termed good ability.—[100]

But one of the most profoundly-read politicians in the Republic—one of the most discerning—a man remarkably like Madison in his grade of Ability—Martin Van Buren—recently wrote me that no approach had yet been to a beginning (thus he *piled up* his idea) of a true Life of Jefferson, & he significantly added that he who wrote it would have to encounter a *"fearful responsibility"* Aye—*"fearful"* was the word.

Now, my friend, at heart I exactly agree with Mr. Van Buren. Professor Tucker's work, usually accurate to the letter in facts—usually fair & liberal too—not without ability of Statement & dexterity in honest defence—yet after all, in my poor opinion, never goes below the *middle* of his subject.—He does not *skim,* but he does not go to the *bottom.* He did not understand the great ethnic features (if I may so term them) of his subject.—He did not understand the *inner* history of parties; the *spirit & soul of the times.*—His investigations were personal. He did not go vastly beyond official records. He did not enter into Jefferson's *feelings* any more than he occupied his stand point in the colder matters of opinion.—It was ice trying to represent fire! Not cowardly, he struck not one *unnecessary* blow; though the explanation or illustration of his Subject would have been oftentimes immensely cleared up by a *swinging blow.*

I am not at all sure I shall do better. But I shall tell a good deal *more.* I have about 300 *family* letters of Mr. J's unpublished, & none of

[100] Tucker, *The Life of Thomas Jefferson,* is referred to many times by Randall, both in his text and in his notes. See Randall, *Life,* I, 31, 32, 310; II, 74, 171, 172, 608; III, 429, 467. Tucker is included among those acknowledged in the "Preface," and in one instance Randall speaks of "Professor Tucker, generally correct, and always candid authority." *Ibid.,* III, 429.

their kind published.[101] I have 50 reservoir of *important facts* from which it is certain Prof. T. never drew one. I believe, between you & I, I have read more *volumes* for my materials, than T. did *tokens* (There's for you, old *Editor!*)—If I do not *see* deeply at least I *feel* deeply; I shall speak out *all* I feel. The north wind which sweeps without is not at this moment more fearless & reckless than *I,* so far as Mr. J's political or personal *enemies* are concerned.—

Now what I propose is this. If you will come out in a Second edn. (which I think an excellent idea) wait for *my facts* in regard to Mr. J. Wait for his family correspondence &c. *In the mean time, swell your materials in regard to all your other main figures, so as to make a plump instead of a thin 8vo. Make it the Pantheon of Virginia Heroes!!!* Let lecturing go for the present. Waste not your powder *thus!* Strike for the glory of something higher—Get my idea now, exactly. Fill up all your portraits a little more elaborately—make your work properly historical—make a vade mecum of all Virginians. Make it the favorite reading book of Va. young people for future time.—[102]

Think this over. But now, in whatever form your new Edn. may take let me request you to strike out a line about Wm. Randolph which 1. is an *error* & 2d. wounds the ideas of a person or two who may be foolish in it. The matter is not of a *figs* importance *per se;* & is not worth a word of controversy pro or con, except among those who would delight in archaeological investigations in regard to the color of Eve's night-gown! It makes no odds whether *you* are convinced of your error or not, So long as the thing is or no importance.—*Respectable* families have good right to consider their own uniform traditions, *which pertain to their own affairs & history,* as good authority as any other peoples traditions can be on *that* Subject. My friend, it is ungraceful to dispute *family* traditions, about themselves when there is no object in it. *You have not done so.* You stated an unimportant fact, on what you considered good testimony. You have *since* found that fact disputed by the settled & uniform tradition of *an ancient & respectable family.* In such a case *I*

[101] "Our deepest and warmest acknowledgments are due to the family of Mr. Jefferson, for their countenance and aid, in preparing this work. . . . They laid before us their stores of private manuscripts, never before opened, without reserve—transferring to us a large and important collection of newly discovered ones, without preliminary perusal. They furnished us their full recollections and opinions on every class of topics. They labored for us assiduously in collecting materials from Mr. Jefferson's surviving friends in Virginia; and they asked his friends in other States to in like manner contribute their assistance." Randall, *Life,* I, xi-xii.

[102] The chief value of Grigsby's work is its fund of biographical and bibliographical information on the personnel of the three Virginia constitutional conventions frequently not available elsewhere.

should omit the fact, & say in a note of ten words, that it was stated So & so in the first Edn. but that I had since learned that the supposed fact was in conflict with those settled family traditions which, in the absence of direct testimony, *ought to be regarded as the best evidence in the premises.* This would commit you to nothing, & be (meo arbitrio) a graceful way of waiving flat contradiction, or discussion—about—nothing!![103]

I am sure you will not be offended at my freedom in talking to you about this as if you were an older brother—

I can *take* as well as *give* plain talk—(where I am among my friends!) If you don't believe it (reasoning from my daring vehemence in pushing forward the ultima ratio with foes) try me! Lay on your cudgel, & see if I don't roar like a sucking dove!—

Heigho! I am weary with the excitements of yesterday, & this feverish night.

How comes our Hugh II the *Saxon* (ha ha ha!) & how the whilom delicate mother? By our Lady, I'll see the *Saxon* tribe ere I die if I live ten years!

Yours cordially

H. S. Randall

[Endorsed by Grigsby]
Henry S. Randall
Cortland, N.Y. Dec. 4, 1856
Answered

[103] The blast is against Grigsby's sentence: "A few old men had heard from their fathers that the original ancestor had some time beyond the middle of the previous century come over from Yorkshire poor, and made his living by building barns; but they also remembered his industry, his integrity, and his wonderful success in acquiring large tracts of land which he bequeathed to his children." Grigsby, *The Virginia Convention of 1776,* p. 77. William Randolph of "Turkey Island" (*ca.* 1651–1711), founder of the Randolph family in Virginia, "came over to Virginia probably between 1665 and 1675, poor, it is said. He accumulated a large estate, and became a member of the House of Burgesses and of the council. He appears to have been intimate with the first Colonel William Byrd, and well acquainted with Lady Berkeley. He settled at Turkey Island on the James River." This information was obtained from Charles Campbell, *History of the Colony and Ancient Dominion of Virginia* (Philadelphia, 1860), p. 629, by Eckenrode, who comments: "If he was an 'undertaker'—that is, a building contractor—when he arrived, it was not many years before he exchanged that profitable but less exalted occupation for the life of a tobacco planter." H. J. Eckenrode, *The Randolphs: The Story of a Virginia Family* (New York and Indianapolis, 1946), pp. 31–32.

[Grigsby to Randall, December 8, 1856]

Norfolk, Dec. 8, 1856

My dear sir,

Of all our statesmen John Adams is the most vulnerable. His slips of memory are outrageous.* I am heartily glad that you take hold of C. F. Adams. Give it to him with gloves off. Still I love old John. He was as brave and true hearted a patriot as ever lived.[104] He is to be handled in a very different manner from Charles.

1. Martin does *not* state where he got his copy, so far as I can recollect. *Hawks* says, I think, that he got it from the western part of North Carolina; *sed vide pro teipso.*

2. Martin's history of N. Carolina was published in 1829.

As a proof of the attachment of North Carolina to Great Britain as late as August 20, 1775, Hooper presented a report to its Congress (legislature) which ended in these words:

"These expressions flow from an affection bordering upon devotion to the House of Hanover, as established by law, from subjects who view it as a monument that does honor to human nature, capable of teaching kings how glorious it is to reign over a free people. These are the heartfelt affusions of men ever ready to spend their blood and treasure when constitutionally called upon, in support of the succession of his majesty king George the Third, his crown and dignity, and who fervently wish to transmit his reign to future ages as the era of common happiness to the people."[105]

Now I am told, that the Mecklenburg delegates voted for this report, as must have been the case, as the report was unanimously adopted.

As far as I can remember, Martin does not say *when* he obtained his copy or *from whom.*

Be careful in comparing my rapid sketch of Hunter's testimony with that contained in my last.[106]

I have not the slightest objection to your quoting Mr. Loyall's re-

* Of course you are familiar with the letters that passed between Mr. Adams and Mr. Jefferson in their old age.

---

[104] See Paul Wilstach, ed., *The Correspondence of John Adams and Thomas Jefferson, 1812–1826* (Indianapolis, 1925).

[105] William Hooper (1742–1790), born in Boston, graduate of Harvard, revolutionary leader in North Carolina, signer of the Declaration of Independence.

[106] Humphrey Hunter (1755–1827), born in Ireland, a Presbyterian minister in both Carolinas, and one of the witnesses on the Mecklenburg Declaration. See William Henry Foote, *Sketches of North Carolina, Historical and Biographical . . .* (New York, 1846), pp. 421–431; Humphrey Hunter to Dr. Joseph McKnitt Alexander, "Mecklenburg Declaration Papers," Southern Historical Collections, University of North Carolina, Chapel Hill.

mark. Quote it as the remark of the "Hon. George Loyall of Virginia."

Remember I have not the slightest desire to gain any merit by *original* discoveries, and wish you to use every thing I send you as freely as you please.

Urge as an argument (irresistible) against the Mecklenburg paper of the 20th that a *Declaration* of Independence which was never *promulgated* but kept back, is an absurdity in itself, of which no men of sense could be guilty of.

I quote a rentente from Mr. Bancroft's letter to me by which it appears that Gov. Swain, the present president of the University of North Carolina, has also had his eyes opened on the subject:[107]

"Gov. Swain, I am told, wrote the preface to the pamphlet published by the N. C. legislature; but he is now convinced that the paper which you condemn is not genuine, and has written a very lucid statement on the subject, of which I have a copy."

This statement of Gov. S. I never heard of until I received Mr. Bancroft's note.

You might mention incidentally that Mr. Force in the Archives in making a synopsis of the Resolutions of the 31st of May, from inadvertence omits the important resolution containing the acknowledgement of the right of eminent domain in the British Crown!![108]

I do not think that we differ materially in our estimate of Tucker's Jefferson. In estimating its value, *we must go back a quarter of a century,* and look at the state of the public mind at that time. It broke the ice. Many read and liked it, who would not have touched a pungent biography of the sage of Monticello. Now with a new generation another order of biography which shall take the reader at once boldly through the career of Jefferson is required. Let me say that the style of Mr. T's book is very faulty in some respects. Still, rightly considered in all its just relations, it was and is a valuable contribution to history. I think I told you that it changed the views of Lord Brougham in respect of the character of Mr. Jefferson.[109]

I thank you for the suggestions you make about my work on the Convention of 1776. It is my intention to enlarge it in another edition. But

[107] David Lowry Swain (1801–1868), governor of North Carolina (1832–1835), president of the University of North Carolina (1835–1868), author of *The British Invasion of North Carolina,* published as a part of Hawks, *Revolutionary History of North Carolina,* and founder of the *University of North Carolina Historical Magazine.*

[108] Force, *American Archives,* 4th series, II, 855.

[109] Lord Henry Peter Brougham (1778–1868), noted Scottish lawyer and Whig leader, supporter of constitutional, judicial, and educational reforms in Parliament and in the *Edinburgh Review.* A founder of the University of London, Lord Chancellor (1830–1834), a vigorous champion of antislavery.

I do *not* believe that I am in error about William Randolph. He *was* a carpenter, and I can prove that he was no more a cavalier than Martin Van Buren or old Roger Sherman was.[110] I have no respect for descendants who are ashamed (quod hoc) of their progenitors. And the moral lesson presented by a young mechanic landing on our shores "with his axe on his shoulder," as one of my witnesses testifies, and, rising in the teeth of an aristocratic society to the highest rank, and founding a family which for a century and a half has filled the highest offices of the colonial, state and federal governments—I say the lesson presented by such facts, should be pressed upon the public for their admiration and imitation. And shame upon those who are ashamed of such an ancestor.

So be careful of your facts, as I shall top them high and dry, and make out William Randolph not an Englishman and a cavalier, but a Scotchman and a puritan. In sober earnest, do not commit *yourself* on the subject, state what you are told by the family, and dwell slightly on the topic, as Mr. J. does himself, who, by the way, evidently had no confidence in the Randolph genealogy. See his Memoirs.[111]

I shall prove that the Colony of Virginia was settled by thousands of Cromwellians—the bone and sinew of the British people, who gave that colony its peculiar caste, aided as they were *by the peculiar circumstances of the colony.*[112] It is a great question in our history untouched by any but myself, and I mean to make it plain, altho' I strip every jack daw of his borrowed plumes, even though those plumes have waved for a century and a half. In the mean time, I have no secrets from *you.* I will answer any question about the Randolphs candidly and as strictly as if I were upon oath, and argue any topic that is doubtful; but my confidence begins and *ends* with *you.* It is not to pass to the Randolphs, who have given me several indirect reproofs on the subject. And it has flashed across my mind that when I called with Gov. Coles to see Mrs. [left blank] of Boston,[113] then staying at Mr. Trist's, she declined our

[110] Roger Sherman (1721–1793), a self-made man, prominent in the legislature of Connecticut, in the Continental Congress, signer of the Declaration of Independence, the Articles of Confederation, and the Constitution, member of the United States House of Representatives and Senate.

[111] Jefferson wrote that the Randolphs "trace their pedigree far back in England and Scotland, to which let every one ascribe the faith and merit he chooses." See Randall, *Life*, I, 7, n. 3. Randall states that William Randolph "brought with him, it is believed, some small remains of a former family fortune, and being a man of sagacity and enterprise he rapidly increased it, and continued to add possession to possession until the day of his death." *Ibid.*, I, 8.

[112] Grigsby, *The Virginia Convention of 1776*, pp. 35–44.

[113] Eleonora (Ellen) Wayles Randolph (1796–1876), married Joseph Coolidge (1799–1879) in 1825. See Reginald Buchanan Henry, comp., *Genealogies of the Families of the Presidents* (Rutland, Vermont, 1935).

visit, in consequence of my remark about her ancestor, when from a note written to Gov. C. that morning, she stated she was quite well. Now I may be deceived in this suspicion; but whether I am or not, I shall not be constrained to depart from the strictest use of my materials, and from my determination to push no argument beyond its fair force.

I am anxious for your book to appear; but repeat the old maxim *festina lente.*

Can you give me a copy of the Turkey island inscription on William Randolph's tombstone? I am very anxious to obtain it. Or can you tell me the date of the birth of William R? He died in 1711. Do try and furnish me with the above.[114]

I now close for the present, as it grows late, and I have not time to write out my notes to Mr. Bancroft. By the way, it took me a full hour to find the date of the publication of Martin's history. I knew that I had noted the fact, but where the note was gave me the labor.

One word about my schemes. My only object in writing at all has been to supply our Historical Society with a discourse on the three great epochs in our history—the Convention of 1776, that of 1788, and that of 1829–30. Two of these objects I have accomplished, and but for my sickness, and the felons on my fingers, I would ere this have finished that of 1788.

I should like to see you in Virginia, and should you depart from home on a visit to the Randolphs, take the Norfolk Steamer at New York, and spend a day in Norfolk, if no more.

I have a high opinion of Mr. Van Buren's talents, and would regard him as an eminently valuable adviser on every political topic but one.

My little boy grows apace, and amid many difficulties is at present quite well. Mrs. G. has been quite well all the summer, though never robust at any time. Though you have never seen her, and though she has never seen you, she is very familiar with your voice, which she heard in your conversations with me.

I trust your family are blest with health, and have nerves strong enough to resist a snowstorm, especially when it rages at night. In this climate the winter has not yet set in. I have not yet worn an overcoat for cold.

In haste

Very truly,
Yours
H. B. Grigsby

H. S. Randall Esq.

[114] See below, Grigsby to Randall, December 15, 1856.

[Randall to Grigsby, December 12, 1856]

Cortland Village
Dec. 12, 1856

My dear Sir,

Your letter & the book came last evening.—I am much obliged to you. I infer from yours that you still expect to send me the Bancroft notes. With this idea, I do not enter upon my *final* handling of my topic, awaiting the notes. If I misunderstood you, or it will be a very considerable trouble to you to get together the disjecta membra, let it go. But *tell me just when you want your tools again,* for being deeply absorbed in a great investigation I will give myself a little delay if certain it will not inconvenience you.

I certainly, my friend, would never again refer to the affair of W. Randolph were it not necessary to answer a request of yours, & did not another consideration, *justice to others,* with regard to whom *I may have been misunderstood,* render it obligatory on me.—

You ask me for W. R. birth year & and his epitaph.[115] By turning to my chapter where genealogy is touched I find I have not given either. It seems to me that I have a copy of that epitaph somewhere, but it eludes my search. My literary debris or *chips* reach to *cords* including the most miscellaneous papers, that one cares but little for, but hardly likes to burn, that you ever saw got together. I *cannot* take time from *mag. op.* to file or put them in order, & so they go on accumulating!—I will look more for the epitaph, & if I have it & can find it, you shall have it. It is only an *impression* that I have it, & I may have confused it with the epitaph of Bradshaw or some other ancient Trojan!—[116]

Now for a correction. I did not *mean* to say, if I *did* say, that *one* of the *Jefferson* Randolphs had the least sensitiveness in regard to their ancestor being pronounced a *carpenter.* I do not know one of them that I believe would care a *fig* whether he was that or any other respectable occupationed man.—I have talked with nearly all of them on *such* subjects & moreover in regard to *your* published assertion on the subject.— I have both in Letters & orally, quizzed some of them in regard to your overthrowing their pedigrees (in the Spirit in which I love to try to tease you about *Saxondom,*) & have heard nearly all of them in reply

[115] William Randolph's dates are given as (*ca.* 1651–1711), by Dumas Malone, *Jefferson the Virginian,* p. 428. See *ibid.,* Appendix I, pp. 426–434, for a genealogy of the Randolph family in five parts.

[116] John Bradshaw (1602–1659), presided at the trial of Charles I and pronounced sentence (1649). For "Bradshaw's Supposititious Epitaph," believed by Jefferson to have been written by Benjamin Franklin, see Randall, *Life,* III, Appendix IV, pp. 585–586.

speak about your assertion—speak in the most unreserved manner—& have not yet heard the first word of disrespect, unkindness irritation or blame towards you. They supposed you accorded with them in your view of at least one ancestor, & have not appeared to imagine that you could have desired to treat them with any disrespect. They thought you simply mistaken, & have appeared to suppose, & I doubt not do suppose, that *their* representations of the facts, in case of your issuing a new edition, would at once be accepted as satisfactory by you.—

In Phila. I heard at least three (yes five or six) descendants of W. Randolph talking freely on this topic when stirred up by some half mischevous jeers of mine, & they all talked in the spirit I have mentioned—The lady you mention as having denied herself to you & Govr. is an exceedingly debilitated person, to my own knowledge *often* up & down *in the Same day.* I have met her in the morning as well as she ever appears to be & been denied to her in the afternoon on account of *indisposition.* Gov. —— *ought* to perfectly well know this fact & if *he* put you on the scent of a different construction, or *countenanced* a different construction in the slightest manner, *I should be thunderstruck to learn it.* I should attribute it to a *most remarkable forgetfulness* of acts which he ought to know as well as he knows that such a person exists as that noble & preeminently gifted woman.

——Furthermore, G. W. Randolph of his own accord, or in answer to some remark of mine, spoke of you as a gentleman of rank & consideration in Va. as one he had heard high representations of as a man of breeding, delicacy & refinement;—& he spoke *decidedly well of your work on the Va. Convention.* If he mentioned the matter of W. R. at all, it was simply as in inadvertent error.—

If I mentioned any one as *sore* on this subject I referred to R. R.[117] & some elderly persons *not of the Jefferson branch of the family.* But I did suppose, & suppose now, that were an onset made, as it were, on their ancestors veracity to establish some point of archaeological curiosity or to "point some moral," they will feel just as you or I would be likely to under the same Circumstances. They have pedigree after pedigree in the handwriting of their ancestors sustaining their version. Mrs. Governor Randolph (the glorious Martha that wrung the brilliant tribute from the cynic of Roanoke)[118] enquired into these particulars, & I have now lying before me in her beautiful handwriting the carefully traced particulars—tracing the family to their home & through different

[117] Richard Randolph.

[118] Martha Jefferson Randolph (1772–1836), eldest daughter of Thomas Jefferson and wife of Thomas Mann Randolph (1768–1828), governor of Virginia (1820–1822). Martha was the devoted companion of Jefferson during the period following the

generations (names all given) in an English county.* They *know,* too, *if their veracity is to be trusted,* that Mr. Jefferson did *not* put the construction on *his* words *you do. That* fact I have particularly enquired into.—[119]

You are entitled to *do* what you please in this matter;—but you *are not* from any thing *I* know or believe, entitled to assume, or act on the feeling, that there has been a particle of *aggression* made on you. And one would think that circumstances had put me in a good attitude to know, when I have freely conversed with those whose confidence has not concealed from me a point of family history.—

And, secondly, Mr. Grigsby, you are *not* entitled from any fact within *my* knowledge or belief, to act upon the hypothesis that the family (the Jefferson Randolphs) have any "Jackdaw" pride in respect to the *mere fact* of what the *occupation* of W. R. was.

When I assume that the branding of their written family records as forgeries or fictions, would be painful to them, I reason purely from the analogy of my own feelings.—I am not aware that one of them has ever thought of a second edition of your work. I am not aware that they know a word has passed between you & me in regard to such an edition or its contents.—I have spoken wholly for myself & never a word for them.—

I addressed you as a friend & currente calamo. If among the scoria & cineres of a volcanic night, I used a word that has tended to exacerbate your feelings (quo ad hoc) I regret it *deeply.* This thing begins to wear a very unpleasant shape to me, & I have felt it my duty as your friend & as the friend of the R's to clear away *every particle of misconception,* 1. which could possibly flow from my mutually friendly interference & 2. which conflicted with my own hardly questionable information—

I have now discharged my duty, & have said out my say.—I do not

* A connexion also traced to the Scotch R. v.

---

death of her mother. After Martha's marriage (1790), she and her husband resided at Monticello. Randall's *Life* has many of Jefferson's letters to Martha. John Randolph of Roanoke (1773–1833), House administration leader (1801–1805), opposed Jefferson after 1805. He paid high tribute to his kinswoman, Martha Jefferson Randolph, in his toast: "I drink, gentlemen, to her—to the sweetest woman in Virginia." Randall, *Life,* II, 224.

[119] "If he attached no special importance to his long maternal pedigree, he never dreamed of throwing any discredit on its accuracy in point of fact—though perhaps he thought *all* pedigrees running back through *ages,* a class of records to place implicit confidence in which required a pretty strong exercise of 'faith!' This was what he meant to express, and all he meant to express, in the remark we have quoted." Randall, *Life,* I, 7, n. 3. Grigsby speaks highly of the Randolphs, although Randall's letters give the opposite impression. Grigsby, *The Virginia Convention of 1776,* p. 77.

quote a particular word from your remarks, as if I thus sought to give them a characterization (can you get at the idea *hidden* under *such* a word?) I *slashed* on freely, I doubt not, for I always do, where I give my confidence; & people who throw stones must not mind if a glass of their own now and then gets *smashed!* If you will hold me quits, in respect to *words,* I will you!—

Now, my friend, don't take it ill of me if I say in Conclusion that I will (*of course*) most freely furnish you the fact you ask if I find it (and I must try to find for *my* use)—but I desire now to step out of *this* controversy. I have neither right nor wish to entangle myself in it. I regret that my well intentioned officiousness has given me *any connexion* with it. God knows I have enough, & serious enough personal controversies on my hands already.—

Truly yours

Henry S. Randall.

[Endorsed by Grigsby]
Henry S. Randall
Dec. 12, 1856
Answered Dec. 15, 1856

[Grigsby to Randall, December 15, 1856]

Norfolk, Dec. 15, 1856

My dear Sir,

I *will* write out the notes on the North Carolina depositions in a day or two.[120] When I wish any thing I send you I will write as you say. By the way, I wish I could give you the North Carolina volume; but, although I *bought* four copies, all of which I have given to public institutions, I have but that one left, which was a present to me.[121]

I have read your letter about William R. most attentively. Let me say that you did not tell me any thing which I did not know before as to your generous views and feelings in the case. I understand your position quite as well as you have explained it; and I have taken you for *my* friend from the beginning to the end of the affair; and I have just thought that you wrote to me in the same spirit in which under the same circumstances I would have written to you. I consider all that you have

[120] Depositions taken by order of the North Carolina legislature are printed in whole in Force, *American Archives,* 4th series, II, 855.

[121] François-Xavier Martin, *The History of North Carolina.*

said as spoken in a spirit of generous magnaminity and friendship; and so it was that I wrote you as I did. Let me be *just* before I proceed farther. Gov. Coles, *so far as I know,* has never heard of the matter in talk between us. He does not know that a human being has taken exception to a single word in my little book, and it only recently flashed across my mind that the lady in question might possibly have felt as I intimated in my letter. But your explanation settles the question forever in my mind. My own wife, who has been an invalid for fifteen years, acts from indisposition just as the excellent lady in question is represented by you to do. I have known my wife cheerful and pleasant in company one hour and in bed a great sufferer the next. Until you wrote I did not know even that Mrs. ——[122] was an invalid. She had spent the preceding evening at the Governor's, and next morning wrote that she had not suffered from the sitting up, and was as well as usual; but I can readily see in such a note a disposition to show her kind entertainers that she had not suffered from her visit. I am as sure as I am busy that Gov. C. never dreamed of any thing out of the way.

And of the *Jefferson* Randolphs I think and believe as you do; but I have reasons to think that some of the other branches have spoken tartly, especially our friend R. R.[123] But, with all possible provocation, you may be sure that, if I touch the subject at all, it will be done in such a way as not to wound the proper delicacy of a single rightminded person.

You must take my remark about the *"Jack daws,"* (did *I* use the word?) in a spirit of playfulness as it was written; and I do assure you that none will receive your genealogies with greater candor than I will.

There was not one word in your letter to wound my feelings, nor have they been wounded; and I think it was because I did express some pain that such a woman as *you* represented Mrs. —— of Boston to be might possibly have been offended by me, that you connected the feeling expressed in that paragraph with my banter about the Jackdaws. And let me tell you that I *"slash"* on just as you say I do, and cannot recall the exact expressions which I use in an unreserved letter to a friend. I do assure you upon my honor, that I have not the least recollection about the figure of the Jack daws, though in the haste of a letter written in the time it would take to read it, I may have used it.

Now, if you *cannot* furnish *me* with the inscription on William of Turkey Island's tomb, I will furnish you, just in the words as given me in

[122] Ellen Wayles Randolph Coolidge, usually appears as Ellen Coolidge.
[123] Richard Randolph.

a letter from Charles Campbell the historian,[124] received since I wrote you:

"Col: William Randolph
of Warwickshire, but late
of Virginia, Gent:
Died April 11th, 1711."

(here the Coat of Arms)
(not given by Mr. C.)
"Mrs. Mary Randolph, his only wife,

Died * * *
she was daughter of Mr. Hen. Isham
by Katherine his wife; he was of
Northamptonshire but late of
Virginia, Gent."

The above is an exact transcript of the record taken from Mr C's letter. He did not state what the asterisks meant; whether an obliteration, or a mere blank designed to be filled at her death. I also understand from the epitaphs that they are on the same stone.
I also add a fact that may be worth knowing, that his eldest son of the same name was born in Nov. 1681, and died in October, 1742, aged 61.

One word more about your concluding paragraph. I differ with you about it *in toto*. You have *not* been *officious;* nor do I see any thing like *controversy* between us. So I don't see how you can "step out" of a controversy which has had no existence; for I certainly cannot call a comparison of views on a disputed question confidentially expressed among friends, *a controversy*.

In the mean time, push on the 'opus magnum;' and let me have at least the first volume for my summer reading. In the mean time let me ask, whether you have ever seen the elegant obituary written by (as I think) a professor of William and Mary on Sir John Randolph,[125] who died in 1736? It will be found in the Va. Historical Register, and the exact page and volume you will find in my discourse where I speak of

[124] Charles Campbell (1807–1876), historian, editor, and antiquarian with a special interest in Virginia. His reputation was established by *An Introduction to the History of the Colony and Ancient Dominion of Virginia* (Richmond, 1847).

[125] Sir John Randolph (*ca.* 1693–1737), son of William Randolph I, sent in 1729 to England to obtain a renewal of William and Mary's charter and returned knighted. Grigsby, *The Virginia Convention of 1776*, p. 55, n. refers to "Sir John Randolph," *The Virginia Historical Register and Literary Note Book*, IV (1851), 138–141. This article is a copy of the obituary which appeared in the *Virginia Gazette,* March 11, 1736/37.

Bland[126] and Nicholas[127]—*in the notes.* I should think you require that article, as well as the inscription on Sir John's marble slab on the wall of the chapel of William and Mary College. Should you think it important to have them, and have them not, I will copy the obituary for you, and will write to Williamsburg for the inscription which I have not complete.

In haste, very truly yours,
Hugh B. Grigsby

Mr. Randall Our Norfolk papers had your note about our young Virginia female riders in their columns some days ago.[128]
P. S. The reason why I do not send the article on the death of Sir John Randolph is because you may already possess a copy, and because it would take me half an hour or three quarters to copy it. But I will copy it for you by return mail, if you desire it.

[Grigsby to Randall, December 17, 1856]

Norfolk, Dec. 17, 1856

My dear sir,

I give you the substance of my letter to Mr. Bancroft as well as I can make it out from my notes.[129]

There are fourteen deponents in all. Of these fourteen *seven* gave their depositions *before* it was important to discriminate between the twentieth and the thirtieth of May, and declare that the Mecklenburg meeting was held "in the month of May, 1775," "towards the end of May," and one of them, "that it was certainly before the fourth of July 1776." The testimony of these *seven,* therefore, is more in favor of "the end of May," the *thirty first,* than the 19th or the 20th, which was but four or five days only beyond the middle of the month.

The remaining *seven* declare as follows:
George Graham, William Hutchinson, James Clark, and Robert Robinson, four of the seven, unite in a joint deposition. This deposition is evidently drawn by some person who detailed on paper all that he could gather about the affair, and who wrote *after* it became important to discriminate between the twentieth and the thirtieth of May. A meeting that happened a year ago could hardly have been sketched with a greater

[126] Richard Bland (1710–1776), Virginia statesman, delegate to Continental Congresses (1774–1775), and a member of Virginia Convention of 1776. See Grigsby, *The Virginia Convention of 1776,* pp. 57–61.

[127] Robert Carter Nicholas (1728–1780), conservative, Virginia patriot, and a member of Virginia Convention of 1776. See *ibid.*, pp. 61–68.

[128] See Randall, *Life,* III, 339–341.

[129] Cf. with Grigsby to Randall, June 11, 1856, above, which contains much the same information.

regard for minute details. And some of these details are plainly at variance with the facts as stated by one of the reputed actors in the meeting of the twentieth, such as a grand signing match [torn edge] in evident imitation of the scene which occurred on the [torn edge] of the Declaration of Independence in Congress on the fourth of July, [torn edge] Now a joint deposition of a number of persons is in itself a suspicious thing; but when that deposition contains so many minute details of a scene which transpired more than forty years before: details which it is hardly probable that four persons disconnected from each other at the time could have seen with the same degree of prominence, or having seen, could recal them with the same vividness, and which differ materially from the statements made by men who are acknowledged to have been present at a meeting, if indeed any meeting were held, a joint deposition, I say, of such a character might well be regarded with suspicion, and I was led to look into it with some degree of scrutiny. And the result is that the four deponents who depose with such minuteness concerning details that transpired five and forty years ago, were, according to the statement of their ages added to their names by themselves, *two* of them but boys of *fifteen*, at the time, and the other two but *twenty two* years old, their ages averaging *eighteen;* and they address their deposition to Col. Polk, a son of the Col. Polk[130] who is said to have read the Declaration of the twentieth at the meeting, and whose son might be supposed to have heard the details frequently from his father, if such a scene had occurred, but who, though a boy of eighteen at the time and present at the supposed meeting, does not venture to give to the public any deposition of his own! Such a deposition is surely not worth the paper on which it was written.

The deposition of Humphrey Hunter, another of the *seven*, written *after* it became important to discriminate between the twentieth and the thirtieth of May, takes for granted that the date of the supposed meeting was the twentieth of May. In order to settle the matter, however, most conclusively he adds an incident of his personal history which was associated with the *date* of the meeting; for he tells us, that "on that memorable day, I was twenty years and *fourteen days of age;*" and in a note accompanying the deposition the exact date of the birth of Mr. Hunter is given; viz, the fourteenth day of May, 1775;—a date that well nigh settles the question; for if we make the calculation, we will find that on the nineteenth of May 1775 (for the meeting is alledged to have *begun* on the 19th) instead of being twenty years and *fourteen*

[130] President James K. Polk was a grandnephew of Thomas Polk (1732–1794), one of the chief founders of Mecklenburg County and the city of Charlotte.

days old, he was twenty years and *five* days only old; but on the supposition that the true meeting was held on the *thirtieth,* the twenty years and *fourteen* days are within *two* days of that date: a mistake he might readily make, if he trusted to his memory alone. Which it is evident from the mistake he did. The deposition then of this witness is most decidedly in favor of the thirtieth. The depositions of the sixth and seventh witnesses, written *after* the interest about the twentieth was excited, include that date, though it is very apparent that the witnesses taking the date for granted, are disposed to recal other things. What strikes us plainly in examining these depositions is the manifest caution and brevity of the deponents who were the reputed responsible actors of the time, and the full, elaborate, and graphic descriptions of those witnesses who were either children at the time, or not old enough to have taken any part on such an occasion.

On the whole subject, looking merely to the fact of the depositions, my conclusion would be, that it is not impossible that a muster of the officers of militia might have been held on the 20th of May, and that they appointed the thirtieth as a day of general meeting; that the meeting of the twentieth, if held at all, was private and informal, and that on the *thirtieth* the great meeting described as the meeting of the twentieth by the deponents did take place at Charlotte, when and where the resolutions of the thirtieth were adopted. The fact that some of the deponents say that numerous bye-laws were adopted on the twentieth, when according to the supposed true account of that meeting no such voluminous byelaws were adopted, or if adopted, were ever heard of, shows that it was the thirtieth, when numerous byelaws were certainly adopted, and published at the time.

The above is the substance of my letter to Mr. Bancroft; but I will now add that, looking at all the facts of the whole case, my conclusion is that there *was no meeting on the twentieth;* and that the proceedings of the thirtieth having been mislaid and lost, the effort to recover them from memory resulted in the so called Mecklenburg Declaration of the *twentieth* of May.

I have written in haste, but I believe that I have filled up my notes substantially as they were written to Mr B.[131]

In great haste for the mail, I am very truly

Yours
Hugh B. Grigsby

Henry S. Randall Esq.
Cortland Village
N. Y.

[131] This Grigsby letter may have caused Bancroft to ignore the May 20 meeting.

[Randall to Grigsby, December 27, 1856]

Cortland Village Dec. 27, 1856

My dear Sir,

Your two last are received. The notes are valuable & clear. I think I shall put them into my appendix in the form in which they stand, if I receive no objections from you.—

I am glad that xxx xxxxx[132] is not responsible for any hint of misdirection in the matter we have talked of. I esteemed him a *good man,* but not without touches of worldliness; & I *thought* once I caught a gleam of a feeling, in a conversation with him, in respect to a certain family,—which I did not choose to define, & which I thought there were *reasons* for *his* not possessing.—

I used the word "controversy" as between you & me simply in a literal meaning, & with no thoughts of attaching to it the semi-invidious import it often bears.—I meant that I had opposed what I understood to be your intentions on a certain point, because I believed it would give deep pain,—but that I had no real right to offer any advice or opinion on the subject, being neither Brau nor Brau's brother—& that accordingly, as you did not seem to entirely accord with me, I would *step out!*

I am glad, my dear Sir, that you so promptly abandon certain prepossessions, which were natural enough under the circumstances; but which I chanced to know were unfounded. This was the frankness & the magnaminity I confidently expected.—

To go to another topic. Mrs. C——[133] is one of the most gifted women I ever met with. G. W. R.[134] has sound ability, but she has, I imagine, far more of the hereditary *genius* than any other member of the family. She writes an offhanded, obviously unstudied, but most beautiful letter, expressed in those particular terms which evince talent, high breeding, & great acquaintance with the world. I shall publish a dozen or two of her letters, giving Monticello pictures—& if they do not sparkle in the direction I have named, "then," as the children say, "tell me so!" She has no idea whatever that they are to be published.[135] But mark, I have a distinct carte blanche from the family to quote *anything* I choose from any of them, & to give the *names* where the writers are males.—I also distinctly apprised *three* of her sisters that I intended to quote those letters entire, & assigned my reasons for not informing her of it. The

[132] Probably Governor Coles.

[133] Ellen Coolidge.

[134] George Wythe Randolph, a brother of Ellen Coolidge.

[135] For Ellen Coolidge's descriptions of Jefferson's life at Monticello see Randall, *Life,* III, 307–351.

first was, she could not write with such easy beauty under the suspicion of publication; & second I was desperately afraid she would come in with a decisive veto.—After showing the letters to her sisters, they told me to consult my own judgment & they would stand between me & blame.[136]

A Phila. gentleman told me he was in China with her. He said that she visited in the English Society at the port—that she always came late & retired early—that while she staid the present Admiral Dundas,[137] Capt. Elliot[138] & others "drew up round her three deep" & that he never saw a woman command so much attention. She was regarded by the English gentlemen as a most remarkable woman.—I have, I suppose, a couple of hundred letters from her more or less. I consider her a decidedly more graceful letter writer than H. T[139] & wherein her genius falls behind his, I have failed to discover. She was his library companion, amanuensis, Secretary &c from infancy until marriage.[140]—But alas, she is aged, & a hopeless invalid, up & down with every change of the wind.—You will please not mention her authorship of the Sparkling letters which I shall publish (after all *sparkling* is not the word—they are too quiet, subdued & unpretending for that). You may however mention it to Mrs. Grigsby (Mrs. Grigsby, I wish you a Merry Christmas!) for since I have learned we are acquaintances through a partition wall I have been smitten with a great regard for her!—And read her all I have said for Mrs ——, because I would have her know what a DonQuixote her other side of the wall acquaintance is to stand up for his lady friends,—aye, after years have stolen the delicate beauty from the cheek & those same years & disease have taken away all but the occasional ela[sti]city of spirit & power to meet & to please friends.—(Don't be jealous, Grigsby,

[136] The daughters of Martha Jefferson were (1) Ellen Wayles Randolph (1796–1876), wife of Joseph Coolidge; (2) Cornelia Jefferson Randolph (1799–1871), unmarried; (3) Virginia Jefferson Randolph (1801–1882), wife of Nicholas Philip Trist; (4) Mary Jefferson Randolph (1803–1876), unmarried; (5) Septimia Anne Cary Randolph (1814–1877), wife of Dr. David Scott Meikleham.

[137] Vice-Admiral Sir Richard Saunders Dundas (1802–1861).

[138] Captain Sir Charles Elliot (1801–1875).

[139] The manuscript at this point is illegible. Probably the initials stand for Thomas Jefferson though Randall might have reference to Nicholas Trist who remained at Monticello during Jefferson's last years (1824–1826), acting as his secretary and nurse. For an able treatment of this period, see Barbara Mayo, "Twilight at Monticello," *The Virginia Quarterly Review*, XVII (1941), 502–516.

[140] Ellen Wayles Randolph was her grandfather's favorite intellectual companion during the last twenty years of his life. In 1825 she married Joseph Coolidge, a young Boston merchant, beginning a connection between the Virginia and Boston families which lasted more than a hundred years, largely through the occasional exchange of correspondence. See Hard Jefferson Coolidge and Robert H. Lord, *Archibald Cary Coolidge* (Boston and New York, 1932), p. 2. Barbara Mayo notes that of the nine remaining children of Martha Randolph "Ellen most resembled her grandfather; she had the fair Jefferson coloring, even temper, and intellectual tastes." Mayo, *op. cit.*, p. 502.

because I feel disposed to *show off* before my other side of the wall acquaintance, but *trot me out* like a good honest body! There is something so piquant & teasing to the imagination in beginning an acquaintance through a course of brick & two courses of plaster! Ha ha ha! pray Mrs. Grigsby don't think I am "cracked" or that this is *just after dinner!* I work, work, work. Writing a letter now & then is nearly all my conversation out side of my own little circle. When my spirits get to effervescing in a letter, they require no after dinner stimulants. I have enough to mourn over. This is the strong occasional rebound of animals spirits.—

Mr. Grigsby *what* have you named your boy? Is it Cedric, or Torquil, or Ulric or Athelstane, or Harold or What? By the by, my father & my oldest son have a good Saxon *sounding* name—Roswell—I think it should be rather spelled Roswal.

There, I think I have written enough nonsense for once! I feel relieved as the boy said after he got his whipping.—

Oh! by the way. I have given many a thought to the slavery questions I put you, since,[141] —& the true way of going between Scylla & Charybdis I think dawns upon me. It is to spread out about the usual amount of canvas, grasp the helm, & hold right forward where duty & manhood point the way!—I am not an "abolitionist." I have no sympathy with the mad & fanatical spirit which controls a portion of our people. I can't please them if I try. I won't *try*. My work won't have so many purchasers by three quarters, seven-eights—I shall probably be denounced & hunted. Be it so. Truly Yours

H. S. Randall

[Endorsed by Grigsby]
Henry S. Randall
Cortland, Dec. 27, 1856

[Penciled letter in Randall's hand, *ca.* 1856]

Among my "Jefferson Gallery" I want the two Tazewells Littleton W & his father Henry. You probably have letters from the Govr. & can't you contrive some excuse to ask him for a letter of his fathers? They belong to the great old breed of Va. & my splendid vol. of Mss. will be incomplete without them.[142]

[141] See above, Randall to Grigsby, June 18, 1856.

[142] Henry Tazewell (1753–1799), chief justice Virginia Supreme Court, United States Senator (1794–1799), friend of Jefferson. See Grigsby, *The Virginia Convention of 1776*, pp. 79–83. Littleton Waller Tazewell (1774–1860), son of Henry, lawyer, United States Senator (1824–1832), governor of Virginia (1834–1836). See Grigsby, *Discourse on the Life and Character of the Hon. Littleton Waller Tazewell* (Norfolk, 1860), *passim.*

1857

[Grigsby to Randall, April 6, 1857]

Norfolk, Va. April 6, 1857

My dear Sir,

Your letter of the 1st instant was received on Saturday morning, and I immediately called on Mr. Leonard of the Argus, and got him to put in type for Monday's (todays) paper the article enclosed in your letter. I wrote the editorial which I enclose, calling attention to the subject.[1]

I regret to learn that there is to be such a competition between your work and Mr. Hildreth's;[2] but one thing is certain, I think, that the majority of readers throughout the Union are conservative, and that your book on this score alone will far outvie the work of your rival. Then there can be no comparison on the score of matter. I can very well see how a life of Jefferson by an abolitionist may be a dangerous book; still I hope to see you triumph in the nonslaveholding states as we will certainly see it in the Southern.

Press forward the work at all hazards, and cancel oversights in the second volume.

I regret to learn from the note of your son that you have been ill. You work too hard while you work. Three or four hours at work and one or two in the fields will accomplish more for the Opus Magnum than six continuous hours employed upon it; that is, *diebus communibus*. Overwork brings on sickness, and the loss of weeks in time and in spirit.

I was much interested in reading the printed communication enclosed, and I am very anxious to see the book. I hope that you are now recovered, and are intent upon your writing.

---

[1] This letter is not in this collection. The article appeared in the *Daily Southern Argus*, April 6, 1857. The *Argus* (Norfolk, 1848–1861) was edited by Abram F. Leonard, joined in 1856 by William Lamb. Cappon, *Virginia Newspapers, 1821–1935*, p. 141.

[2] Richard Hildreth (1807–1865), *The History of the United States* (6 vols.; New York, 1849–1852). The work is strongly pro-Federalist. For his treatment of Jefferson, see *ibid.*, VI, 138–141. His antislavery writings were popular: *Despotism in America: or, an Inquiry into the Nature and Results of the Slave-Holding System in the United States* (Boston, 1840); *The Slave: or Memoirs of Archy Moore* (London, 1836); *The White Slave—Another Picture of Slave Life* (London, 1852); *Archy Moore, the White Slave: or Memoirs of a Fugitive* (New York, 1855). Lewis Tappan described Hildreth as "not a member of the Anti-slavery Society, but is an independent thinker, a friend of human rights & a fearless writer." See Lewis Tappan to John Scoble, New York, May 5, 1840, in Annie Heloise Abel and Frank J. Klingberg, *A Side-Light on Anglo-American Relations, 1839–1858* (Washington, 1927), pp. 69, 319. Hildreth published no life of Jefferson.

I leave Norfolk *on the 1st of June* for Charlotte, so that from that date my address will be "Charlotte C. H., Va."

In haste and with kindest regards,

I am truly
Yours.
[no signature]

Mrs. G. is quite well, and my little boy can almost walk. He seems to have an historical taste; for, if he be put down in my study, he instantly crawls to the foot of my table and turns over with evident gusto a set of Hening's Statutes that I have on the floor for convenient reference.[3]

In fear of accidents I enclose your last letter to me.

The Richmond Enquirer of the last mail contained the article in extenso.

[Randall to Grigsby, April 29, 1857]

Cortland Village, N. Y.
Apl 29, 57.

My dear Sir,

I have nothing special to say, but like a horse off from his feed, I am off from writing this afternoon; & I drop you this note to say I am pretty well recovered again, & am fairly at work. But this afternoon I accidentally got some papers badly mixed up together, & it has thrown my thoughts into "pi." When I am well enough to sit up, these *pi* fits don't attack me oftener than once in six weeks. I hear people talk about writing when they are "in the mood."—I am *always* in the mood!

But it is comical that when I get tired & weak I can't tell whether I have got in all the words I want & have not the faintest conception whether they are spelled accurately!

It was my daughter, not a son that wrote you, when I was on my back. My boys are far away.

By the by, I advise you to be cautions how you let Hugh II begin so early in the Statute books!—Those that don't begin until they are eighteen or twenty, often get *too sharp.* If he begins before he is two, the Lord ha' mercy on him.

Well I have worked out that *slavery* problem in my mind! Nous ouvrons! I have got the *religious* problem about solved. I am on the 3d chapter from the end, & they once blocked out.—Still I don't expect to

[3] W. W. Hening, ed., *The Statutes at Large: Being a Collection of All the Laws of Virginia* (13 vols.; Richmond, 1809–1823).

get to printing before June or July. I suppose it makes little difference provided all is ready for fall.—

Pray fire off a long letter at me about matters & things in general, whenever you feel in the spirit of it. How comes on your work? When will you publish? What do you do on your summer estate? Do you confine yourself to literature & social matters, or do you supervise & "bang about" out of doors?

Please present me respectfully to Mrs. Grigsby (for I am determined not to surrender her as an acquaintance though our introduction was none the closest) & please make a low bow for me to Hugh II & tell him I presume to modestly suggest that he had better let *law* books alone for the present.

Truly yours
H. S. Randall

P. S. I think I have already written you to thank you for your attention in respect to the Newspaper article. I started this under the impression that you left Norfolk for Charlotte May 1, instead of June 1.
H. B. Grigsby.
[Endorsed by Grigsby]
Henry S. Randall Esq
Cortland Village N.Y.
April 29, 1857

[Grigsby to Randall, May 28, 1857]

Norfolk, May 28, 1857.

My dear sir,

I received your letter a few days ago, and was much gratified to learn that you had recovered from your severe attack. It must be imprudence in some of its more fascinating guises that has led to your indisposition. Nature has been most bountiful to you in bestowing a stalwart form and especially a pair of lungs that are qualified to perform their manufacturing duties for a century; and if such a machine is allowed to get out of order in a fine healthy atmosphere, it must be from a sad neglect of ordinary care on him who is entrusted with its management.

You have a great advantage over me in respect of lungs. Mine actually pain me at this moment from having written the lines on the opposite page. Indeed but for a life of attention to little things, I should have been in my grave before my twenty fifth year.

As it is, I am tiring to tell you that Dr. Hawks made on the 20th instant at Charlotte in Mecklenburg county, N. C., a speech of three hours and a half in favor of the authenticity of the Mecklenburg Declaration of the 20th of May, 1775, and completely demolished the arguments of those who opposed the truth of that instrument, at least in the opinion of the writers for the newspapers. A reporter for the N. Y. Herald was present, I am told, and you must look out for the report in that paper. I have heard nothing as yet of the scope of his argument; but I sincerely wish that your book had been in the press, that I should have the chance of first following the ingenious writer in the mazes of his argument.[4] I predict that his speech will present one of the most elaborate and admirable specimens of special pleading ever seen outside of the courts of law. But our friend must rest assured either that he has broken my limbs beyond all reach of the medical art, or that his own will be broken in a similar manner. My mode and temper of discussion will depend upon his on the 20th instant. Thus far I have spoken with high-toned courtesy, and if he has adopted a different note, as I suspect from a report in the Columbia S. C. paper he may have done, I may be apt to follow the example of so high an authority. To be candid, such a question can be described best by those *in the negative with a rough tongue.* To call a forgery is more to the point than any mere paraphrase.

We all continue well. My little boy sleeps as soundly as if the Mecklenburg declaration was true, or as if you had finished your work, and was breathing free. What a sad medley are the letters of Webster published in his so called Correspondence? There are, of course, some that are good; but there is no connection and the very letters which we know he must have written on trying occasions are evidently kept back for another generation.[5]

Should you write to me before the tenth, address your letter to Norfolk: after that time to "Charlotte C. H. Va."

Do let me hear of the progress of the "Life."

I write in haste to tell you of the recent demonstration on Mecklenburg.

With kindest regards,
I am truly yours,
Hugh B. Grigsby

Mr. Randall

---

[4] The Grigsby-Randall letters on the Mecklenburg Declaration imply that Grigsby's arguments are incorporated almost verbatim by Randall. *Life,* Appendix II, pp. 570–581. All parties agree on the genuineness of the May 31 document. When Grigsby mistakenly uses the date May 30 he means May 31.

[5] Fletcher Webster, ed., *The Private Correspondence of Daniel Webster* (2 vols.; Boston, 1857).

P. S. Professor Tucker spent two hours with me two weeks ago. He has returned to Philadelphia. His *third* volume is out.[6] His second is good on the commercial difficulties of Jefferson's and Madison's administrations.

[Grigsby to Randall, June 27, 1857]

"Charlotte C. H. Virginia"
June 27, 1857

My dear Sir,

Do I owe you, or do you owe me, a letter? or do each of us owe the other? Well, I have read Dr. Hawk's speech at Charlotte, Mecklenburg County, N. C. on the 20th ult., and have written a deliberate reply which I shall deliver in Philadelphia or elsewhere; as soon as a pamphlet copy with his authority appears. You perceive he could get out of all the dilemmas in which I place him, and avert all my objections, if he had my speech in reply to his newspaper speech before him, when he undertook to prepare a copy for publication.

I think I have riddled the resolutions of the 20th of May pretty thoroughly, and have dealt with the reverend doctor as his shameful misrepresentations and falsifications deserve.

As I wrote you an abstract of my notes on the Mecklenburg question, I must refer you to a more critical analysis of the testimony to my forthcoming speech, which has been prepared with greater care than my letter, and with all the documents in full before me.

I reached here with my family five or six days ago, and shall remain until frost. So remember my post Office.

How comes on the Opus Magnum? How has your health been since your attack? and how and where do you intend to be during the summer?

Let me know all. We are well; though my little boy is suffering from the effects of teething.

With kind regards,

I am, very truly,
Yours
Hugh B. Grigsby

To/
H. S. Randall Eq.
Cortland Village
New York

[6] Tucker, *The History of the United States.*

[Randall to Grigsby, July 26, 1857]

Cortland Village N. Y.
July 26, 1857

My dear Sir,

I wrote you a long letter from N. Y. City a few days since. On reaching home I found it in my trunk *effete!* I write such rattle to bang letters to *friends* that they always sound flat, when they get cold: & if kept till then, they are never sent.

My literary craft is sliding down the stays into the water—publishing. Oh how I wish I had you & Dr. D.[7] & a friend or two more to bore by turns. You would be invaluable in the critical department. I am pressed too hard (not being strong or well) for deliberation or clear headedness. How often have I wished for you.—

Derby & Jackson publish[ers] [are] the most enterprising young firm in N. Y. I suppose I could have chosen. I chose them in preference to one of the two great firms who have too many irons in the fire to *crowd* one. Oh bon-a-vie! the work stretches to 3 vols. 800! printed in Small pica but notes & extracts in finer type. It is stereotyped as we go along—(on new type.) They furnish 3 steel engravings & more if I want them, & fac-similes ad lib. They expect to do it all in the best style. Their first offer to me was the same Mr. Irving received for his Washington[8] & I accepted it of course.*

I discover that *in print* it is a wonderfully outspoken book; but God knows it is an honest one, & I believe it is a *fair* one.

As the work is considered "authorized" I felt it my wish to submit my summing up on slavery to Mr. J's family. G. W. R.[9] writes me that he "neither wished to add, subtract, or alter a word." So, the Lord be thanked, "*somebody* is suited! I presume the fanatics will crucify me, for *telling the truth!* Greeley[10] told one of my publishers just before I visited the city that the work "would be able but very one-sided!!!" There yelled the pack, only they will conclude, when it appears, that it is *not* "able!"

I am glad you propose to give Rev. Dr. H. "special Jesse," when you get him on paper. I was talking with Dr. Cogswell of the Astor Library

* They also declined to have a page of the Mss. Exd in advance taking all on trust.

---

[7] Dr. Robley Dunglison.

[8] Washington Irving (1783–1859), *The Life of George Washington* (5 vols.; New York, 1855–1859).

[9] George Wythe Randolph.

[10] Horace Greeley (1811–1872), used the *Tribune* as an antislavery medium.

about Dr. Hawks.[11] Said C. "He has the most unlogical mind of any man of any pretensions I ever knew. He can't reason any more than a *woman!*"

(My friend through the wall: if you look over your husband's letters, understand that this was Dr. Cogswell's abominably ungallant speech, not mine!—)

I have answered H. in extenso, in Appendix. Wow! I never shall write another word on that subject. You must do the final pulverising.—

I think it will take a couple of months to get clear through. I have to work rather slow for me—for I find a good deal of trimming & paring yet to do.—

I shall be about dead when I get through. I wouldn't wonder if I peeped in on you by & by in Norfolk. I mentioned to you that I promised to visit Gov. Allston of S. C. this fall.[12] I found I could not & so wrote him. He now again writes urging me to come with my wife & daughter & recruit up with him at the time of the holiday, &c.—My family will be other wise engaged. But I have half made up my mind to go myself. If I do, I shall of course visit Richmond, Edgehill, &c. I should hate to go out of the Old Dominion without taking off my hat to you & yours.—Heigho! I have grown ten years older this Summer.

Pray present my compliments to Mrs. Grigsby & Hugh II. I expect the latter grows like a young cedar!

Cordially Yours
H. S. Randall

[Below in pencil]
T. B. Macaulay wrote me the *juiciest* attack on our govt. I ever read. If I had time I would send you a copy.[13]

Mr. Grigsby.
[Endorsed by Grigsby]
Hon. H. S. Randall

[11] Joseph Green Cogswell (1786–1871), librarian and bibliographer, helped John Jacob Astor establish the Astor Library, served as its superintendent (1848–1861), and compiled an *Alphabetical Index to the Astor Library . . . and of the Proposed Accessions* (New York, 1851). Cogswell received his Ph.D. from Goettingen in 1819 and used his knowledge of that library in his work in American libraries. For a recent account of Cogswell, see Orie William Long, *Literary Pioneers, Early American Explorers of European Culture* (Cambridge, Mass., 1935), pp. 77–107.

[12] Robert Francis Withers Allston (1801–1864), governor of South Carolina (1856–1858), rice planter, and scientific agriculturalist.

[13] The famous letters of Lord Macaulay were particularly irritating to Randall and to Grigsby because of their indictment of the whole career of Jefferson. Not American independence, nor American institutions were in Macaulay's opinion in any way responsible for the wealth and greatness of the country. Indeed, had the British monarchy continued in the new world, or had the Hamiltonians had an even greater

[Grigsby to Randall, August 1, 1857]

Edgehill, Friday, Aug. 1, 1857

My dear sir,

Your letter of the 26th, received last evening, was very cheering to me. The intelligence that the Opus Magnum was "sliding down the *stays* into the water," (barring that the metaphor is not strictly nautical,— it should be "ways") was most gratifying. I looked to three volumes from the first; and if Washington's purely *military* life has four volumes,[14] why ought not Jefferson's entire career be entitled to three?

So you have been in New York, and perhaps about the very time that I was on a flying visit to Philadelphia. I was in that city on the 7th, 8th, and 9th of July and on the last mentioned night deliver'd a speech before the Penn: Historical Society, on the Mecklenburg affair in reply to Dr. Hawks. It is not yet printed, and I am not certain when it will be. I am very anxious that you should look it over, as I may possibly have misled you in my Bancroft letter, which was written *currente calamo.*[15] The Penn Historical Society is too poor yet to print its papers; and it is a very heavy task on me to prepare laborious papers, and then to print them at my own expense. I think I have answered the Doctor on every point, and have settled the matter—but *nemo debet esse iudex in sua causa.*

I disagree with Dr. Cogswell about Dr. H. I think the Doctor is a very astute reasoner. His characteristic is not his illogical turn of mind, but an inveterate stubbornness, which will not take in the truth, and an unconquerable prejudice which he is determined to cherish. His hatred of Mr. Jefferson is at the root of his defence of the resolutions of the 20th of May, 1775; and as a free declaration of that prejudice would be unbecoming to him as a Christian and as a politician, he is compelled in his fight against your hero to hoist the flag of state-love and state-

---

triumph, the development of the country would have been equally rapid and the future more secure. Since Randall and Grigsby hated Federalism and ardently believed that American independence was a key to the country's prosperity and power, they smarted under the stinging indictment of Jefferson. Macaulay's reading of the three volumes of the *Life* did not change his mind. The reader will remember that Lord Macaulay's position against increase of popular power was that of leading statesmen, such as Lord John Russell and Lord Palmerston, between the two Reform Bills of 1832 and 1867. The letters ably describe the differences of a century ago between the aristocratic structure of Great Britain and the more democratic society of America. See Sir George Otto Trevelyan, *The Life and Letters of Lord Macaulay* (2 vols.; New York, 1875), II, 407–412. Pertinent extracts of these letters are quoted in Appendix A.

[14] Marshall, *Life of George Washington.*

[15] See above, Grigsby to Randall, December 17, 1856.

pride. Did you ever look at the slur which I think he sought to cast on Mr. Jefferson in relation to that statesman's "Act concerning Religious Freedom,"? You will find it in the Doctor's "Contributions to the Ecclesiastical History of Virginia."'[16] Do you remember the anecdote about the first sentence of the preamble of the act concerning Religious Freedom?[17]

I congratulate you on the terms which you have accepted for your work and sincerely hope that it will bring in a round hundred thousand in less than ten years to your exchequer. It would afford me sincere pleasure to be with you in looking over the sheets. By the way, I have just received a letter from Lippincott & Co. of Philadelphia, informing me that they had forwarded to me by mail, at the Bishop's request, the first volume of Bishop Meade's work on our Old Va. Churches, and religious history, in sheets. It will appear in six or eight weeks, unless kept back from booksellers' reasons. It will make two huge octavos of four or five hundred pages, with sundry engravings, and an Appendix. I wrote the Bishop freely during its publication in numbers. I will certainly be mentioned in the work by quotations and perhaps otherwise; and as you have intimated that you have made a quotation or two from me, I shall have the honor of being kept alive hereafter by two sets of people of my acquaintance of very opposite character, the sacred and the profane.[18]

I saw Dr. D. in Philadelphia during my late visit. He was suffering

[16] In the words of Hawks: "That these various classes should have been protected, both in person and property, is obviously the dictate of justice, of humanity, and of enlightened policy, but it surely was not necessary in securing to them such protection, to degrade, not the establishment, *but Christianity itself* to a level with the voluptuousness of Mohammed, or the worship of Juggernaut: and if it be true that there is danger in an established alliance between Christianity and the civil power, let it be remembered that there is another alliance not less fatal to the happiness, and subversive of the intellectual freedom of man—it is an alliance between the civil authority and infidelity: which whether formally recognized or not, if permitted to exert its influence, direct or indirect, will be found to be equally ruinous in its results. On this subject, revolutionary France has once read to the world an impressive lesson, which it is to be hoped will not speedily be forgotten." *Contributions to the Ecclesiastical History of the United States* (2 vols.; New York, 1836–1839), I, 177–179. For Jefferson's own remarks, see Thomas Jefferson, *Writings,* ed. by H. A. Washington (9 vols.; Washington, 1853–1854), I, 36–37.

[17] An amendment was proposed to the preamble inserting the name of "Our Saviour" before the words "the Holy Author of our religion," which was voted down. Hawks, *Contributions . . .*, I, 177–179. For a copy of the act, including the changes made by the Assembly, see Randall, *Life,* I, 219–220.

[18] Bishop William Meade (1789–1862), third bishop of the Protestant Episcopal Church in Virginia (1841–1862), wrote his *Old Churches, Ministers and Families of Virginia* (2 vols.; Philadelphia, 1857) under the title of "Bishop Meade's Recollections," in serial form for *The Protestant Episcopal Quarterly Review and Church Register* (New York, 1854–1856). Its original publication in numbers enabled Grigsby to correct numerous mistakes before the book appeared.

severely from the gout, though sitting up. His attack is the severest which he has ever encountered; but he is cheerful, and we had some pleasant talks together. I saw Gov. Coles for a few minutes the evening of my arrival. He left town next day. He is very well, and is in better plight than usual. He and Dr. D. also inquired respecting you. I also saw Mr. Gilpin for an half hour.[19] He left the day after I saw him. Professor T. is now engaged on the General Index of his book, to be appended to the fourth volume.[20] I think I told you that Mr. Tucker spent an hour or two with me in my library some weeks ago.

By the way, Edgehill is the name of the estate on which I reside—the patrimonial estate of my wife. It has been so called ever since the beginning of this century. In fear of misleading my correspondents I head my letters with "Charlotte C. H. Va."; although I live five miles from that place.[21]

I sincerely hope to have the pleasure of meeting with you in Norfolk on your proposed jaunt. The best plan is to take the Norfolk boat at Baltimore, and then pass to Richmond from Norfolk. You ought certainly to unbend and relax, or, as Shakespeare Says, "*pause* and live like a gentleman"[22] for a month or two after the publication of the life. You richly deserve a decent holiday.

You *cannot be* ten years older than you were last year. Figures forbid it. It is overwork and over-anxiety that sinks your spirits for a season. You sit and labor too much at one spell. You sit too long and too "solidly on your centre." You must do as Mr. Jefferson did, ride in the open air *daily*.[23] My fear is not that you will grow prematurely old, but that you will be stricken with apoplexy or paralysis; hence my frequent allusions to exercise and vegetable diet.

I suppose you saw the communication of Miss Ellen W. Randolph on the subject of Pocahontas, who was misrepresented in Kingsley's novel of Amyas Leigh. It was read before the Penn: Hist. Society.[24]

By the way, once more. In a volume of the New York Historical Society Collection—ad finem—you will find the account of the sitting of the full house of Burgesses of Virginia in which a Mr. Jefferson is a

[19] Henry Dilworth Gilpin.

[20] Tucker, *The History of the United States.*

[21] Edgehill was also the name of a Randolph estate near Shadwell, the estate of Peter Jefferson. Thomas Jefferson Randolph resided at Edgehill following Jefferson's death and built a new house on that estate. The name "Edgehill" was taken from the site of one of the battles of the English Civil War. Eckenrode, *The Randolphs*, pp. 147, 258.

[22] Misquotation.

[23] Jefferson "continued to ride a little on his favorite horse to within three weeks of his death." Randall, *Life*, III, 538.

[24] Amyas Leigh is the hero of Charles Kingsley's *Westward Ho.*

member. Do look at it. Jefferson is also a chairman of a committee of the House, if I mistake not. The paper was communicated by Bancroft. An extract might do well in the Appendix for our meridian.[25]

Mrs. Grigsby would like to have the pleasure of seeing as well as of hearing you on your next approach to her vicinity. Our boy is cutting teeth. He is now seventeen months old—runs about the yard, hollows after the calves, barks after the dogs, but can only say má and pá. He takes to human talk slowly. I trust your wife and daughter are well. Do they look over the proofs? If you insist upon their doing so, would you not be indictable under that section of our bill of rights, which forbids "cruel and unusual punishments" to be inflicted even on the guilty, much more the innocent?

[no signature]

[Written at top of letter]

If Macaulay is vexed with this country on public grounds, it must be on the score of filibustering, or Pennsylvania financiery. As for the first, whisper to him the word "India;" and as for the second, ask him when has England ever paid the principal and interest of the money shut up in the Exchequer by Charles the Second & William and Mary agreed to pay half; but where is the other half? and does not Mr. M. know that some of the victims of British financiering emigrated to Pennsylvania? So Pennsylvania may be only paying England in her own coin.[26]

[Randall to Grigsby, August 24, 1857]

Aug. 24, '57
Cortland Village

Oh, now, mon ami, wouldn't you be reckoned the *modestest* man on earth! How complacent you must have looked when you wrote you expected to be remembered because I & Dr. —— Somebody[27] had put you in our books! Why, man alive, I have *booked* you as much, I should

[25] "Proceedings of the First Assembly of Virginia, 1619. Communicated with an Introductory Note, by George Bancroft," New York Historical Society *Collections*, 2d series, III (1857), 329–358. Among the list of delegates is this entry: "For Flowerdieu Hundred: Ensign Rossingham, Mr. Jefferson." *Ibid.*, p. 336.

[26] Grigsby may have had William Walker (1824–1860), in mind as an irritant to Macaulay. Walker engaged in filibustering from 1853 to 1860, first in Mexico and then in Central America. John A. Quitman's (1798–1858) interest in the liberation of Cuba belongs to a somewhat earlier time. Whether Macaulay paid any attention to these activities is unknown. For a recent study of Anglo-American financial relations with numerous references to Pennsylvania, see Ralph W. Hidy, *The House of Baring in American Trade and Finance, English Merchant Bankers at Work* (Cambridge, Mass., 1949), *passim.*

[27] Bishop William Meade.

say, as five times,[28] & placed your name second in the list of those to whom acknowledgements are made in Preface.*[29] I have kicked out all that could raise a bruize about old William Randolph's occupation, on purpose to let there be peace between your people and my people. I have been more than liberal to G. T.[30] partly on your account, partly on Dr. D's acct (& partly on his own.)—All this I have done purely for *my own* interest—to let the trogolydites [*sic*] know what good company I keep! And now you come simpering up with a meek face & tell me that *you* expect to be remembered, because I & Dr. What do you call 'em have booked you! Wasn't you a bad *rogue* when you was young? I shall ask Mrs. G. about it when I come to Norfolk next winter! That I will!—The stereotypers have got nearly to close of Vol. 1. I shall, as soon as they begin to print, direct sheets to be sent to you—By the by, one thing is a little awkward. My pub's have concluded to issue by subscription. This will send out first vol. a month or two first.—

I have treated the Slavery fire brand like all other questions—*chronologically*—that is given *some* of his passing expressions with the occasion that called them forth. The summing up is in the 3d. vol.[31] I mentioned to you that the Randolphs & even Pryor[32] was *satisfied* that I had handled this topic justly & prudently—that they were *satisfied.* Still, some fiery sons of—(guns) of Editors *might* fancy from these earlier excursions (necessary to show a decent regard for biographical truth or accuracy) *and in the absence of the summing up,* that the tendency of the work was to favor the present foolish agitation; & raise a fuss that would injure me severely.—Now my wiser friends must pass round the word quietly, but not in a shape that it will come back in some cantankerous newspaper, to give my opponents *here* a deadly advantage of me by saying that I have submitted my work to *"Southern dictation"* &c. &c. If a word is necessary in Norfolk I will rely on you to Speak it—& safely.—

I would like much to have you review the work in a series of shorter or longer papers in the Enquirer perhaps, or if you don't feel free there,

* Second to J. C. Cabell's, & he is dead.

---

[28] See above, Randall to Grigsby, November 14, 1856, n. 88.

[29] Joseph Carrington Cabell (1778–1856), next to Jefferson the founder of the University of Virginia, which he helped shape for thirty-seven years as rector, visitor, and legislative supporter.

[30] George Tucker.

[31] See Randall, *Life,* III, Appendix XXXIV, pp. 667–669.

[32] Roger Atkinson Pryor (1828–1919), associated for a time with Thomas Ritchie on the Richmond *Enquirer.* In 1857 he founded the ultra-Southern newspaper, *The South* (March, 1857–November, 1858) and became an ardent secessionist. In late 1858 he moved to Washington to edit *The States* and serve as a Virginia congressman (1859–1861). Cappon, *Virginia Newspapers, 1821–1935,* p. 184.

in your Norfolk paper. Entre nous, my entire reliance is on the democracy, & there are few of them in the north. If my work sells merrily, why I am in clover.—otherwise, oh bon-a-vie!

I sent you a circular just recd from my publishers. I would have omitted some of the last sentences from the Comml. Advertiser article but these publishers will have their own way.[33] Now send me a list of names (I care not how large) to whom it would be well to have my publishers send this circular—*all classes of men*. I should by all means have given them your article in Norfolk Arg. to include, & I looked for it *hours*, but it was irrecoverably mislaid.—Let your list scatter as widely as your local acquaintance extends over the State. Seeing what "the South" says will help guard against the fears I have named. And the Com. Advertiser & the Phil. N. Am. are about as much against agitation.—

You may use the sheets sent you just as you please.

Your worn out, tired out, half blind, three-thirds sick

humble Servant
H. S. Randall.

Remember me to Mrs. G. & Saxon Hugh. I shall make my bow to the former & shake a rattle at the latter *this winter*, if I am alive & well.—

I *was* in N. Y. when you were in P. I would have gone across in less than no time had I known it.

Burn this foolish letter as soon as you read it.

[Endorsed by Grigsby]
Hon. H. S. Randall
Aug. 24, 1857
Answered Sept. 8, 1857

[Grigsby to Randall, September 20, 1857]

Charlotte C. H., Virginia
September 20, 1857

My dear sir,

I hope to read your books through a dozen times before my history of the Va. Federal Convention of 1788 will be given to the public.[34] What I shall say about the reported sayings of Mr. Jefferson mentioned by Webster will be just what you would say and with the same love of

[33] *New York Commercial Advertiser*, March 24, 1857.

[34] This discourse was delivered before the Virginia Historical Society, February 23, 1858, but a published version did not appear until 1890–1891.

St. Thomas as yours.[35] It will be explanatory. Thus when Mr. J. wonders where Henry obtained his polished language, I will refer to his early instruction by a Scotch teacher critically skilled in Latin, in that language reading under such a guide even Virgil and Livy. This is the true explanation, and one applicable to all, on some scale, who have shown a mastership of phrase.[36] *Et sic omnia.* I will also dwell upon the *onus* of Webster's report, which is that, taking Henry all in all, "we could not have done without him:"—a Compliment whose brilliance would hide a thousand flystains.[37]

I wish I could put you *en rapport* with my friend, John Henry: but he is so peculiar, and so unable to correspond by letter with anybody, that I fear it will be impossible without a personal interview. He is sixty one or two, reads the papers, and hardly any thing else, has not one scintilla of genius, has hardly common sense, is so odd as to attract the attention of the children by the queerness of his behaviour, sometimes does not see the point of a jest until half an hour after it was uttered, and then when the point of it has gradually worked its way into the brain, bursting out in an explosion which shakes the house, and acts in other ways so queerly that you could only know him kindly at his own house or at the house of some intimate friend. *I* always endeavour to *put down* unkind and funny observations about him by some such talk as this: "Gentlemen, if we think that John Henry is not such a son as Patrick's son ought to be, we ought to remember that his family has produced *one* Patrick, and before other families have returned the compliment, they ought to have the grace to keep their mouths shut at least."[38]

---

[35] See Randall, *Life*, I, 490–491; III, 505–509: Fletcher Webster, ed., *The Private Correspondence of Daniel Webster*, I, 364–373.

[36] Henry's "father was a Scotchman and a teacher, and was so well versed in the Latin classics, that no less a judge than Samuel Davies pronounced him, Scotchman as he was, more intimately conversant with his Horace than with his Bible. As it is well-known that the Scotch teach their children Latin at an early age, it is probable that Henry was in his early youth skilled in the rudiments of that tongue." John Adams recorded that Henry had stated at the 1774 congress that he had read Virgil and Livy, at fifteen, but had not read a Latin book since. Grigsby, *The Virginia Convention of 1776*, p. 145. See *ibid.*, pp. 144–154, and Grigsby, *The History of the Virginia Federal Convention of 1788*, I, *passim*, for sketches and penetrating evaluations of Henry. See also William Wirt, *Sketches of the Life and Character of Patrick Henry* (Philadelphia, 1817); M. C. Tyler, *Patrick Henry* (Boston, 1887); William Wirt Henry, *Patrick Henry: Life, Correspondence and Speeches* (3 vols.; Boston, 1891).

[37] "We could not have got along in the Revolution without him . . . he was a man of enlarged views . . . he was a truly great man" were some of the expressions Jefferson used when speaking of Henry. Randall, *Life*, III, 508.

[38] John Henry (1796–1868), youngest child of Patrick Henry, lived the life of a planter on the "Red Mill" estate, the last homestead of his father, and although only two years old at the time of his father's death, he was steeped in family lore. Grigsby, *The History of the Virginia Federal Convention of 1788*, I, 4.

But with all my love for him, I cannot but see that he is at times ridiculous to the last degree, nothing but his personal virtue and respectability of position, and, above all, his enthusiastic devotion to the memory of his father, redeeming him from social outlawry.

I will show him or read to him parts of your letter when I see him, and in that way kindle the flame of kindness between you. You could accomplish every thing by a visit, and when you visit Norfolk, I will go to Charlotte with you if you have five or six days to spare. I will take you to my house and thence drive in my buggy to Red Hill. The visit will be of intense interest, but will cost you about four days and fifteen or sixteen dollars in travel; but it will repay it all. And although I consider it disgraceful that such a man as John Henry should not procure the earliest copy of your work, yet, as he is slow in the book-line, if you had a spare copy for him it would be received as an heirloom, and I think, under the peculiar circumstances of the gift, will soften him towards our common saint.

Now, as I have written to you on a matter strictly confidential and which, if seen by others must lead to painful results to ladies as well as gentlemen, I must ask you to burn this letter.

With kindest regards and in the greatest haste, Very truly

Yours,
[no signature]

[Randall to Grigsby, September –, 1857]

Cortland Village
Sept. 1857

My dear Sir,

Yours came yesterday.—

I write immediately to make a suggestion to you & to Mr. Henry.[39] His modesty as regards his own family has led him, I apprehend, not to sufficiently realize one certain & undoubted fact. You might as well attempt to pluck Washington & Jefferson from the *hearts* of the American people as Patrick Henry. You might as well attempt to push the Alleghanies from their bases! He was *the* Southern torch bearer of the Revolution. He was *the* orator of his whole country. He never has been even approached in the latter particular.

The whole conversations recorded by Mr. Webster are just enough colored or discolored to be made caricatures.—I have particularly

[39] John Henry.

alluded to Mr. Websters Memoranda & cited *better authority than my own* to show that they are (unintentional) exaggerations[40]—If directly attacked, in detail, in respect to Patrick Henry, it would probably call out controversy, & you would have all of Wirt's private statements to Judge Carr, conspicuously paraded &c.[41] My impressions are clear & positive that Jefferson had not a particle of ill-will towards Mr. Henry—on the other hand that he admired & was *attached* to him. I have proceeded on this supposition throughout my work. I presume I have in all given nearly 50 pages to Patrick Henry.[42] Next to Madison, & John Adams I think I have given him the most important place among my dramatis personae, after my "hero." I *love* Patrick Henry. I would deviate two hundred miles from my road to shake the hand of the man who can call him father. I respect John Henry's sensitiveness. It is the sensitiveness of filial piety. I wish very much I had the honor of his acquaintance. I hope I may hereafter have that honor.

I have not taken Wirt's *public* model of Henry. I consider it dressed up & untrue to the original. I think he has made a different man, & in reality a *less*[er] man.—I speak freely of Henry's peculiarities, of what I esteem his foibles. But I *believe* I have presented a picture of him which will show that I *love* him—& that will make others *love* him—not as a Roman stalking round majestically in a toga, & talking blank verse, but as

"the forest born Demosthenes.—"[43]

as the magnificently gifted child of wild nature—as the true lyrical & transcendantly first orator of his country.[44]

I am free to say I think any issue made between him & Jefferson would be founded on misconception; & I believe is wholly uncalled for. I know you would not place an explanation on erroneous grounds, but I would

[40] Fletcher Webster, ed., *The Private Correspondence of Daniel Webster,* I, 364–373, has Webster's "Memorandum of Mr. Jefferson's Conversations." Randall drew upon the recollections of Jefferson's family and of others to correct Webster. See Randall, *Life,* III, 505–510.

[41] Wirt (1772–1834), attorney-general under Monroe and John Q. Adams, wrote his *Sketches of the Life and Character of Patrick Henry* while engaged in a busy legal career. Much of Wirt's material was obtained from those who had known Henry. Wirt's close friend, Dabney Carr (1773–1837), was the son of Jefferson's sister, Martha. Randall undoubtedly was familiar with John P. Kennedy, *Memoirs of the Life of William Wirt* (2 vols.; Philadelphia, 1850), and has reference to the correspondence between Wirt and Carr which appears in that work. See Kennedy, *passim,* for an account of Wirt's life of Henry as well as for his correspondence with Carr, Jefferson, and others.

[42] See Randall, *Life,* III, Index, p. 698, for his references to Henry.

[43] "Henry, The forest-born Demosthenses, Whose thunder shook the Philip of the seas," Randall, *Life,* I, 37–38. Ernest H. Coleridge, ed., *The Works of Lord Byron* (13 vols.; London, 1898–1905), V, 560.

[44] For Randall's evaluation of Henry, see *Life,* I, 20, 37; III, 508.

most respectfully suggest that all explanations be deferred until you see what view Mr. Jefferson's *family* take of the Webster Memoranda.—A month or two will bring it before the public in my third volume.—[45]

I wish there was some way for me to make the acquaintance of John Henry. I am half a mind to write to him. You are at liberty to show him my views.—I would like you to bring us into some kind of contact. I would rather know the son of Patrick Henry than the President.

Yours in haste,
H. S. Randall

Burn this Postscript

P. S.

The Circular was designed only as an *introduction;* to set men talking or thinking; & *incidentaly* to show that the work comes from no *abolition* quiver. I presume no extensive orders by mail are expected & please have no reference whatever to that idea, in the list you send.—Send a list of the thinkers & talkers & prominent men.[46]

By my word! I *would* like to know John Henry—I care not whether he is a talented man or not. Cannot you get him to write me on the strength of my letter? Would it do for me to write to him? Cannot you contrive an acquaintance on paper? I have fallen *in love* with his father since I have studied him out of Wirts *ridiculous* dressing up. It is the least life-like biog. I ever read without one exception. And Wirts grinning confessions to Carr, don't leave *him* in my judgment *exactly* in a position where *I* would like to stand! I don't believe in two squeaks in a voice—one for the public & one for private ears!!

Cordial regards to Mrs. Grigsby & *young* Cedric of Rotheswood.

By the by, if your wife interests herself in your private & literary corr. I wish you to understand that no injunction to confidence, or to "burn" is to cut *her* off from any thing *I* write. Tell Mrs. G. I have *imagined* about her, until I have made her out a particular acquaintance & particular *friend!* I won't say any more as you called me a *young* man in your last! Again cordially.

H. S. R.

[Endorsed by Grigsby]
Henry S. Randall
Sept. 1857
Answered Sept. 21, '57

[45] *Ibid.*, III, 506–508.

[46] See above, Randall to Grigsby, August 24, 1857, in which a list was requested.

[Grigsby to Randall, October 6, 1857]

Charlotte Court, Va.
October 6, 1857

My dear Sir,

I send you some names on the other side. I wish I had it in my power to send you their dollars instead of their names. I suppose that, as the nights are getting longer, your volumes will soon appear. I am eager to greet them.

Let me say in reference to your opinions about Wirt's life of Henry that I do not coincide with you in some important respects. That there is much bad taste in the writing, that the work was hastily and imperfectly executed, and that the fame of Henry deserves a fitter record, I cheerfully concede, but with all these deductions the "life of Henry," or rather, as he modestly calls his book, The Sketches of the life of Henry," are a most worthy and particular contribution to our biographical literature. It has done great good, and will do great good for years to come. I have said this much lest by my silence I should appear to approve your wholesale condemnation of that work.

John Henry lives twenty five miles from my house, and I rarely see him unless when we visit each other. When I see him, I shall speak with him on the topic of your last letter.

I suppose the day of your freedom is at hand. We are all well. My little boy is thriving, and seizes the reins in driving with a gee-up to the horse.

I have been compelled to cut my tobacco crop green because it *fired;* but hoping that you will never be a tobacco-planter, and that, if you should be, your tobacco may never *fire,*

I am, very truly,
Yours
Hugh B. Grigsby

Henry S. Randall Eq.
Cortland Village
New York

[The following document appears on second folded page of letter dated October 6, 1857, but bears date of September 6, 1857—since the two sheets are attached (really one sheet of paper) the list seems to have been made earlier and not sent until the October date, or a mistake in the date written "September" may have been made. The letter is endorsed in the writing of Randall, "Hugh B. Grigsby, October 6, 1857.]

Charlotte C. H. Va. Sept. 6, 1857

Dear Sir,

I send a list of names at your request, with the post offices of the persons mentioned.

Massingford P. O. Charlotte Cy. Va.

Capt. Wm. M. Watkins,	Wm. B. Green.

Charlotte C. H.

Col. J. P. Marshall,	Wyatt Cardwell,
William T. Scott,	William Cardwell,
Joel W. Marshall,	Col. Wilcher Cardwell,
H. H. Marshall,	Thomas Watkins,
W. O. Bouldin,	Dr. Joel Watkins,
David Morton, jun.,	John F. Edmunds,
R. J. Gaines,	Nicholas Edmunds,
R. V. Gaines,	Henry Scott,
W. W. Read,	James Scott,
David Comfort,	John Edmunds,
William Smith,	William J. Watkins,
John Smith,	Capt. McGehee.

Roanoke Bridge, P. O. Charlotte Cy. Va.

Capt. Jam. D. Morton,	John Spencer,
Capt. Jacob Morton,	Alex. Spencer.
William Morton,	

Richmond, Va.

Wm. H. Macfarland,	Gustavus Myers,
Conway Robinson,	John M. Patton.
John R. Tucker,	

Norfolk, Va.

George Loyall,	Harrison Robertson,
John B. Whitehead,	Myer Myers,
Conway Whittle,	Littleton W. Tazewell, Hon:
Col. George Blow,	John N. Tazewell,
Gen. John S. Millson,	Tazewell Taylor,

John T. Francis,
Mallory W. Todd,
R. Chamberlaine,
Alex. Tunstall,
R. W. Bowden,
James H. Behan,
Walter J. Doyle,
John E. Doyle,
Henry Irwin,
J. J. Moore,
T. J. Cornich,
William T. Hendren,
William P. Stewart,
Thos. J. Corphew,
J. Marsden Smith,
George MacIntosh,
Cincinnatus Newton,
Dr. Thos. Newton,
Dr. D. C. Barraud,
Otway B. Barraud,
Charles H. Shield,
Hon. Francis Mallory,
James Southgate,
Dr. E. O. Balfour,
Dr. William Selden,
Dr. Tunstall,
William W. Sharp,
Charles Sharp,
Dr. G. W. Cowdrey,
John Higgins,
Dr. Nash,
Hardy & Brothers,
Finlay Ferguson,
William P. Griffith,
John D. Ghizelin, jun.,
John Williams,
Boerum & McLean,
William Southgate,
Geo. W. Camp,
Duncan Robertson.

[Endorsed by Randall]
Hugh B. Grigsby
October 6, 1857

[Randall to Grigsby, November 3, 1857]

Cortland Village, Nov. 3d

My dear Sir.

This is election day. We must doubtless be beaten; but we shall make heavy gains on the Sectional & Anti Constitutional party.[47]

We have had a commercial earthquake "up here." Have you heard of it? Nor is it quite over. The ground yet shakes, & fissures constantly open swallowing up this & that poor devil.

St. Thomas goes on stereotyping—but his appearance is deferred for an uncertain period—perhaps two weeks, perhaps two months. You will receive sheets as soon as we commence printing. I enclose you 3 pages of plate proof. It looks like t——r, being printed on dry paper.—I send

[47] This election was a Democratic victory. Gideon J. Tucker was elected Secretary of State; Sanford E. Church, Comptroller; Lyman Tremaine, Attorney-General; Hiram Denio, member of the Court of Appeals. Information obtained in correspondence with Edna L. Jacobsen, Associate Librarian, New York State Library.

it to you to let you see my farewell to Patrick Henry.[48] It is a little more in the "Spread Eagle" fashion than I often indulge in: but the moment I start on "old Pat," my pen takes the bit & prances away at its own gait. Can't help it. I am a thorough lover.—I love no man or woman by halves!—You see *about* my manner of treating him generally. I refer to him 20, maybe 50 times. Now I hope, on my Soul, that the *Son* I take so deep an interest in because he so devoutly cherishes his fathers fame, will appreciate my quo animo & not feel hurt because with manly freedom I mix the unpleasant with the pleasant truth. You may, if you please, enclose the pages entire or in part to J. H. & tell him something about my feelings towards his father throughout my work. Write so as to *draw out an answer* from him & let me see the answer. No matter if it is "over the left." Patrick Henry's Son cannot offend me. I know not why I feel so strong an interest in the singular man you described to me.—

These are me[l]ancholy times for authors in the book selling way. Heigho! Heigho!

How is Mrs. Grigsby & Saxon Hugh? Have you had a pleasant summer of it? By the by, what's become of that queer Randolph whom you once told me of?[49] You told me something very interesting of his connexion with J. of Roanoke & his peculiarities but I have suffered it all to fade into dimness in my mind. What think you of J. R. of Roanoke? I expect some of you "f. f. v's" will think I have been severe on him. I confess I have no admiration for him.—I have given him a full-length picture where I record his defection from the Republican party. What an infernal liar (politely speaking) is that melo-dramatic biographer of his? How carefully he slurs telling the truth![50]

Yes, I shall here & there step on *several* toes! I have no where been consciously vindictive. I have never intentionally traveled out of my

---

[48] "Except in his divine gift of oratory, there were other perhaps greater than he; but not one was so indispensable. He was the Tribune of the People—the exponent of their innermost hearts—the master of the magical key which unlocked and gave the control of their minds. He was the first—incomparably the first—orator of his country. None approached him but (in his great moods) titanic John Adams." Randall, *Life*, II, 494.

[49] St. George Randolph, a nephew of John Randolph of Roanoke. Eckenrode refers to him as a "hopeless lunatic." *The Randolphs*, p. 187. For a fuller treatment, see Marion Harland [pseud. Mary Virginia Terhune], *Autobiography, the Story of a Long Life* (New York, 1910), pp. 320–324. This deaf and dumb Randolph was a local celebrity of Charlotte, Virginia, about "whom clung a glamour of romantic importance." *Ibid.*, p. 323.

[50] John Randolph of Roanoke (1773–1833), a great-grandson of William Randolph I, was the subject of a biography by Hugh A. Garland, *The Life of John Randolph* (New York, 1850). For Randall's analysis of Randolph's character and ability, see *Life*, III, 152–159. For Grigsby's estimate, see *The Virginia Convention of 1829–30*, pp. 41–45.

path to blame.—But I have recorded the honest convictions of my own mind. Of course then I have not whitewashed *everybody*. I would rather be a dog & bay the moon than write in that sickly, silly, adulatory, mutual-admiration-Society, mutual scratch-back, tickle-me Billy-&-I'll tickle-you-billy spirit in which most of our American biographies have been written. Yet I spurn the man who will carry a conscious personal or partisan resentment into a book *intended* for preservation.—

Remember me most respectfully to Mrs. G. & the Saxon.

With Cordial regards
Henry S. Randall

Hugh B. Grigsby E.
[Endorsed by Grigsby]
Henry S. Randall,
Cortland Village, N. Y.
Nov. 3, 1857
Answered Nov. 12, 1857

[Grigsby to Randall, November 12, 1857]

Charlotte C. H. Virginia,
Nov. 12, 1857

My dear sir,

Your letter of the third instant was received last evening. We, too, have had the tempest in the money market in our cities; but such things have but little weight with thrifty and economical planters who live on their estates. It must, however, prove serious in many respects in all business affairs. My neighbour, Mrs. Terhune, the wife of the pastor of our Presbyterian church, tells me that your publishers, who are also hers, remain firm, and will probably weather the storm. You know she is the Marion Harland of "Alone," "The Hidden Path," and "Moss-Side".[51]

I returned last week from a visit with Mrs. G. and her infant to some friends on Staunton River, and, among others, to John Henry and his family at Red Hill. I spoke of you to him. He is, as I think I informed you, inclined to be hostile to Mr. Jefferson, and has spoken freely about him to others; but he has never spoken a word against him in my presence. I spoke to Mr. Henry of yourself and of your forthcoming work, and gave him a copy of your publisher's circular. I also took the liberty of showing him a part of one of your letters to me. When he had read

[51] Marion Harland (1830–1922), a popular romantic novelist, wrote many books mostly concerned with the South before or during the Civil War. A pioneer in home economics.

it, he said that you had a warm heart, that there must be no controversy about his father and Mr J., and that he would be happy to see you at his house. More than once during the visit he repeated to me that he would be most happy to see you, and requested me to say so to you when I wrote you again. I shall transmit to him the proof contained in your last; but from the peculiar caste of his habits and character I cannot expect any acknowledgment in writing of the opinions which he may draw from your remarks. He cannot but be gratified with your manner of treating the memory of his father. One word before I go further, though I fear it comes too late. Garland's speech put into the mouth of John Randolph is *wholly* apocryphal. Randolph had a cold and could say but a few words.[52] See my sketch of J. R. in the discourse on the Va. Convention of 1829–30[53] and the article of Dr. Archibald Alexander who was present at the time, in the Va. Historical Register.[54]

I will probably make my movement Norfolkward in a few days; so *hereafter* my address will be the city of Norfolk.

My papers lead me to believe that we have carried New York.—I think you need not fear any thing from your remarks on John Randolph. The warm friends of Randolph are the warm foes of Jefferson, and their hatred must follow necessarily.

Mrs. Grigsby and our boy have been well during the summer. He is growing finely, though small, taking after the mother's side of the house. Mrs. G. is much gratified at your kind recollections and good wishes.

I trust the money atmosphere may clear up, if it were only that your volumes might run their course under favorable circumstances.

I await the proofs with deep interest. Be kind enough to request the publishers to address them to me at Norfolk.

With kind regards, and in great haste,
I am very truly Yours,

Hugh B. Grigsby

Henry S. Randall Eq.

Cortland Village
[Endorsed by Randall]
Hugh B. Grigsby,
November 12, 1857

[52] Randall, *Life*, II, 494–495, has a brief reference to this affair and cites Garland, *The Life of John Randolph*, I, 129–130.

[53] Grigsby, *The Virginia Convention of 1829–30*, pp. 41–45.

[54] Archibald Alexander (1772–1851), Presbyterian clergyman, educator, and author "Reminiscences of Patrick Henry," *The Virginia Historical Register and Literary Note Book*, III (1850), 205–213. This reprint from the *Princeton Magazine* mentions an encounter between Randolph and Henry which is further commented on by a reader in "Patrick Henry and John Randolph," *ibid.*, IV (1851), 34–36.

[Randall to Grigsby, December 24, 1857]

C. V. Dec. 24, '57

My dear Sir.

D. & J.[55] wrote me they have sent you my 1st vol.—(of a small edition got out in advance for printers &c)—I discover it contains a number of typographical errors. These don't mar the sense, but they do the grammar, &c. I shall have them corrected so far as discovd. before an edition goes to press.—I was overworked & ill, & relied too much, of necessity, on proof readers.

I observe the N. Y. Papers are opening their mouths. The Herald seems to think it is a pretty good book, but it might have been made better by *omissions*.[56] The Post (Bryants paper) give me credit for great "fervor, Clearness & vigor of expression rising sometimes into eloquence"—& he insinuates I am decidedly honest—but he complained too that I have inserted irrelevant matter and pitches with great fury into typographical blunders (*making* two of them himself) & verbal criticism.—When he sees more of the work he will be *severer* yet![57]

The truth is the work cannot suit sectionalists—or anybody affected with the Southern-phobia. That disease rages now in the north. Greeley was in this town yesterday. He said I was a "worshipper" &c.—& intimated that I would *catch* it in the Tribune. I unquestionably shall.

My "superfluous matter" consists principally of two things—a *history* of Jeffersons Governorship—and that puts the whole South & Virginia especially in a position of honor in regard to the Revolutionary Contest, which is wormwood to our sectionalists.[58] They literally hunted Gilmore Simms out of N. Y. City for defending the conduct of his own State, (S. C.) in the Revolution.[59] Second, considering Jeff. the founder of the Democratic party, I could not give his life without giving his connexion with that party. This involved some outlines of the history of that party & consequently of its antagonist.[60] I make out a very bad *parentage* for the present sectional party!! Hence those tears. This I believe is a fair interpretation of their motives. And they will display more fury as more vols. are pubd.

[55] Derby and Jackson, Randall's publishers.

[56] The New York *Herald*, December 20, 1857.

[57] The New York *Evening Post*, December 19, 1857.

[58] For Randall's account of Jefferson as governor of Virginia, see *Life*, I, 238–361.

[59] William Gilmore Simms (1806–1870), Southern novelist and journalist. In 1856 he defended the South in a series of lectures in New York but was forced to abandon his talks.

[60] For Randall's account of Jefferson as founder of the Democratic party, see *Life*, I, 632–645.

Between you & I, my defence or overthrow will be *practically* a question of politics. I always told you I could hope for nothing, finally, but for the approbation of old fashioned State right democrats.—Virginia & Pa. papers (but most especially the former) will give the *cue* among the democrats of the Union.—

I hope they will assume no controversial tone at the outset with respect to northern criticisms or notice them. That is not the best way to help me. But I hope if I have given faithful history, it will be recognized as such. Why should we have four vols. to bring Washingtons life down to his presidency—every part worked out to minute detail[61]—& then not have the history of Jeffersons *governorship* because forsooth it does justice to his State! And why should we not have, for once, *the other side of the medal,* in political history? And where could it be appropriate if not in a life of J?—

My letter book says I wrote you on the 13th.[62] I utterly forget *what.*—Perhaps I to some extent covd. the ground I am now covering. But I apprehend not. I am *worked* out of all recollection! I merely go like a machine.—

I shall make no hestitation in saying in your friendly ear that my fate, in the life of J. hangs mainly on Va. If the presses of that state *vigorously* sustain me, I shall "flourish" despite all else: if not, I am—am—"up a stump!" (The name of the Enquirer sounds biggest abroad)—but I *hope* to see more than one Spear couched.—*If you believe I have done the fair & the true thing* I shall rely more on you than any body else. But I must stop writing for the mail.—Burn this swift and incoherent scrawl.

Your friend
H. S. Randall

[Endorsed by Grigsby]
H. S. Randall,
Dec. 4, 1857 [*sic*]

[Grigsby to Randall, December 29, 1857]

Norfolk, Dec. 29, 1857

My dear sir,

I received your last letter a few moments since, and I drop you a line to say that I received the first volume of the Life of Jefferson two days

[61] Marshall, *Life of George Washington.*
[62] This letter is not in this collection.

ago. I have gone into it as far as the administration of Jefferson which I have not yet finished, but I have read enough to see that you have given us a most excellent book which deserves the cordial support of every Virginian of every shade of party. Your fullness in Virginia history during Mr Jefferson's term is a great recommendation of your work, as you fill a chasm which has always been bewailed by me. Of course, there will be severe animadversions of the friends of Harry Lee[63] and others, but when you recal what those friends have written of Jefferson you calculated upon such results when you undertook faithfully to do your duty to your subject. I think there is a material improvement in the style as you advance. But I am yet unable to tell what will be the full effect of your book on my mind until I have read it. Thus far I am full of hope and courage.

The South must support your work; but the South is slow to purchase. You must make up your mind that the day of ultimate success will certainly arrive, without indulging too sanguinely the belief that the time will be short. I am convinced that no Virginian could have dared to do that justice to Mr. J. which you have done. And the vindication of Mr. J. has an additional force in coming from one beyond our limits.

I will drop a line to the Enquirer to ask whether the editors will undertake to review the work themselves, or will receive a notice from me. The younger editor is very clever and able, and may prefer the task for himself.[64]

I have written this letter in great haste merely to acknowledge the receipt of your work and your last two letters.

I should think that the virulence of the Tribune will tell favorably in the South; but it may affect the sale in the nonslaveholding states.

I thank you for the kind recognition of my name in your preface; and had I been near you, I certainly would have done all that was possible for me.

Should you ever have a circular for a new emission, I will at any time suggest what occurs to me. About Henry you are mistaken; that letter

[63] Henry Lee (1756–1818), "Light-Horse Harry," *Memoirs of the War in the Southern Department of the United States* (2 vols.; Philadelphia, 1812), indicted Jefferson's civil and military administration of Virginia. These *Memoirs* were republished by his son, Henry Lee (Washington, 1827), and by another son, Robert E. Lee (New York, 1869). The revised edition is friendly to Jefferson's administration. See Randall, *Life*, I, 102–103, 153–157, 210–212, 301–304, and III, Appendix XXXII, pp. 660–664, which has the correspondence which passed between Jefferson and Henry Lee, the son of "Light-Horse Harry" shortly before Jefferson's death. See also H. Lee, *Observations on the Writings of Thomas Jefferson, with Particular Reference to the Attack They Contain on the Memory of the Late Gen. Henry Lee* (New York, 1832).

[64] William W. Dunnavant is probably referred to.

of Charles Lee set you wrong.[65] I know that letter well. But it is distinctly stated by Edmund Randolph that Henry advocated the resolution for independence on the floor of the Convention with unrivalled powers of eloquence.[66] In a memorandum on page 203 of my discourse on the Va. Convention of 1776, beginning *"Dec. 12, 1855."*[67] This is one of the class of trifles when compared with the great object of your work, which I would have pointed out. But I see a noble spirit of justice and magnaminity in all your statements, and an utter incapacity on your part to act unkindly or ungenerously by any one. I think you pressed too hard upon Richard Henry Lee on the subject of the headship of the Declaration Committee, but this is a matter which you have a right to decide upon for yourself; and it may be that something to come hereafter in the work may be founded upon it.[68]

You see I must write very unsatisfactorily to you at this stage of my perusal of the "life," as I have not read the half of the first volume yet.

Should a notice of the first volume appear in the Enquirer *before* the other volumes appear?

In great haste,

Yours truly,

Hugh B. Grigsby

H. S. Randall, Esq:
[Endorsed by Randall]
Hugh B. Grigsby
December 29, 1857

---

[65] By relying on a letter of Charles Lee (1758–1815), a brother of Henry Lee, printed in Force, *American Archives*, 5th series, I, 96, Randall gives the impression that Patrick Henry was hesitant about making the resolution for independence. See Randall, *Life*, I, 128. After consulting Grigsby the error was corrected in an Appendix. See *ibid.*, III, Appendix XXXVIII, pp. 679–680.

[66] Edmund Randolph (1753–1813), member of the Continental Congress (1779–1782), governor of Virginia (1786–1788), member of the Constitutional Convention, United States attorney-general and secretary of state. See Grigsby, *The Virginia Convention of 1776*, pp. 76–79.

[67] Grigsby states: "It is due to the reputation of Pendleton, Henry and Nelson to state a fact which I accidentally discovered some days ago in the Virginia Gazette of Nov. 2, 1803. It is there reported that Edmund Randolph in his address at the funeral of Pendleton stated that the resolution instructing our Delegates in Congress to declare independence was drawn by Pendleton, was offered in convention by Nelson, and was advocated on the floor by Henry." Grigsby, *The Virginia Convention of 1776*, pp. 203–204.

[68] Richard Henry Lee (1732–1794), on June 7, 1776, introduced the resolution that "These united colonies are, and of right ought to be free and independent states; . . ." in the Continental Congress. Question raised, why then was he not made a member of the committee of five, which drafted the Declaration of Independence. See Randall, *Life*, I, 102–103, 144–161.

[Grigsby to William Foushee Ritchie, December 30, 1857]

Norfolk, Dec. 30, 1857

My dear sir,[69]

I have just read with great pleasure your notice of Mr Randall's life of Jefferson, and highly approve of the judgment shown in making interesting extracts from the work. I wish to speak to you in confidence. This book is the truest and most fearless life of our great Statesman which has been published or can ever be published. No Virginian could have performed the work so fearlessly and therefore so effectually. What I have to ask is that you will allow me editorially to review this first volume some-what in detail in a spirit of historical criticism. My interest is excited in the work from the fact that it is essentially a southern book; and *par excellence* a *Virginia* book. The review of Jefferson's gubernatorial term is the most full account of that period in existence, and is our best history for that epoch.[70] These things should be handsomely acknowledged by Southern men, and in a mode that shows the worth of the author is fully appreciated by us. And yet all this should be done in a spirit of history.

I think I will not require more than two thirds of a column for a number, and not more than two or three numbers, probably not so much; and I will write in continuation of your own capital article on the subject.

As I have not written a line or even cast the proportions of the review, I must speak vaguely; and indeed I will not undertake the task until you inform me whether my labors would be acceptable to you.

I know the tenor of the succeeding volumes, but of course I shall not touch them until they appear.

I congratulate you and would cordially congratulate your dear father[71] if he were living, on this noble and first great defence in the forum of history of our noble chief of Monticello. The South and the South alone must sustain my friend Randall. He does by Jefferson what northern

[69] William Foushee Ritchie (1813–1877), son of Thomas Ritchie and editor of the Richmond *Enquirer* following his father's death. Cappon, *Virginia Newspapers, 1821–1935*, p. 171.

[70] Randall, *Life*, I, chaps. vii, viii, and ix.

[71] Thomas Ritchie.

federalists have done by Washington, Jay, Hamilton, Ames, Adams, & *id omne genus.*[72]

With high regards, and in haste. I am very truly,
Yours
Hugh B. Grigsby

To William F. Ritchie, Esq.
P. S. I have addressed this note to you, as I do not know personally your talented junior, and he is too young to know me. Indeed I am only afraid that you are too young to know the friendly relations which existed between your father and myself.

[Endorsed apparently by Ritchie]
Hugh B. Grigsby
Dec. 30, 1857

[72] Marshall, *Life of George Washington;* John Church Hamilton, *The Life of Alexander Hamilton* (2 vols.; New York, 1834–1840); and John Church Hamilton, ed., *Works of Alexander Hamilton* (7 vols.; New York, 1850–1851); Seth Ames, ed., *The Works of Fisher Ames* (2 vols.; Boston, 1854); Charles Francis Adams, ed., *Works of John Adams* (10 vols.; Boston, 1850–1856).

1858

[Grigsby to Randall, January 1, 1858]

Norfolk, January 1, 1858

My dear sir,

Your note informing me of your New York visit was received by the last mail.[1] I had written to you a day or two before in acknowledgement of the two last letters which I received from you.[2] In that letter I expressed the pleasure which your work gave me as far as I had gone. I have now traced Mr. J. until the adoption of the federal constitution, and my pleasure in perusing the Life is more and more enhanced. You have done a noble work for which every liberal American ought to thank you.

In the Enquirer of Tuesday appeared a most favorable notice of the Life, the notice and the extracts filling three entire columns.[3] It is all that you could wish for the readers of that paper. But I have written to Mr. Ritchie to request the privilege of continuing his review editorially in one or two numbers, and I expect to hear in a day or two.[4] A mere communication has comparably but little effect.

Be assured that the day of your triumph will come; but whether the time be long or short, I am not able to say.

I write in great haste, in the midst of the New Year amusements. Wishing you and yours a happy New Year, and many returns, I am very truly yours,

Hugh B. Grigsby.

P. S. We are all well. You must take things easy now. Remember that it is a great deal better that every paper in the Union should abuse the Life than be silent on the subject, and that no good author was ever written down by any pen but his own. You may expect warm friends and bitter and unappeasable enemies. The Randolphs are nearly all bitter federalists. Even they hate Mr Jefferson. As I have told you in my last letter, no Virginian could have written the life of Jefferson without having slain half of his friendships. And this is an additional reason for our obligations to you.—John Randolph's personal friends

[1] This note is not in this collection.
[2] See above, Grigsby to Randall, December 29, 1857.
[3] This issue is not available.
[4] See Grigsby to Ritchie, December 30, 1857, *ante.*

remain twisted to this day. Capt. John Marshall,[5] Judge William Leigh,[6] and many others have ever hated the democratic party, and especially Thomas Jefferson and Thomas Ritchie.
[Endorsed by Randall]
Hugh B. Grigsby
Jan 1, 1858

[William F. Ritchie to Randall, January 2, 1858]

Richmond
Jan 2d 1858

To
Henry S. Randall Eq.

My dear Sir

I have been waiting for my wife[7] to acknowledge the many kind & agreeable things in your last favor—but she is seized with a fit of diffidence and I seize a spare moment to thank you in her name and to say that she will prize very highly any autographs which you can spare from your treasures—Since I last wrote she has partaken with me in the pleasure of reading your charming book which, from the opinion of good judges formed upon the extracts I made in last Tuesday's Enquirer, is surely destined to eminent popularity. I am indeed most glad that my critique was acceptable to such men as Hugh Blair Grigsby and I enclose his letter as among the most valuable compliments that you must appreciate.[8]—I wrote him promptly thanking him for his kind offer & urging him to write as extended & full editorial criticisms as his

[5] Probably the Jack Marshall referred to by Marion Harland: "Many of the stories that clung to the Parsonage had to do with the Orator of Roanoke. The house was at one time the home of Captain 'Jack' Marshall, the father of the late Judge Hunter Marshall. The latter was, during our residence in Charlotte, a near neighbor and charming acquaintance. His father, 'Captain Jack,' was one of the cronies whom John Randolph's eccentricities and fits of violent rage had not estranged. Politically, his constituents adored Randolph." *Autobiography*, p. 318. See W. W. Paxton, *The Marshall Family* (Cincinnati, 1885), and William C. Bruce, *John Randolph of Roanoke* (2 vols.; New York, 1922) II, 637.

[6] William Leigh, a brother of Benjamin Watkins Leigh, and the friend and executor of John Randolph of Roanoke. He was a widely known Halifax lawyer, member of the General Court of Virginia, and a member of the Constitutional Convention of 1829–1830. See Philip Alexander Bruce, *History of Virginia* (6 vols.; New York, 1924), VI, 562.

[7] Anna Cora (Ogden) Mowatt's (1819–1870) husband died in 1851, and on June 6, 1854, she married William Foushee Ritchie, after thirteen years on the stage in England and America. A novelist and playwright, she left Ritchie permanently in 1861 over the issue of secession.

[8] See above, Grigsby to Ritchie, December 30, 1857.

time would allow—I shall publish them with the sincerest pleasure, as I feel that he is worthy to do justice to the subject—

I wish I had the time & the tact to write you something worth reading, in return for your very agreeable letters—the first of which, you will have observed, I turned to a valuable use—But my pressing engagements only allow me to thank you most heartily for the rare pleasure you have given to myself & to all true Virginians by your able, interesting & delightful book—

I have the honor to remain
Truly your friend
W. F. Ritchie

[Endorsed by Randall]
W. F. Ritchie,
January 2, 1858
[In pencil] Husband of Anna Cora

[Grigsby to Randall, January 11, 1858]

Norfolk, January 11, 1858
—Monday—

My dear sir,

I have just read your last letter from New York.[9] I despatched by the vessel that brought it (though I did not get your letter until *this morning*) a review for the Enquirer under the editorial head.[10] You may imagine it is highly favorable. Still it is discriminative, and I explain away the imputation upon Henry, because from the very high character of your work the blow would be felt *now*, and *by posterity*, and the antidote should instantly follow the bane.[11] You may well suppose that I am in the highest degree courteous, and give that full appreciation of your work which I feel, and which will be felt by every intelligent reader.

I am now about to begin my preparations for the 23rd of February next, when I shall appear before the Historical Society at Richmond on the Convention of 1788.

Had I received your note earlier, perhaps I would have modified the first two or three paragraphs of the review; but as they come editorially

[9] This letter is not in this collection.
[10] Grigsby's review of Volume I of the *Life*, appeared in the Richmond *Enquirer*, January 14, 1858, and was widely republished.
[11] *Ibid.*

from a professed party paper, they are in proper keeping with their position.[12]

I need not say to you that I did not dream of the publication of any part of my hasty note to Mr. Ritchie; or I would have given another turn to one or two of its sentences; and as little of the republication in the Argus.[13]

Send on the work as soon as practicable to Richmond, to catch the legislature which is *biennial,* and which will adjourn in February some time.

Mrs. G. is obliged to you for your kind remembrance, and the young Cedric has looked with admiring eyes on the face of Jefferson and the view of Monticello in the frontispiece of the "life."

In haste, very truly,

Yours.

Hugh B. Grigsby

Henry S. Randall Eq.
New York

P. S. I have requested Mr Ritchie to send you two copies of the Enquirer containing the notice which, I suppose, will appear on Wednesday or Thursday next;

By the way, when you have finished my copy of the Lecture of Dr. Hawks, please let me have it, as it is important that I should be able to refer to it.[14] But retain it as long as you think it is necessary for your purposes. I wish you could have seen my late argument on the Mecklenburg question, which would have canceled some minor errors on the subject in my previous writings.

[Grigsby to Randall, January, 1858]

Norfolk, January, 1858

My dear sir,

The note from New York and the letter of the 10th are received.[15] I will prepare a brief letter immediately in allusion to the error about

[12] The Richmond *Enquirer,* the organ of the Richmond "Junto" lead by Thomas Ritchie, editor, supported Jefferson, Van Buren, and Polk. Ritchie edited the administrative paper, *The Union,* in Washington (1845–1851).

[13] Grigsby to Ritchie, December 30, 1857.

[14] Grigsby addressed the Pennsylvania Historical Society, July 9, 1857, rebutting Hawks's May 20, 1857, address at Charlotte County, North Carolina.

[15] Neither of these communications is in this collection.

Henry, which you can publish or use as you please; and will forward it to you forthwith.[16]

I do not know a single member of Congress with whom I am congenial enough to write about the "Union" matter except Gen. Millson,[17] and I shall write him by this mail such a letter as will show what I think and feel, and which the "Union" gentlemen may see.

I suppose the "Review of the Life of Jefferson" will appear in tomorrow's (Thursday) Enquirer, and you will see my notice of the Henry error.[18] As Ritchie had already made quotations, and my article is a continuation of his, I make no selections; and I think my cursory summary of the chapters will perform the main office required by a review for Virginia.

In haste, very truly,
Yours,
Hugh B. Grigsby

Mr Randall
New York

P. S. I have just written the strongest letter I could frame to Gen. Millson, who is an old playmate and lifelong friend of mine, requesting him to communicate with the Union on the subject. What he may do I know not; but I know his confidence in me as a politician and a man.

[Endorsed by Randall]
Hugh B. Grigsby,
Jany 11, 1858

[Grigsby to Randall, January 15, 1858]

Norfolk, January 15, 1858

My dear sir,

I send you the above letter which makes the correction about Henry, and which you requested me to write.[19]

I wrote you today, informing you of the appearance of the Review of the Life in the Enquirer of last Thursday. It has several grave mistakes, but the two I corrected—relating to the omission of the name of Henry, and using the word *declined* instead of "destined"—were the most important.

[16] This letter appears in Randall, *Life*, III, Appendix XXXVIII, pp. 679–680. A recent authoritative contradiction of Grigsby is presented in Irving Brant, *James Madison* (New York, 1941), I, pp. 216 ff.

[17] John S. Millson (1808–1874), Norfolk lawyer, member of the Thirty-first to Thirty-sixth Congresses from Virginia, and of the House Ways and Means Committee (1858–1860). He was never a Senator. John Sherman, *Recollections of Forty Years in House, Senate, and Cabinet* (2 vols.; New York, 1895), I, 195.

[18] Richmond *Enquirer*, January 14, 1858.

[19] For letter, see Randall, *Life*, III, Appendix XXXVIII, pp. 679–680.

If you do not receive the Enquirer, let me know and I will hunt up a number for you. I always bind my own.

Yours.
H. B. G.

Mr R.

[Grigsby to Randall, January 15, 1858]

Norfolk, January 15, 1858

My dear sir,

I have just glanced over the Review of the Life of Jefferson in the Enquirer of Thursday.[20] It fills nearly five columns. There are one or two capital errors; as for instance in the sentence that Pendleton,[21] Nelson[22] and Henry bore certain parts in relation to the Virginia resolution of Independence, *Henry's* name is left out. Read the sentence as follows; "and was supported against all opposition *by Henry* with that astounding energy and eloquence of which he was the master." The printer left out the word "by Henry, with" and ruined the sense. While I speak of the Convention of 1776 becoming the first house of Delegates under the Constitution, for the words "*declined* to act as the Full House of Delegates," read "*destined*" to act &c &c.

The other errors I think will be detected and remedied by the reader.

I have borrowed the Daily Enquirer of Thursday from an editor, and will return it immediately, or I would send it. I trust that Mr Ritchie has not forgotten to send you two copies as I request him to do.

In great haste,

Very truly
Yours
Hugh B. Grigsby

Mr. Randall
Cortland Village
New York
[Endorsed by Randall]
Hugh B. Grigsby,
January 15, 1858

[20] Richmond *Enquirer*, January 14, 1858.

[21] Edmund Pendleton (1721–1803), governor of Virginia (1774–1776), presiding judge of the State Court of Appeals (1779–1803). Randall describes Pendleton in Jefferson's glowing tribute, found in his *Memoir:* "Mr. Pendleton, taken all in all, was the ablest man in debate I have ever met with." Randall, *Life*, I, 198. See also Grigsby, *The Virginia Convention of 1776*, pp. 45–54.

[22] Thomas Nelson (1738–1789), wealthy merchant, signer of the Declaration of Independence, brigadier-general, governor of Virginia, played a key part in the Virginia Convention of 1776 by introducing the resolutions drafted by Edmund Pendleton and supported by Patrick Henry asking Congress to declare the colonies independent. The resolutions, passed on May 15, 1776, were taken by Nelson to the Congress in Philadelphia.

[Grigsby to Randall, March 23, 1858]
[Written in pencil]

American Hotel, Richmond,
March 23, 1858, Tuesday—

My dear Sir,

Your kind letters addressed to Norfolk have been read, but [not] with me now, and I know not how long all thought of literature is gone.[23] On the evening of the 3rd of the present month, I was knocked down on Broad Street, Richmond, by a swift omnibus, the wheels of which passed over my body, crushing my ribs on to the intestines, and separating them from the vertebral column. My state was distressful at first; I am now unable to move in bed without assistance. In a few days it is thought that I will be strong enough to be carried to the Norfolk steamer, when I will take up my abode in my own home.

I cannot foresee when I shall be able to *read* even, much less to write; such is my extreme exhaustion, and confinement to one position by my growing bones. By the way, my wife, who came from Norfolk last evening, and brought me your letters, does not know of any volume having been sent me from you or the publishers. It is probably that the Norfolk agent Ghiselin[24] has it in his possession ready to send it on my arrival in Norfolk.

Is not my fate sad? Yet, on the other hand, how wonderful has been my escape! Since the wheel of the omnibus crushed my poor body on the cords of Broad Street, and yet I live and breathe.

Still I rejoice at your success which you so richly deserve.

Mr. W. C. Rives[25] spent an hour Saturday evening with me. He told me he had procured the second volume of your work.

I am incapable of reflection on business at present. I am now propped in an easy chair, and scribble this note from the back of a book. I am too unwell to read it over.

Very truly,
Yours,
Hugh B. Grigsby

Mr. H. S. Randall
Cortland Village
N. Y.

---

[23] These letters are not in this collection.

[24] John Dyson Ghiselin (1820–1906), life-long resident of Norfolk, book dealer, publisher, importer, and stationer. See *Virginia Pilot*, April 29, 1906.

[25] William Cabell Rives (1793–1868), Congressman and United States Senator from Virginia, twice minister to France, member of the Confederate Congress. Studied law under Jefferson and wrote the unfinished, to 1797, *Life and Times of James Madison* (3 vols.; Boston, 1859–1868).

[Grigsby to Randall, March 29, 1858]
[In pencil]

Norfolk, March 29, 1858

My dear sir,

I was removed from Richmond to Norfolk last Friday. I am still a great sufferer—cant move in my bed without assistance—cant read, or think on affairs. Swain is of the highest character as a gentleman, politician, president of the University of North Carolina, &c.[26] He is a correspondent of mine. I have not yet seen your second volume, but hope to receive it in a few days. I cannot yet look forward to any time when I shall be able to read or write.

In haste, truly Yours
Hugh B. Grigsby

Mr Randall
Cortland Village, N. Y.

[Grigsby to Randall, April 15, 1858]
[In pencil]

Norfolk, April 15, 1858

My dear friend,

I thank you for your kind and most welcome letter of the 12th.[27] It was most cheering to me. Not that my spirits ever give way; but the near prospect of the conclusion of your great work, to say nothing of the strain of affection running through the letter, was refreshing to me.

I am recruiting generally beyond doubt; but two nights ago I endured as much pain from my right side as I have done since my hurt; but that is better today. I walk about our level streets a square or two of a fine day, creeping slowly and bent low. I sometimes think quantum mutatus ab illo & &.[28]

Now for your second volume. I received it *six* days ago, and, feeble as I am, I have read to the 551st page, beside the whole affair of Bayard and Smith's depositions &c.[29] You have performed your task gallantly,

[26] See above, Grigsby to Randall, December 8, 1856, n. 107.

[27] This letter is not in this collection.

[28] How changed from what he once was.

[29] James Asheton Bayard (1767–1815), Federalist representative from Delaware (1797–1803), was the intermediary, who secured an understanding with Jefferson resulting in Jefferson's election. Samuel Smith (1752–1839), Jeffersonian republican representative from Maryland (1793–1803), acted on behalf of Jefferson. For the text of their depositions, see Randall, *Life*, II, 606–623; III, Appendix XIX, pp. 623–626. For a sketch of Smith and some of his correspondence with Jefferson, see *ibid.*, III, Appendix XX, pp. 626–630.

skillfully, triumphantly. You have not only defended your subject, but you have scattered death and destruction among your enemies. The Miranda affair is a masterly episode.[30] The position of Washington, untouched by the wave of federalism, is admirably delineated.[31] Among the lesser things none pleases me more than the conclusive letter from Sparks about "the pigeon hole slander."[32] Do you know that I alluded to that note of his which you quote, *and which clearly shows the current of his belief, when it was written,* when I spoke in my review of his having cast a nettle on the grave of Washington [*sic,* i.e., Jefferson.][33] But I know not where to begin to point out the worth of your second volume. It is masterly and it is original. You have achieved a permanent fame by that volume alone. I am pleased with the courtesy of which you speak of Marshall, while you point out his errors and misrepresentations.[34] I hope you speak of Wickham in the same way.[35] This is, separating the politician from the person, where the person is pure.

But I am exhausted with writing. I cannot bend or stoop to a dish, and scribble these lines on the back of a book.)

Mrs. Grigsby and my son are well. She feels very sensible of your kind notices in your letters, and says that she would be rejoiced to see you in Virginia.

Bancroft treats the Mecklenburg affair too carelessly. He is afraid of offending some prominent North Carolinians. The subject is the Alpha & Omega of Carolina history in the estimate of Carolinians, and merited a full notice from Bancroft.[36]

Mr W. C. Rives told me in Richmond that he had obtained your second

[30] Francisco de Miranda (*ca.* 1750–1816), Venezuelan patriot, sought the support of England and the United States in his crusade for the independence of Venezuela. See *ibid.*, II, 434–442. For an excellent short account, see William Spence Robertson, *The Diary of Francisco de Miranda* (New York, 1928), pp. xiii–xxxvi.

[31] Randall, *Life,* II, 518–520.

[32] The Sparks letter appears in *ibid.*, II, 370.

[33] "Even Sparks, in his life of Washington, flings a nettle most wantonly on the grave of Jefferson." Grigsby, review of Volume I of the *Life,* Richmond *Enquirer,* January 14, 1858.

[34] Randall charges that Marshall in his *Life of Washington* attempted "to prove that the 'great party' which he [Jefferson] had so long led and which carried with it all the sympathies of his heart, was but an organization of demagogues and dupes, and that he was only the greatest demagogue." Randall, *Life,* II, 39. Jefferson countered Marshall with the publication of his *Ana* which gives information on Jefferson's service as secretary of state. *Ibid.*, II, 35–42.

[35] John Wickham (1763–1839), distinguished Virginia lawyer, counsel for Aaron Burr in his trial of 1807. See *Ibid.*, I, 217; III, 204, 205.

[36] As mentioned earlier, George Bancroft ignores the meeting of May 20, 1775, and carefully leads up to the May 31 meeting. See above, Grigsby to Randall, August 18, 1856, n. 77, and this correspondence and notes, *passim.*

volume, and he further told me that he had your work on sheep raising.[37] I did not know before that you had tried your hand upon the inferior animals before you undertook Saint Thomas. By the way, I knew that you had written on agriculture, and that you deserved Swift's compliment; but I did not know that you had published a valuable work on the rearing of sheep.

I thank you sincerely for the present of the second volume, and the elegant dress which it wears. I shall treasure your work for my boy, to say nothing of myself. I only regret that I am unable to write a notice of it for the Enquirer; for I cannot look ahead to any time when I can use a pen. I see the second volume has already been favorably noticed in the Enquirer.[38] With kind regards to all yours, I am with the highest respect,

Very truly,
Yours,
Hugh B. Grigsby

Henry S. Randall Eq.
Cortland Village
N. Y.
Hugh X Carrington Grigsby—his mark—
My boy sends his mark, and has been
pulling at my paper all the time that
I have been writing.

P. S. The letters "N. R." represent T. M. Randolphs name, viz: "Man*n Re*—"[39]

[Grigsby to Randall, June 8, 1858]

Norfolk, June 8, 1858.

My dear sir,

I have just returned to Norfolk from a trip on business; and hasten to acknowledge the receipt of the volume containing Hawks's discourse, and your last letter.[40]

Thursday and Friday last I attended the meeting of the Board of Vis-

[37] Randall, *Sheep Husbandry in the South: comprising a Treatise on the Acclimination of Sheep in the Southern States, an account of the different breeds; also, a complete manual of breeding, summer and winter management, and of the treatment of diseases . . . in a series of letters to R. F. W. Allaton . . .* (Philadelphia, 1848; Philadelphia, 1851; New York, 1852).

[38] Richmond *Enquirer*.

[39] Thomas Mann Randolph. See Randall, *Life*, II, 224–225; III, 327–328, 564.

[40] This letter is not in this collection.

itors of William and Mary College held in the Governor's office in the Capitol at Richmond. Mr. Tyler presided as Rector,[41] and we had Mr. Wise who is a Visitor,[42] Mr Boulware, formerly minister to Naples,[43] Bishop Johns,[44] Macfarland,[45] Lyons, the brother in law of Wise,[46] and some ten others who were fair specimens of the gentlemen of our good old Commonwealth.[47] Wise spoke two hours Thursday, and as many hours Friday in support of a report which he presented and which concluded with a resolution establishing all the professorships anew and from the foundation. I had never seen him before when under full speech, and was much interested in his manner. He is very clever, very bold, and, I think, a much abler man than he is supposed to be. In private life he is most amiable, and devoted to his friends. I could not, however, approve his programme, which was too revolutionary for my taste, and was compelled to oppose it. I thought I should stand alone in the opposition, and spoke with some seriousness about the probable effects of the new scheme; but to my surprise my resolution which was

[41] John Tyler (1790–1862), ex-president, reëntered political life with the outbreak of the Civil War. The rector was chosen from the visitors.

[42] Henry Alexander Wise (1806–1876), while governor of Virginia (1856–1860), broke the strength of the Know-Nothing party in the South and held the Virginia delegation to Buchanan. Wise wrote *Seven Decades of the Union . . . , illustrated by A Memoir of John Tyler . . .* (Philadelphia, 1881). See Barton H. Wise, *The Life of Henry A. Wise of Virginia,* 1806–1876 (New York, 1899).

[43] William Boulware (d. 1870), graduate of William and Mary, appointed Minister to Naples by President Tyler, resigned his position as visitor in 1870. See Alfred Bagby, *King and Queen County Virginia* (New York, 1908), p. 325; Minutes of the Board of Visitors, College of William and Mary, July 22, 1870, p. 97; Elizabeth Hawes Ryland, "The Roanes of King and Queen and King William Counties," *William and Mary Quarterly,* 2d series, XVIII (1938), 287.

[44] Bishop John Johns (1796–1876), president of William and Mary College (1849–1854), fourth Protestant Episcopal Bishop of Virginia.

[45] William Hamilton McFarland (1799–1872), lawyer, legislator, churchman, president of the Farmers' Bank of Virginia (1837–1865), member of the Secession Convention of 1861, member of the counsel for Jefferson Davis on the charge of treason. See Landon C. Bell, *The Old Free State* (2 vols.; Richmond, 1927), II, 310–311; A. J. Morrison, *College of Hampden Sidney* (Hampden Sidney, Va., 1921), pp. 193–194; Mary Wingfield Scott, *Houses of Old Richmond* (Richmond, 1941), pp. 199–200; Elizabeth Wright Weddell, *St. Paul's Church, Richmond, Virginia* (Richmond, 1941), pp. 451–453.

[46] James Lyons (1801–1882), a prominent Richmond attorney and legislator, a "States Rights Whig," succeeded to John Tyler's place in the Confederate House of Representatives in 1862. Thomas H. Ellis called him "not only one of the ablest lawyers, but one of the most elegant and accomplished gentlemen in the commonwealth." See *Richmond Portraits. In an Exhibition of Makers of Richmond,* 1737–1860 (Richmond, 1949), p. 108; Mary Wingfield Scott, *Houses of Old Richmond,* p. 200.

[47] In addition to those specifically named by Grigsby, the Board of Visitors included Colin Clarke, Dr. Edward P. Scott, William B. Harrison, Tazewell Taylor, the Rev. George Woodbridge, Edward T. Taylor, Dr. Nathaniel M. Osborne, Judge William W. Crump, David May, and George W. Lewis. *The History of the College of William and Mary, from its Foundation, 1693 to 1870* (Baltimore, 1870), p. 69.

designed to kill his report was adopted, and the college in my view saved from a perilious experiment. I am afraid Wise will not like me the better for it; but at his table where the Board dined we had much pleasant and friendly conversation.

I doubt whether Wise is a hearty lover of Jefferson. His father was turned out of the Speaker's chair of the Ho: of Delegates in 1799 by the republicans,[48] and Wise himself is a U. S. Bank man; but I have only suspicions to base my opinions upon.

As soon as I see the sheets of the third volume I will give them my prompt attention, and you will soon hear from me about them.

Did you ever hear the ditty that was current at Burr's trial: "Aaron Burr is come to town," &c. Dr. Osborne[49] and Mr. Tyler quoted it to me at the Exchange in Richmond last Friday evening. Dr. O. gave me some wonderful instances of the intensity of the excitement in 1799 et seq. in Petersburg. These we may talk over some day.

All are well. My little boy, though only two years and three months old, can walk a mile. His father at one time could walk fifty without effort in a single day.[50] So, like yourself, I can sing: "Ilium fuit—fuimus Troes."[51]

With kind regard, I am truly

Yours

Hugh B. Grigsby

Mr. Randall
Cortland Village
N. Y.

P. S. On the 21st I leave for Williamsburg as the chairman of a committee to examine into and determine what changes, if any, may be wisely made in the professorships &c. Bishop Johns is my colleague.

[48] Major John Wise (*ca.* 1763–1812), a Washingtonian Federalist, served in Virginia House of Delegates (1791–1802), speaker of that body (1794–1799). For a genealogy of the Wises in America, see Jennings Croffer Wise, *Col. John Wise of England and Virginia* (Richmond, 1918). John Wise appears on, pp. 90–95.

[49] Dr. Nathaniel M. Osborne, a resident of Prince George County and a College visitor, he gave more than five hundred dollars toward the repair of the College chapel damaged by the 1859 fire. *The History of the College of William and Mary, from its Foundation, 1693 to 1870*, p. 69.

[50] In his biographical sketch of Grigsby, R. A. Brock states that Grigsby made "a journey on foot to Massachusetts, through several of the New England states and the lower portions of Canada, and back to Virginia." See Grigsby, *The History of the Virginia Federal Convention of 1788*, I, viii.

[51] Troy has been and is no more.

[Grigsby to Randall, June 28, 1858]

Norfolk, June 28, 1858

My dear sir,

I have read the third volume with all the pleasure which I anticipated, and have written a review of it for the Enquirer which may have appeared yesterday.[52] I requested the Editors to send you a couple of numbers. My review is written in the warmest temper of appreciation, and my main design was to spread such a canvass before the country readers of Virginia and the South as will impel them to buy the book. I indulge in no disquisition which I could have done in a quarterly. It is one of the inconveniences in writing for a paper published in another city that you cannot see the proofs; but I ever hope for the best.

I returned from Williamsburg last Friday, where I had gone to meet Bishop Johns to reconstruct the professorships of William & Mary College. While there I saw beneath the chapel floor the vaults of Sir John Randolph, of his son Peyton Randolph, the President of the first Congress, and John Randolph, the father of Edmund who was the successor of Jefferson as Secretary of State.[53] The scene is full of charming associations, and I hope to visit the old city with you some of these days. Ghizelin, the agent of your work here, has gone up to over ninety copies I believe.

I have not heard from you since I wrote last—and my main purpose now is to say that about the 10th of July I shall leave town for my home in Charlotte Address "Charlotte C. H. Virginia."

The weather here is piping hot. Fortunately I suffer from neither heat nor cold.

By the way I think you say that John Randolph of Roanoke had fought a number of duels.[54] He challenged and was challenged repeatedly, but fought twice only: the first when at William & Mary College with Gen. Robert B. Taylor of Norfolk,[55] a fellow student whom he

[52] Grigsby's review of Volume III of the *Life* appeared in the Richmond *Enquirer*, probably on June 27, 1858, and was reprinted in the Norfolk *Southern Argus*, June 30 and July 1.

[53] Sir John Randolph was the first person buried in the College chapel; his sons, Peyton Randolph, and John Randolph, attorney general for the Crown for Virginia, were also buried in the chapel. *The History of the College of William and Mary, from its Foundation, 1693 to 1870*, p. 38.

[54] "His courage was combined with quarrelsomeness. He was more than ready to put every dispute on the footing of personal offence. He was fought a number of duels for words which were uttered in parliamentary debate, and which were characterized by less than his own habitual personalities." Randall, *Life*, III, 150. H. J. Eckenrode, states that Daniel Webster was among the various men challenged by Randolph. *The Randolphs*, p. 209.

[55] Robert Barraud Taylor (1774–1834), brigadier-general in the Virginia militia (1813–1814), later a judge of the Virginia general court.

wounded putting a ball in his thigh which he kept there till he died at the age of sixty odd; and the duel with Clay.[56]

There is one thing which I suggest *entre nous*. In revising your preface, I advise the substitution of "I" for "we." You are speaking distinctly in the first person, and the plural is ungracious and stiff.

My little boy took up the fine copy of your third volume which was sent me by your publishers, and seemed to be proud in having so grand a book in his hands.

In great haste and with sincere congratulations on the close of your great work, I am, most truly,

Yours,
Hugh B. Grigsby

Henry S. Randall, Eq.
Cortland Village, N. Y.

P. S. I thank you for your kind recognition of me in the article on the Mecklenburg Declaration,[57] and in the preface of my letter about Henry.[58]

By the way the second you close rather too abruptly the last chapter.[59] You should have put yourself forth in a masterly outline of the life and character of your subject, and have made a lasting impression of Jefferson as a whole. But I well know your arduous labors; and it is very easy for me to sit down at my ease and put hard, and, perhaps, superfluous work upon you.

In great*er* haste, I am yours,

H. B. G.

[Grigsby to Randall, July 20, 1858]

Norfolk, July 20, 1858

My dear sir,

I have been delayed in Norfolk up to this time, but shall depart Thursday evening for my home in Charlotte. I write this note lest you may have written to "Charlotte C. H." (my post office until November next,) a letter requiring an immediate acknowledgement. My review of

[56] A reference to the "corrupt bargain" led to a duel between Clay and Randolph, April 8, 1826.

[57] See Randall, *Life*, III, Appendix II, p. 582.

[58] Randall pays tribute to Grigsby as "one of the most candid and accurate historical investigators and critics of our country." *Ibid.*, III, Appendix XXXVIII, pp. 679–680.

[59] The last chapter covers the period 1826–1848 and takes up the topics of Jefferson's religious views, the sale of his estate, and his descendants. It is true, as Grigsby protests, that there is no interpretative conclusion on Jefferson. See *ibid.*, III, 553–565.

the third volume was copied at full length in the Argus of this city,[60] and your book is selling well. More than *one hundred* copies have been taken, when I feared that not a third of that number would have gone off so soon.

My friend Dr. E. O. Balfour has presented to me for your acceptance a hickory cut from the grave of Jefferson, which I have received most courteously on your behalf. The tribute is the more valuable as it comes from a most worthy gentleman who is rarely stimulated to such overt acts in behalf of authors. He is my neighbour being directly opposite to me in Norfolk.[61]

My little son has been seriously ill, but is beginning to walk a few paces. His indisposition has kept me thus far in this city, where, by the way, the summer can be as pleasantly spent on the score of health and comfort as elsewhere. Mrs. G. continues pretty well.

I have had a siege at William and Mary. Our board sate two days, Wise putting forth all his great powers to kill my scheme of studies which was built on the destruction of his own, and losing the day altogether. I suppose we both spoke some twenty times, and our last session was protracted until 2 o'clock A. M. still we all parted kind friends.

Yours truly,
Hugh B. Grigsby

To Henry S. Randall Esq.
Cortland Village, N. Y.
[Endorsed]
Hugh B. Grigsby, presenting cane from Dr. Balfour, &c.
July 20, 1858

[Extract typed on the back of stationery bearing letter head of the United States Navy Yard, Norfolk, Va.]

Extract from the letter of Hugh Blair Grigsby to Henry S. Randall, dated the 25th of July 1858:—

"By the way, in the event of my death, all your letters to me will be at your service. They are scattered according to their dates in my correspondence. All those which you desired to be destroyed, were instantly burned."

[60] Grigsby's review of Volume III of the *Life*, written for the Richmond *Enquirer*, appeared in the Norfolk *Daily Southern Argus*, June 30 and July 1, 1858.

[61] In his biographical sketch of Grigsby, R. A. Brock states: "The relics treasured by him were many and varied. Perhaps as endeared as any, approaching the claims of a collection, was that of canes which had belonged to great men and cherished

[Grigsby to Randall, July 25, 1858]

[Endorsed]

H. B. Grigsby—say my letters will be at my command in case of his death &c—opinions on Life of J. July 25, 1858

Charlotte C. H. Va., July 25, 1858

My dear sir,

I have just reached my country home where I find among other letters yours of the 7th instant.[62] I am sorry to say that the letter containing inquiries about certain parts of your work, and especially relating to Mrs. Coolidge, never came to hand. Respecting the lady in question I have only to say that every suspicion was banished from my mind as soon as I learned that she was an invalid; still I was gratified to learn from you that there was no foundation for such a suspicion. I am not apt to take offence unless offence is intended; and I could hardly deem it probable that a descendant of Thomas Jefferson would fall out with me because I spoke what I believed to be true and honorable of another branch of her family.[63]

I think you have done the Mecklenburg question very fairly for the general reader; but evidently with haste.[64] When your twentieth edition is about to be issued, I will prepare a letter, if I am living. It is not unpleasant to think of taking passage in the ship Thomas Jefferson, H. S. Randall, Commander.

You have done the Lee topic very well. You have said all that was necessary. More would have wounded severely the feelings of innocent relatives; and though any thing you might say would have been justifiable, it is better the whole affair should stand as you gave it.[65]

---

associates, or had grown in spot historic and sacred. These supporting staffs he was, with jealous impartiality to the memory of the donor or departed friend, in the habit of using in turn, thus one day he was assisted in his walks with the cane of a loved uncle, Reuben Grigsby, another with that of his revered friend, Governor Tazewell, another with a staff from the Mount of Olives, and so through more than a score of reverential exercises." Grigsby, *The History of the Virginia Federal Convention of 1788*, I, xi–xii.

[62] This letter is not in this collection.

[63] Grigsby refers here to his belief that Ellen Coolidge refused to see him when he and Coles called on her in Philadelphia because he refers to the first Virginia Randolph as a "builder of barns" in *The Virginia Convention of 1776*. Randall persuaded him that Mrs. Coolidge was an invalid. See this correspondence and its notes for December, 1856.

[64] Randall, *Life*, III, Appendix II, pp. 570–582.

[65] Jefferson's relations with the Henry Lees, father and son, is discussed in *ibid.*, III, Appendix XXXII, pp. 660–664.

As I have just arrived, I have not seen John Henry; and indeed months may pass before I see him, as I shall be closely engaged at home during the summer.

The ground was delicate about Webster. The fact is that he and Mr. J. were not *congenial;* and he has remembered every thing as a lawyer remembers the testimony of his opponent's witness.[66]

About Wirt I do not think that we differ as much in reality as appearance. We regard his book from different points of view. You regard it as a biography of Henry simply; while I regard it as the tribute of an adopted son to the memory of our great orator. In my view the *intention* is half the battle. But apart from this, I, as a Virginian, look at the effect of his book on our young men. Moreover I am grateful to him for having saved much which, if he had not saved; would have perished altogether. Wirt lived with men who knew Henry, and he has collected much from them. His entire exoneration of Henry from the shedding of Philips' blood by act of attainder is most valuable to the reputation of Henry.[67] Strip Wirt of many instances of false taste and bad writing, and you still have a mass of important facts which he has saved and made familiar. Then what are the pretensions of his book? Nominally and really *mere sketches,* as you will learn from the title page. Popularity is no infallable test of worth; if it were the question would be settled in Wirt's favor; as almost every intelligent man in the United States has read him. Even By[r]on has immortalized Henry in his verse through Wirt. Remember that Charles Lee's letter is lately brought to light.[68] About Jefferson and Jackson, speaking from a general recollection; I think you have acted honestly. I forget whether you gave an account of the Lynchburg dinner at which Jefferson gave the memorable toast: "Honor to the man who has filled the measure of his country's glory." If you have, you have given the facts of the case, and may safely allow them to speak for themselves.[69]

[66] Jefferson was unfavorably presented in Fletcher Webster, ed., *The Private Correspondence of Daniel Webster,* a presentation refuted by Randall. See *Life,* III, 505–509.

[67] Josiah Philips, leader of a gang of banditti in Norfolk and Princess Anne counties in 1777, was attainted for treason by the legislature, but Edmund Randolph, the attorney general of Virginia, indicted him for highway robbery, and Philips was convicted and executed on that charge, not for treason. See Wirt, *Sketches of the Life and Character of Patrick Henry,* pp. 234–241.

[68] Charles Lee to Patrick Henry, May 7, 1776, used by Randall, *Life,* I, 128, n. 4, gives the impression that Henry was backward in supporting the resolution for independence. Grigsby presented evidence to the contrary and Randall corrects his early statement by publishing Grigsby's statement. See *ibid.,* III, Appendix XXXVIII, pp. 679–680.

[69] Webster presented Jefferson as having a highly critical opinion of Jackson. For Jefferson on Jackson, see *ibid.,* III, 506, 508–509. There is no account of the Lynchburg dinner in Randall.

I do not write in the Messenger. I reviewed Bishop Meade's "Old Churches" &c. at his request in that periodical;[70] but I have written nothing since. Some years ago I wrote an account of the library of John Randolph for that publication[71] at the request of Mr. Thompson.[72] Indeed I write nothing that I am not compelled by some strong consideration of public or private interest to strike off. By the way, the floor of the Chapel of William and Mary was taken up some weeks ago, and the vaults examined. Three attorneys general of Virginia were seen resting side by side—Sir John Randolph,[73] his eldest son Peyton, the president of the First Congress,[74] and his brother John who went over with Dunmore.[75] I gave the article to my young friend William Lamb of the Argus who will publish it in a day or two.[76] It is called "The Dead of the Chapel of William & Mary."[77] Perhaps you may like it; perhaps not, unless you indulge in the mood of the article at times yourself. I will try and have a copy sent to you. I have received no letter unless your last in any way alluding to the Messenger.

I am glad that you heard from Dunglison and Gov. C. I sent a copy of my last review to Gov. C.; but have received no acknowledgement. Perhaps he had left the city, and my letter and paper had not reached him.

I am gratified that you receive the approbation of the surviving relatives of Mr. J. Had they been lukewarm in their appreciation of your great services to the fame of their ancestor, I should have argued against their good sense and their goodness of heart.

I am no great planter. I have just returned to my plantation after

[70] For Grigsby's review, see *Southern Literary Messenger,* XXV (1857), 161. The *Messenger,* published from 1834 to 1864, served as a channel for Southern talent.

[71] "The Library of John Randolph of Roanoke, *Southern Literary Messenger,* XX (1853), 76. In his sketch of Grigsby, R. A. Brock notes that Grigsby's library of some six thousand volumes "contained many volumes from the choice library of the erratic John Randolph, of Roanoke, to the auction sale of which Mr. Grigsby, with much self-satisfaction, liked to tell that he trudged on foot." Grigsby, *The Virginia Federal Convention of 1788,* I, xi.

[72] John R. Thompson (1823–1873), editor of the *Southern Literary Messenger* (1847–1860), poet, and Southern propagandist during the Civil War.

[73] Sir John Randolph (1693–1737), son of William Randolph I, attorney general, speaker of the House of Burgesses, and the only Virginian knighted in the colonial period.

[74] Peyton Randolph (*ca.* 1721–1775), a man of wealth, attorney general and speaker of the House of Burgesses, he, nevertheless, joined the revolution.

[75] John Randolph (*ca.* 1727–1784), trained in the Middle Temple like his brother, Peyton, he took the Tory side and lived in England (1775–1784). His daughter returned to Virginia with her father's remains.

[76] William Lamb (1835–1909), editorially championed the states' rights position (1856–1861), supported Breckinridge.

[77] Grigsby's article appeared as an editorial with no name ascribed on the editorial page of the *Daily Southern Argus,* July 31, 1858.

eight months absence, and find every thing about the crops referable to human action pretty fair; but a dreadful drought has put things terribly aback. I am not an active manager. I am away too much. Our home is pleasantly situated. It is the birthplace of my wife, and the seat that was founded by her father.[78] The house is of brick, large and in fair repair. The estate is considered valuable. We have a wood fifty yards from the front door extending for miles. It has all the capacities of a delightful home; though our long absences must account for the want of embellishments that attract the eye. My wife was an invalid for fifteen years; and we have hardly resided here an entire year at one time in that interval. Withal it is a home well worthy of the love of both of us. Our neighbourhood is excellent in society. Almost all my neighbours are educated men. Three relatives of my wife have called this morning. One of them, Henry Carrington, and son of Paul Carrington,[79] Sen., is a graduate of Princeton is an able and thoroughly intelligent man, and is the only uncle of my wife's now living.[80] He is six feet, large in proportion, and is one of our most valuable and high minded gentlemen. He was accompanied by his son in law William Read, a relative of my wife's, a graduate of Hampden Sidney, familiar with the best productions of the day, and a most successful planter.[81] The third was an eminent physician of Mecklenburg, another relative of my wife, an own cousin, now on a visit to his sister Mrs. Read, my next neighbour one mile off.[82] Either of these gentlemen could do honor to any society in this country or in Europe. Ex pede Herculem.[83] By the way, I forgot to say that Mrs. G. is obliged to you for your invitation to

[78] Edgehill, Charlotte County, was founded by Clement Carrington (1762–1847), the father of Mary Venable Carrington. He was the second son of Judge Paul Carrington, the elder, a revolutionary soldier, and Virginia magistrate. See *William and Mary Quarterly*, 2d series, X (1930), 88–89.

[79] Grigsby's sketch of Henry Carrington (1793–1867) is available in Alexander Brown, *The Cabells and Their Kin* (Boston, 1895), pp. 558–559.

[80] Paul Carrington (1733–1818), the founder of the Virginia Carringtons, emigrated to Virginia from Barbados early in the eighteenth century. A jurist and planter, he played an important role in uniting the colonies for independence and served as a member of the committee on the Declaration of Rights in the Virginia Convention of 1776. For a biographical sketch, see Grigsby, *The Virginia Convention of 1776*, pp. 97–105; Bishop Meade, *Old Churches, Ministers and Families of Virginia*, II, 28–30, treats of the Carringtons who intermarried with the Reads and the Cabells.

[81] William Watkins Read (1821–1889), a graduate of Hampden Sydney, a lawyer, married Paulina Edmonia Carrington (1825–1904), in 1845. He was a descendant of Colonel Clement Read who in conjunction with Paul Carrington associated with Jefferson, Washington, and Henry in the independence movement. Read's mother, Anne Mayo Venable (1784–1869), was a Venable as was Mrs. Grigsby.

[82] For genealogical information on the Read family see, Alice Read, *The Reads and Their Relatives* (Cincinnati, 1930), pp. 530–32.

[83] One can judge the size of Hercules by the size of his foot.

visit you. The letter containing the first invitation did not reach me.[84] Our country has the Blue Ridge in view and is as healthy in summer as in winter. And should you ever come as near as Richmond, you need not apprehend any malarious disease from our atmosphere. It is quite as safe as Albermarle, whither our friend Coles goes with his family to spend the summer.

I read to my wife the passage relating to the Carrington family in the third volume at the time I was reading your work. She is obliged to you for the kind notice. The Cabells and the Carringtons are closely connected by blood and marriage. The gentleman first named above of my visitors married Louisa Cabell,[85] the eldest daughter of Judge Cabell, the life-long friend of Wirt.[86] Cabell and Wirt married sisters, the Misses Gamble;[87] and my friend Henry Carrington aforesaid knew Wirt and regarded him as a personal friend. They enjoyed together the hospitality of Monte Video, the seat of Judge Cabell on the James. Mrs. Henry Carrington is still, although over fifty, one of the loveliest women of her sex, as she was the great belle of her youthful days. She was the contemporary of Laura Wirt, who was her bridesmaid. Mr. Henry Carrington's charming family reside five miles directly south of me—the third plantation from me on the banks of the little Roanoke which runs through my plantation. If you turn to my Convention of 1776, page 119, Note, you will see an allusion to Henry Carrington's son William Cabell Carrington, who was a son of Henry & Louisa Carrington.[88]

I hope your health will continue to improve. You are blessed with a colossal constitution; and you have only to adopt a farinaceous and saccharine diet, instead of animal food "except as a condiment," abstain from all liquors whether malt or otherwise, and work hard with your hands one day in seven, to attain a long and late healthy old age. My injury has left its mark upon me. It affects my breathing. I bend with difficulty. But I am grateful that I am alive. All the chances were against my recovery. But my temperate habits enabled me to weather the gale. Have I told you that I never tasted a glass of grog of any kind in my life?—I walk as erectly as ever.

I think I have now gone through with all the topics alluded to in your letter. By the way, in the event of my death, all your letters to me will be at your service. They are scattered according to their dates in my

---

[84] This letter is not in this collection.

[85] Henry Carrington married Louisa Elizabeth Cabell (1798–1865), whose graciousness as described by Grigsby is quoted in Brown, *The Cabells and Their Kin,* p. 558.

[86] William H. Cabell (1772–1853), president of the Virginia Court of Appeals.

[87] William H. Cabell married Agnes Sarah Bell Gamble (1783–1863). William Wirt married Elizabeth Washington Gamble (1784–1857).

[88] See Grigsby, *The Virginia Convention of 1776,* pp. 113–119, for information on the Cabells and the Carringtons.

correspondence. All those which you desired to be destroyed were instantly burned:

I shall devote this summer to the finishing my work on the convention of 1788. I am pledged to the public and to the Historical Society for its completion, having read portions of it at the last annual meeting of the Society.

By the way, should you ever visit me at Edgehill, if you will take the Steamer *Roanoke*—not the Jamestown—at New York, and continue in her from Norfolk to City Point, then take the City Point road to Peterby, then the South Side railroad to the junction with the Danville, then the Danville to Drake's Brand Depot, then the hack five miles to Charlotte C. H., you will reach me in eleven hours from Norfolk; that is, you will leave New York at five o'clock P. M., reach Norfolk at five P. M., and my house next day at 11 A. M. This is rapid travelling from Norfolk.

Having thus written you a letter fully as long as your last,[89] I must bid you adieu.

I wrote you a note from Norfolk two or three days ago.

In haste Truly Yours
Hugh B. Grigsby

Henry S. Randall Esq
Cortland Village

P. S. I have just received a very kind letter from Gov. Coles at Saratoga. He is in excellent health. He has not yet had time to read the third volume. He has fears of the success of the life in Philadelphia; but he should remember that Philadelphia is devoted to the name and federal policy of Hamilton; especially those whom he ordinarily meets with. But that any man who liked Jefferson and his policy dislikes your book, or will treat it coldly *credat Iudaeus Apello, non.*[90] But the *bitter* imprecations of the friends of Hamilton you expect and will certainly receive; and receive in the proportion of your success in delineating the life and character of Jefferson. Moreover, in the cities especially, *time* is an element in calculating the success of your work, and the voice of the country at large must first react upon the cities. I think I told you that more than *one hundred* copies have been sold by my young friend Ghiselin of Norfolk; and if there were as efficient an agent in Richmond, Lynchburg, Petersburg, &c, as you have in Norfolk, I think the sales would have been, and will be, in the same proportion.

I have just received a letter from Ellen Randolph; very kind and encouraging.

[89] This letter is not in this collection.
[90] Let the Jew Apello believe, no!

[Grigsby to Randall, July 31, 1858]

Edgehill, July 31, 1858

My dear sir,

Your letter enclosing a note for Dr. Balfour was received by the last mail.[91] I immediately enclosed the letter to Dr. B. to him with a note of my own, and I am sure that he will be gratified to receive it.

You have wounded past forgiveness all the great friends of Hamilton and the banking interest of the country; and you must expect their *bitter persecution.*[92] This you knew beforehand; but let me tell you that you will see this hostile influence *cropping out* in a thousand ways big and little as long as you live. But it was important that Virginia should speak decisively and instantly, and throw her agis over your enterprize. Hence my exertion in the premises. I have always thought with the Enquirer. Thomas Ritchie was a personal friend; yet I never wrote an article for that paper until I received your first volume in its columns. As I have said to you again and again, *time* will be your avenger and your treasurer; and though I wish you a hearty present reward, it is to the future you must look for a thorough triumph.

I have painfully felt that too much for my happiness, and, perhaps, even should he survive too much for the happiness of my boy, rest on the brittle thread of a single life; but I make it a point not to anticipate powerful events further than to endeavour to brace myself against their power.

I wrote a long letter in reply to your letter that awaited me here. You have doubtless received it ere this.

I don't think the programme of studies of William and Mary will be published. I revised the old programme purely because I was so required to do by the nature of my resolution which defeated Gov. Wise's scheme, and for no other purpose. It is a three years' course, and is in no respect worthy of remark.

Charles Campbell is preparing a new edition of his History of Virginia for the press, and is anxious that I should peruse his manuscript.[93] I sent him yesterday a long and critical letter detailing the errors in his full edition and pointing out some important sources of early historical intelligence. Can you tell me whether the Historical Society publications of New York are for sale or not? I am anxious to obtain the volume

[91] This letter is not in this collection.

[92] For a discussion of the United States Bank Bill and of Hamilton's character, see Randall, *Life*, I, 628–645.

[93] Charles Campbell, aided by Grigsby, revised his *An Introduction to the History of the Colony and Ancient Dominion of Virginia* (Richmond, 1847), thoroughly. The revised edition appeared in Philadelphia in 1860. For an earlier reference to Campbell, see above, Grigsby to Randall, December 15, 1856, n. 124.

which contains the account of the first meeting of the House of Burgesses in Virginia prior to any recorded by Hening. I have read the article in your transactions, but cannot name the volume containing it. It was communicated by our friend Bancroft.[94]

I have just worked over my tobacco, and stacked permanently my oats; and today begin threshing my wheat.

Did I ever tell you that the wife of our Pastor here is Marion Harland, one of the friends of your friends Derby & Jackson? We are Presbyterians, and her husband Mr. Terhune gave us an excellent sermon last Sunday.[95] She is not pretty; but is a very pleasant lady. A lady who can write books which sell to the tune of forty thousand copies must experience even in our retired country the "monstrali digito."

In haste truly Yours
H. B. Grigsby

P. S. All are well. My little boy is carried at the rate of five miles an hour in his little carriage by some twenty or thirty little darkies, who seek no greater fun than to pull him and shout after him in the yard and in the forest.

P. S. A second thought. The letters of Mr. Jefferson to his daughters ought to be prefaced with a graceful sketch of the lives and characters of his daughters—their surviving children &c. Imagination and exquisite taste should mark this preliminary essay. Plates should adorn it. A view of Monticello, a portrait of Jefferson, a portrait, if possible, of both daughters. The essay should fill some thirty or forty pages of the work.[96]

---

[94] New York Historical Society *Collections,* 2d series, III (1857), 329–358. See above, Grigsby to Randall, August 1, 1857, n. 25, for the complete citation.

[95] Edward Payson Terhune (1830–1907), pastor of the Presbyterian church at Charlotte Court House, Virginia (1855–1858), removed in 1858 to First Reformed Dutch Church, Newark, New Jersey, where he remained until his death. See Marion Harland, *Autobiography,* pp. 491–496.

[96] Jefferson's correspondence with his daughters runs through Randall's work. The letters began when his daughters were very young and continued with Maria Jefferson Eppes until her death in 1804 and with Martha Jefferson Randolph until his own death even though Martha resided at Monticello. See Randall, *Life,* I, II, III, *passim.* The descendants Jefferson left at his death are listed in *ibid.,* III, 563. Randall apparently never compiled a separate volume of the letters of Jefferson and his daughters. This scheme was carried out by Sarah N. Randolph, *The Domestic Life of Thomas Jefferson compiled from Family Letters and Reminiscences* (New York, 1871). The author admits: "I am well aware that the tale of Jefferson's life both public and private, has been well told by the most faithful of biographers in 'Randall's Life of Jefferson,' and that much of what is contained in these pages will be found in that admirable work, which, from the author's zealous devotion to truth, and his indefatigable industry in collecting his materials, must ever stand chief among the most valuable contributions to American history. I propose, however, to give a sketch of Jefferson's private life in a briefer form than it can be found in either the thirteen volumes of the two editions of his published correspondence, or in the three stout octavo volumes of his Life by Randall." *Ibid.,* preface.

Bis dat qui cito dat, is as true of the public as of individuals, and the work ought to be prepared at once for the coming Christmas. Or it will be anticipated and the "shine" will be taken off, and much of the profit too. And you cannot prevent it; for the *letters* are not copyrighted. In haste, Yours

I presume the lady is Mrs. Trist.[97]

I am reading Curtis's second volume of the History of the Constitution of the United States.[98] He defends Hamilton from charges of monarchical views in a note, and glorifies him at the end of the volume. Hamilton is the god of federal idolatrys but it is absurd to bestow upon him the praise of being the author and finisher of the federal constitution. That praise is Madison's. Madison drew the resolution of Virginia convoking the Convention at Annapolis, which by adjournment may be said to have made the General Convention that sate at Philadelphia. While the Convention held its sessions in Philadelphia, it is absurd to impute a leading influence to Hamilton, who attended its sessions but a short time. If the numbers of the Federalist persuaded the people to adopt the new scheme, Madison deserves as full praise on that account as Hamilton. And if Hamilton is to be deified for his exertions in the New York federal Convention, Madison deserves still more credit than Hamilton, as he was the main means of bringing in to the aid of the Federal Constitution (at the time) a much greater and more important state in every respect than New York, as Virginia then unquestionably was. Yet Madison makes but a slight figure in Mr. Curtis's book. He does not even scan *the authorship* of the "Virginia" plan, which was the basis of the general action in Convention, but leaves the reader to infer that it was Randolph's who prepared it; whereas *Madison* was its author. Had *Hamilton* been the author, we should have seen an elaborate attempt to show the features of the plan which were ultimately engrafted upon the constitution. Mr. Madison himself in a letter performed this office, and this letter may be found in those published by a gentleman of Washington whose name begins with a Mac.[99] I hope Mr. Rives will

[97] Virginia Jefferson Randolph, wife of Nicholas P. Trist.

[98] George Ticknor Curtis (1812–1894), distinguished lawyer and constitutional authority. In addition to strictly legal works, he published a *History of the Origin, Formation, and Adoption of the Constitution of the United States* (2 vols.; New York, 1854–1858); a *Life of Daniel Webster* (2 vols.; New York, 1870); and a *Life of James Buchanan* (2 vols.; New York, 1883). His work constitutes the classic treatment of the Constitution from the Federalist, Websterian point of view. He vigorously defends Hamilton against monarchical charges. Grigsby is a precursor of Max Farrand in attributing the major role in the drafting of the Constitution to James Madison.

[99] J. C. McGuire, *Selections from the Private Correspondence of James Madison, from 1813–1836* (Washington, 1859).

see these things, and expose them to the public.[100] I must say in candor that the second volume of Curtis' work is very able, and altogether superior to the first. *Will you answer me this question? Is George W. Curtis the judge of the federal court who resigned his seat some time ago?*[101] Please answer me carefully.

Thus it is that the leaven of federalism is introduced into our literature to poison the minds of youth.

H. B. G.

[Endorsed by Randall]
H. B. Grigsby
July 31, 1858

[Grigsby to Randall, September 3, 1858]

Edgehill, September 3, 1858

My dear sir,

Your letter of the 27th ult. was received last evening.[102] Would it not be better that you give me the address of some friend in New York, say Derby and Jackson, with whom one of our Norfolk merchants could deposit the cane from Dr. B? Let me have the name and address in your next, and I will write the Doctor to send the cane accordingly. By the way, I have told you that it is a small twig from the grave of Jefferson, and is very plain. Its whole value is in its history and in the motive that led to its remittance to you. I am sure the Doctor would feel highly pleased to receive from you an autograph of Jefferson.[103]

Frank Cabell is a second cousin of my wife's.[104] His mother,[105] whom I knew intimately and who was one of the cleverest women in literature and even in politics I have ever known, was an own cousin to Mrs. G's, having been the daughter of my wife's father's sister Mary.[106] But Frank, who lives on the James, I have met with personally but once I believe; but I know him and I think it probable he believes he knows me, as well as if we were near neighbours. He is a planter, the nephew of the late

[100] William Cabell Rives was then engaged on a biography of Madison.

[101] George Ticknor Curtis's brother, Benjamin R. Curtis (1809–1874), was a justice of the United States Supreme Court (1851–1857) and leading counsel for Andrew Johnson during the impeachment proceedings.

[102] This letter is not in this collection.

[103] See above, Grigsby to Randall, July 20, 1858.

[104] Nathaniel Francis Cabell (1807–1891), wrote on religion, genealogy, and agriculture; edited *The Early History of the University of Virginia as contained in the Letters of Thomas Jefferson and Joseph C. Cabell* (Richmond, 1856), and collected documents for a history of agriculture in Virginia which are now in the Virginia State Library, prepared family memoirs of the Cabells and the Carringtons.

[105] Margaret Read Venable Cabell (1782–1857).

[106] For the involved history of the Carringtons and Cabells consult Brown, ***The*** *Cabells and Their Kin.*

Joseph C. Cabell, and married a daughter of Gen. John H. Cocke.[107] He is a fine scholar, a capital writer, and is thoroughly conversant in matters appertaining to men and things in Virginia. Withall he is in every respect a high minded, honorable man. In religion he is rather twisted, being a Swedenborgian; and he has written quite an able review of the doctrines of his high priest. I sincerely wish that he was my neighbour. Have you not felt that in the proportion that a man advances far in the pursuit of any literary project, he isolates himself from the mass of even intelligent men? Few can sympathise with him, and you are compelled to move in other men's circles rather than in your own. This may be well enough as a general thing; but a little literary commixture at times might be agreeable.

By the way, I have just quoted the letter of Mr. Jefferson to Gov. C. of August 25, 1814.[108] My object was to show the precise nature of the motion he made in the H. of B. in 1769, when he followed Col. Bland. I was chosing the different notions in the Colony and in the Commonwealth in respect of manumission &c. I have the letter in manuscript, but I refer to your work as to the only book in which it can be found in print.

I have changed much in appearance since you saw me. My hair is nearly as gray as Frank Cabell's who, by the way, has marriageable daughters, though he is about my age only. I should be ashamed to put my face in a daguerreotype; and how my old lady's high cap would look when blasted on a metal plate by the sun, I cannot well conceive. However, I should like to possess the likeness of Mrs. Randall and yourself, and as I can only procure them on reciprocal terms, my old woman and myself will primp up when we get to town. For our county daguerreotypists make sad work even of the prettiest faces, much more of those that are past and drooping, and require tender handling.

I predict that a shark *will bite into* the electric cable in less than six months, let in the water, and spoil it. Have you ever seen a shark's teeth in his head?

In great haste very truly Yours

Hugh B. Grigsby

Henry S. Randall Esq.
[Endorsed by Randall]
Hugh B. Grigsby
Cane—pictures &c.
Sept. 3d. 58

[107] Anne Blaws Cocke (1811–1862), daughter of John Hartwell Cocke (1780–1866), a planter and a brigadier-general in the War of 1812. He believed slavery and tobacco culture the curse of Virginia and was senior vice-president of the American Colonization Society (1819–1866). With Cabell and Jefferson he was a founder of the University of Virginia.

[108] See Randall, *Life*, III, Appendix XXVII, pp. 643–645.

[Grigsby to Randall, September 27, 1858]

Charlotte C. H. Virginia
Sept 27 1858

My dear sir,

I have your last note,[109] and hope that the glories of the Fair are past, and that you are once more restored to the quiet of home. So you see the shark did bite into the cable after all. I have written to Doct. Balfour suggesting the mode of sending the cane to the address mentioned in your letter.

John Henry made me his annual visit last week, and spent a day and night with me. I gave him one of your volumes to look over, and he read it most carefully. I also showed him my letter in the Appendix, and told him that it was at your suggestion that it was written.[110] He read it with evident satisfaction. He is, however, no Jefferson man. In my presence he says nothing against him, but to my wife he lets things out that show the strong current of his prejudices. If he were to read your volumes critically, he might change his views; but I fear that with his large family and pressing wants to be supplied only by the sale of his tobacco that he will never purchase them. When a man can purchase a good book, and is willing to go down to the grave without doing so, the fault and the curse be on his own head.

My article on the Dead of the Chapel of William and Mary has brought out Robert Randolph M. D. of Clarke County. The editors of the Argus sent the printed letter to me; so when I replied I had no knowledge of the name of the author, I did not like his tone, and, though not departing from courtesy, have answered him very differently from what I could have done, had he written in a different spirit. I send you an Argus containing my answer, which, you will see, is, like the original article, editorial.[111]

---

[109] This letter is not in this collection.

[110] Randall, *Life*, III, Appendix XXXVIII, pp. 679–680.

[111] The article on "The Dead of the Chapel of William and Mary" appeared in the *Daily Southern Argus,* July 31, 1858. It served not only as an interesting description of the burial plot but also as a forum for Grigsby's theme on the humble origins of the Randolphs and other first families of Virginia. As a result, Dr. Robert Randolph of Clarke County, sharply dissented on September 21, 1858, in the columns of the *Argus* in a letter signed "Isham." His challenge incited Grigsby to write a rejoinder which appeared in the same issue: "Our correspondent inquires whether we 'intend to convey the idea that William Randolph was a man of low degree.' We confess we do not precisely comprehend what he means by 'Low degree.' With us every man stands on his own worth; and in fixing the 'degree' of a citizen we no more regard the character of his immediate ancestors than in discussing the merits of one of the fine pears sent us the other day by a friend in Smithfield we inquired whether it grew in the orchard of an Anglo-Saxon or a Norman, or a descendant of Confucius, or of one of

I think of getting on my horse in a few days and riding ninety miles to see an aged uncle in the Valley of Virginia.[112] I will spend a couple of days with him, and ride back again—180 miles on horseback to pay a visit of two days! The truth is I have been writing closely and require some exercise in the open air continuously for a week or two. It may turn out that I shall stick at home.

I have to examine every item in the Journals of the House of Delegates, from 1776 to 1790, without the aid of an index. It is fearful labor. I intend to give a sketch of the history of the sessions for the purpose of refuting the notions advanced by Mr. Madison and others of the state of affairs at the time of the formation of the federal constitution. It is a new view, and it is demanded by a due respect of our greatest statesmen.[113]

I have just finished the session of 1786–7, when the members of the General Federal Convention were appointed.

We had a rain Sunday night but not enough to enable us to break the ground for turnips. No corn and a wretched crop of the meanest tobacco are the results of our summer campaign.

Present Mrs. Grigsby and myself kindly to Mrs. Randall, and believe me very truly,

Yours,

Hugh B. Grigsby

Unless Mr. Rives and myself communicate before publication, there will be sad clashing in our review of the period from 1785 to 1790.[114]

---

the peers of Charlemagne." Grigsby chided his protagonist's sources for everyone knew the expression "to lie like an epitaph" and observed that "great men rarely beget great men." The controversy was carried over to the September 27, 1858, issue when the belligerents had their final say.

[112] Possibly Reuben Grigsby, a "loved uncle" whose cane he owned. See above, Grigsby to Randall, July 20, 1858, n. 61.

[113] *Journals of the House of Delegates of Virginia* (*1776–1790*) (4 vols.; Richmond, 1828) were consulted by Grigsby to substantiate his conviction that there was much propaganda in favor of a more powerful central government which deliberately exaggerated adverse conditions under the Confederation. See Grigsby, *The Virginia Federal Convention of 1788*, I, 8–23, and the Introduction to this volume of correspondence, for a fuller discussion. Grigsby's view has received documentation in recent years in the works of Max Farrand, Charles A. Beard, and Marcus W. Jernegan.

[114] Rives published first and Grigsby subsequently drew upon his *Life of James Madison* for *The Virginia Federal Convention of 1788*.

[Grigsby to Randall, November 12, 1858]

Edgehill, November 12, 1858

My dear sir,

I have just received your letter of the 6th instant,[115] and have glanced hastily at the correspondence between Professor Tucker and yourself. I deeply regret that it should have taken place, and especially the spirit of the Professor's letter. It was essentially a declaration of war, especially in the language in which he puts forth the charge of your having got your views or facts from his book, and then of your roving abroad for authorities to conceal your obligations. The most that he could have done in relation to this charge was to express a suspicion of its truth; but the direct and unqualified allegation, which he could not but know might possibly be erroneous, was not consistent with friendly feelings on his part.

On the supposition of friendly relations existing between you, it seems to me that Mr. Tucker ought to have called your attention courteously to his main charge, and afforded you an opportunity of explanation and correction; more especially as your reasoning was contained in a note, which ordinarily, as I judge from my own experience, is usually written rapidly and without the full deliberation which is usually accorded to the text.

On the other hand, supposing other than friendly relations between you, I can easily see that the mode of treating his positive testimony to a particular fact might be offensive to him, as he has no doubt of its exact truth and time as stated by him. But you mentioned it argumentatively, and he should have pointed out the error of your argument, if any, argumentatively, and without a suspicion that unkindness or injustice was intended.

Other expressions in the letter of Mr. T., such as his allusion to your panegyrick, and his reflection upon the relatives of Mr. Jefferson, show that he wrote with excited feelings. Of your reply I will only say that it is written in a most commendable spirit, and reflects the highest honor on you.

Indeed my friend Mr. T. is very old, and has a spirit of pugnacity becoming earlier years. We must make great allowances for extreme old

[115] This letter and its enclosures are not in this collection. Tucker protested that Randall had surreptitiously plagiarized his *Life of Thomas Jefferson* (1837), under the guise of prior permission. Randall specifically credits Tucker with the detection of errors in Marshall's *Life of Washington* and cites Tucker's work in many other places. See above, Randall to Grigsby, December 4, 1856, n. 100, for an exact statement of his use of Tucker.

age, which is apt to excite certain minds on particular topics in an unwonted way.

I will tell you a little affair that occurred last summer between the Professor and myself. He and Mrs. T. were on a visit to a friend in Norfolk; and as in duty bound, I was very attentive to both. The Professor called to spend an hour with me frequently, and I had much instructive conversation with him. As he was an old Virginian by adoption, and had spent his prime of life in our borders, I thought a neat notice of his visit to Norfolk and his honored career in the State would be generally acceptable to his friends and not ungrateful to himself. Such a notice I prepared for my friends of the Argus, and was received with much favor. In the conclusion, let me add, I alluded to the fact that the Professor had written a valuable history of the United States in four volumes in the last seven years of a life that trenched upon 85. Some days afterwards I received a letter from him which began by saying that he had finished a tract on some subject, and then added: "Now I have a crow to pick with you." "How came you to say that I was 85? By that saying you have undone every thing favorable which you had before said," &c. He then went into an argument to show that *two* years made a great difference with old men, etc. I laughed at his argument, but my wife thought it was no laughing matter, and that Mr. T. really took my article in bad part. A lady who was present and who read the letter was of the same opinion. Accordingly I replied argumentatively on my defence in some such way as this: Did you not *with your own pen* tell the public that you were an old man? Did you not say that you had known nearly all the actors in federal affairs since the adoption of the constitution? Did you not put forth this argument in order to show the superior value of your history as the work of a contemporary of the men whose actions you record? And in stating your age, was I not acting on the very ground you had chosen for yourself whereon to exhibit the superiority of your work over those of your younger historical brethren? &c&c&c

I received a reply in a few days in which he stated that he had written wholly in a jest &c &c; but I am inclined to believe that Mr. and Mrs. Tucker both were offended at the mention of the age of Mr. T. who argued in his letter to me that he was only 83!

I am glad that the little tribute of Dr. B. has come to hand. The summer has been a more pleasant one in this region to the feelings, but abominable to the crops. My little boy has wonderfully improved during the past four months.

I spent an evening with Bishop Meade at a neighbour's in the early part of the present week. I then saw the Rev. West who had purchased your book and had been reading it with deep interest. He is a wealthy planter on the Staunton, some twenty miles from my house in Charlotte.

I too was called from home two weeks ago to attend my mother,[116] who was taken ill in Pennsylvania. I did not go farther than Norfolk where I met her in a convalescent state. I trust your mother[117] will gradually improve until she reaches such a state of health as may make life comfortable.

In conclusion let me say that the spirit of your first correspondence with Mr. Tucker is freshly remembered by me; and that the patience and kindness which it breathed show explicitly that you have done all that an honorable and Christian gentleman could well do to preserve pleasant relations with him. I congratulate myself, and I think I ought to congratulate Mr. Tucker, on the part I performed towards bringing you amicably together. He little dreams of the difficulties he has avoided by blunting the edge of your pen as it traced the pages of your life of Jefferson.[118]

With kindest regards, I am, very truly,

Yours,
Hugh B. Grigsby

Henry S. Randall Esq.
Cortland Village
N. Y.

P. S. I will forward the correspondence in a day or two.

[Endorsed by Randall]
H. B. Grigsby
Nov. 12. 58

[Grigsby to Randall, December 21, 1858]

Norfolk, December 21, 1858

My dear sir,

I heartily rejoice that your affair with our old friend Professor T. has been amicably arranged. It would have been sad, in the event of another chance meeting of us all in Philadelphia, that he should have been absent from all our conferences, more especially as in the course of nature he has but few years to live.

---

[116] Elizabeth McPherson, maiden name of Grigsby's mother.

[117] Harriet Stephens Randall.

[118] As stated earlier, Grigsby was responsible for Randall's meeting with Tucker in 1856 in Philadelphia where Randall went to obtain information on Jefferson from Coles, Dunglison, and others.

You do well in classifying your manuscripts, and in arranging them in volumes. They may thus serve an important purpose in your hands or in those of your children hereafter; and must, at least, prove a becoming memorial of your industry and research.

I wish I could help you to some of the missing or wanting autographs; but with us there is no taste in that department, and only to a limited extent the means of gratifying it. Philadelphia, New York, and Boston, and, I may add Charleston, are the abodes of the lovers of autographs.

One word about the collection which you promise me. I have no collection of autographs, and do not propose to make one; and it were better that you retain what you may feel inclined to give me for your own purposes of preservation in your general volumes, or of exchange for others. Unless the letters contain facts of historical importance, they would be of no use to me; and if they did, they were equally useful to you, and worthy of a place in your archives. In this view, though thankful for your kindness and courtesy, I decline them in favor of others who would value them more highly. In the mean time I will hold your wishes in mind, and will endeavour to obtain all I can for you.

My wife is familiar with the "litter" of literary people, and can appreciate your employments; although from my casual writing of a morning she cannot form a notion of literary labor. By the way, Charles Campbell of Petersburg is about to publish a new edition of his history of Virginia from the settlement at Jamestown to the siege of York, and I have written a notice to the public in favor of the forthcoming work, and on the duty of subscribing to it.[119]

I shall certainly keep in mine the daguerreotypes, and when the weather is fair, will have them taken.

Dr. Balfour showed me your letter to him which I read with pleasure.

I have just received a letter from Mr. Rives accompanied by my review of the first volume of your work, which (the review) he had heard of and begged me to lend him. He purchased your volumes as they appeared, and in his letter speaks highly of them.

I enclose an invitation recently received to the wedding of a daughter of John Henry.[120] I could not attend, as I was in Norfolk at the date.

I have not written a line of my history of the Convention of 1788 for two months, but hope to begin my work in a week or two. The inducement to write with us is exceedingly faint. I have no congenial people

[119] The revised edition of Campbell's *History* appeared in 1860.

[120] Emma Cabell Henry was married, December 22, 1858, to Major James B. Ferguson of Richmond, later an agent for the Confederate government in Europe where he was visited by his wife in 1864.

to talk with; and I know that when I finish my book, no bookseller will take it, and I will be compelled to print it myself, and risk a thousand dollars, all the profits going to the bookseller instead of the historical society, for which I have written it.

I have not seen Mrs. G. since I received your letter, or she would have spoken for herself.

With the kindest regards to Mrs. Randall, and your family, I am very truly Yours

Hugh B. Grigsby

Henry S. Randall Esq.
Cortland Village
New York

P. S. I went into our parlours yesterday, and I found Master Hugh with one of your volumes which he had taken from the centre table, busily inspecting the face of the "Apostle." I soon put an end to his reveries. Pictures and apples seem to be his favorite food. I have been looking over Pepys' Diary for a few days past, and my boy has found out that there is a face of Pepys in the work. I made him salute Mr Pepys with the words: *"Mr Peps,* (so pronounced in England) *how do you do?"* The words struck his ear, and his mother heard him frequently repeating them during the day to his doll dog. All this to us with one bairn was amusing enough. By the way, I see in Pepys that words were pronounced in Charles the Second's time just as we now pronounce them in the interior of Virginia. He invariably writes *"chaw"* for *"chew," Barkley"* for *Berkeley,"* &c.

[Endorsed by Randall]
H. B. Grigsby E.
Dec 21, 1858.

1859

[Randall to Grigsby, January 1, 1859]

Cortland Village N. Y.
January 1, 1859

My dear Sir,[1]

I have nothing "on my mind" worth saying,—but I can't let this day slip over without sending you the compliments of the New Year.—I, my wife & my children join cordially in wishing all your household "a happy New Year."

In turning back to your last letter[2] to see if there is anything to answer, I observe your remarks about Mr. Rives. You say he speaks well of my life of Mr. Jefferson. Now let me tell you something queer. When I was writing my work, & came to the place where Mr Jefferson's plow is spoken of,[3] I remembered a paragraph which I had seen in the papers describing Mr Rives' introduction to an agricultural Society in France (if I remember aright) & his remarks on that occasion about Mr Jefferson's plow. I thought I would like to see the truth of the newspaper paragraph verified or contradicted by Mr. R. before I used it, & I thought if I wrote him on the subject he might add other interesting particulars. I did write him. True, I had never met him. But he was a public man—he had written & talked about Mr Jefferson publicly—& I presume, indeed, I cannot doubt, that I either declared or intimated to him that I was what is termed an authorized biographer. I remember now that I told him that I wrote to him directly & did not wait to obtain & enclose an introduction from Col. T. J. Randolph[4] for the purpose of saving time. Should he not as a gentleman & friend of Mr Jefferson have answered me? *He never did so!!*

I had been a particular respecter of Mr. Rives.[5] The youngest regular delegate of a State in the Baltimore Convention of 1835, I had stood up like a game cock in the private caucus of the N. Y. delegation for him,[6]

[1] This is the first Randall letter in this collection since his letter of December 24, 1857.

[2] See above, Grigsby to Randall, December 21, 1858.

[3] Jefferson's journal of his progress from Strasbourg to Nancy gives a mathematical formula for shaping the mouldboard of a plow. See Randall, *Life*, I, 501.

[4] Thomas Jefferson Randolph (1792–1875), eldest son of Jefferson's daughter, Martha, and Thomas Mann Randolph, and the favorite grandson of Jefferson. This grandson served as Jefferson's chief executor. He published the *Memoir, Correspondence, and Miscellanies from the Papers of Thomas Jefferson* (4 vols.; Charlottesville, Va., 1829).

[5] See above, Grigsby to Randall, March 23, 1858, n. 25, for information on Rives.

[6] In 1835, Randall was twenty-four years old.

for the V. Presidential nomination, against that large majority who decided to cast the vote of the state for R. M. Johnson.[7]—My letter to him about the plow was intended only as a beginning to a correspondence on other topics of my biography. For example, I wished to draw from him a letter in regard to Mr Jefferson's connection with his law Students &c. &c. & place it in the text of my work, not only to give fullness to my picture of Mr. J. but to honor his supposed friend Mr. Rives.

Now on what ground could Mr. R. have declined to answer a *civil* letter from an authorized biographer of Mr. J? The thing is unexplainable—unparalleled. I confess I have *felt,* though I have not *shown,* strong resentment, at his conduct.—

You say he speaks well of the book. It has occurred to me that it is barely possible he never received my letter. I directed to Charlottesville, Albemarle Co., & I requested the P. M. to put on the proper address & forward it, if necessary. If I had waited to write to Col. R.[8] for his address, I might as well also have obtained a letter of introduction—but I did not suppose either to be necessary. I doubt whether you could find a P. M. in this State who would not have forwarded a letter to *me,* under like circumstances.—There is a *possibility,* however, my letter did not reach him, & it is not *fair* perhaps to cherish a resentment without *knowing* you have had provocation.

I wish there was some way to ascertain the facts. Are you well enough acquainted with him to do this? If so, *I* care not if you put the question bluntly to him.

Again renewing the compliments of the Season to you & your family I remain

Cordially your friend
Henry S. Randall

P. S. I also wanted particularly to compare notes with Mr R. in respect my account of the intercourse & friendship between Jefferson & Madison, & my comparison between their characters—because I understood Mr. R. was writing M's life[9]—

[Endorsed by Grigsby]
H. S. Randall
January 1, 1859

[7] Richard Mentor Johnson (1780–1850), member of both the United States House and Senate (1819–1829), distinguished in the War of 1812, ardent Jacksonian, vice-president (1837–1841).

[8] Thomas Jefferson Randolph.

[9] See Randall, *Life,* III, 308–314. For a recent original and valuable interpretation of the interplay of the minds of Jefferson and Madison, see Ardienne Koch, *Jefferson and Madison: the Great Collaboration* (New York, 1950).

[Grigsby to Randall, January 26, 1859]

Norfolk, January 26, 1859

My dear sir,

I send to Messrs. Derby & Jackson, New York, by the Express of this day, a daguerreotype of Mrs. Grigsby and her son, and another of myself. They are not very good specimens of the art, but they are the best that could be obtained here. The general opinion of our friends is that I appear at least ten years older than I am, and that Mrs. G. is rather more venerable than she is entitled to be; but on the whole they must be considered accurate, perhaps painfully so to the individuals represented on the plate. My little boy moved at a critical time, and spoiled his mouth, and does not appear as we delight to see him with his ruddy complexion and bright dark eyes. In honor of your efforts in the cause of Sheep Husbandry[10] your essays on which subject I saw for the first time some days ago for a few moments) my little boy procured a sheep at the toyshop, and was soothed into perfect repose by the possession of so fine a present.

I have just shaken hands with Expresident Tyler who is on a visit to Norfolk, and is looking quite well.

There is nothing stirring here. I visited Gov. Tazewell a few days ago. He is quite well; and entered into an argument instanter about the probable burial place of Lord Botetourt in the Chapel of William & Mary.[11]

Mrs. G. presents her cordial regards to Mrs Randall and yourself; and will be gratified to see you both even in the forms which village daguerreotypography may give to your persons.

In haste, Very truly Yours.

Hugh B. Grigsby

Henry S. Randall Esq.
Cortland Village,
N. Y.

P. S. My age is fifty two and two months; that of Mrs G. is seven years less; and Carrington's age will be three years on the 13th of February Next.

[Not endorsed]

[10] Randall, *Sheep Husbandry in the South*, published in 1848, went through five additional printings before 1880.

[11] Baron de Norborne B. Botetourt (*ca.* 1718–1770), a popular governor of Virginia (1768–1770), sought unsuccessfully for harmony with the House of Burgesses. A marble statue, erected in his honor, now stands in the quadrangle of William and Mary College. Grigsby maintained that Botetourt was buried in the Chapel of the College in the same place as was Sir John Randolph.

[Randall to Grigsby, February 14, 1859]

Cortland Village, N. Y.
Feb. 14th 1859.

My dear Sir,

Last evening (I mean Saturday evening), the papers brought the news of the burning of William & Mary & the total destruction of its library, apparatus, collections, &c. Oh—oh—oh! what a disaster! What a miserable sense of insecurity for every physical thing we treasure up, does such a circumstance force home upon us? One hundred & fifty years of diligent accumulation swept away in fifteen minutes! We must build our valuable repositories more securely. We must make them fire proof. It is only tempting a more rapid destruction to bring together costly books & works of art in any other kind of building.[12]

You & Gov. Tazewell were yesterday disputing about the buryal place of Lord Botetourt in that old Chapel. Now there is no chapel—no tomb! Probably the graves are obliterated and the bones calcined to ashes, of the Chiefs & heroes who slept there. What a sad & miserable train of reflections this gives rise to. Verily we are dust, & to dust we *must* return.

The three strangers—i. e. strangers to this *place*—who have been since the 26th ult. on their way here from Norfolk have not arrived, though the latch string has been constantly out for them & the fatted calf ready.[13] I presume they could not have lost their way. They probably stopped with D & J. in New York, & in the hurry of affairs have forgotten to start again. (Hope they are not dissipating in the great city!) I shall write D & J. herewith & then if I don't hear of them I will "make a fuss."

You beat me a little on the score of age. I am 47 & my wife is 45—the same age with Mrs. Grigsby. Tell *her* I think it is *cheating* & *taking advantage* for gentlemen of 52 to have wives of the same age with gentlemen of 45.

[12] "On the night of 8th February, 1859, . . . the College building, with most of its interesting antiquities, were destroyed by accidental fire. The Library, containing many curious and rare books, with some manuscripts, chiefly presented by Kings, Archbishops, Bishops and Governors, and the cabinet of apparatus in which were instruments more than a century old, the gift of the Colonial House of Burgesses were consumed. The mural tablets in the Chapel to the memories of Sir John Randolph and Bishop Madison in Virginia were also destroyed." *Historical Sketch of the College of William and Mary* (Richmond, 1866), pp. 19–20. In 1849, Grigsby demanded that the library of the Virginia Historical Society be fire proof within and without and offered a hundred dollars towards the construction of such a building. See Grigsby to William Maxwell, corresponding secretary of the Virginia Historical Society, Charlotte County, Virginia, December 29, 1849, in the *Virginia Historical Register and Literary Note Book*, III (1850), 52–55.

[13] Daguerreotypes of Grigsby, Mrs. Grigsby, and their son, Hugh Carrington.

Wight Carrington finds his good fortune in his parent having *sheepish* acquaintances. It is curious what a thorough hobby sheep & sheep raising is with me.

Apropos, I am glad you call your boy by the maternal name. It is always *due* to the mother. And then Carrington is such a mouth filling & fine sounding name. It sounds *gentleman* all over.—When this young Virginian comes to see me, I can show him the letters of some of his ancestry. I have one written by Judge Paul Carrington[14] & one by Col. Edward.[15] Your wife's father I believe was Col. Clement. How does he stand connected with preceding?—[16]

I don't remember whether I ever mentioned my wife's family name to you. It was Polhemus.[17] The first of the name in this country settled at Flatbush (he was a clergyman from Holland) & his coat of arms is, or was a few years since, attached to his old pulpit.[18] The family spread on Long Island, & a portion of them passed over to New Jersey. They were usually rich & influential. They divided in the Revolution, as did most of the old Long Island families.—some of them fighting for the king & others for their country. My wife's direct ancestors all took the patriotic side. Her father was a Captain in the Revolution. One of her great uncles followed Braddock to DuQuesne (commanding a company if I remember aright)—marched with Wolfe to Quebec—rose rapidly to the rank of Major in the continental line in the Revolution—fought in many of the hardest fields of the Revolution—was the Senior officer

---

[14] See above, Grigsby to Randall, July 25, 1858, n. 80.

[15] Edward Carrington (1749–1810), member of his county committee (1775–1776), revolutionary soldier, member of the Continental Congress (1785–1786), marshall of the United States District Court of Virginia in 1789, foreman of the jury in the Richmond trial of Aaron Burr. Randall quotes at length from two Jefferson letters addressed to Carrington, one on Shays' Insurrection, the other on the Federal Constitution. See *Life*, I, 463–464, 488–489.

[16] Mrs. Grigsby's father, Clement Carrington, was the second son of Paul Carrington, the brother of Edward Carrington.

[17] Jane Rebecca Polhemus, daughter of Henry and Jane (Anderson) Polhemus, [Paul K. Randall], *Genealogy of a Branch of the Randall Family*, p. 60.

[18] The Reverend Johannes Theodorus Polhemus (c. 1598–1676), served the ministry of the Dutch Reformed Church successively in the Palatine, in Westphalia, in Dutch Brazil (1637–1654) during its temporary occupation, and at Flatbush and Brooklyn in New Netherlands. His ministry at Flatbush was between 1662 and 1665 and that at Brooklyn lasted until his death after fifty-five years of service to his church. He and his family began the history of the Polhemus family in America. For more information on this early Polhemus, see Louis P. DeBoer, "Pre-American Notes on Old New Netherland Families," *The Genealogical Magazine of New Jersey*, III (July, 1927), 102–108; Teunis G. Bergen, *Register in Alphabetical Order of the Early Settlers of Kings County, Long Island, N.Y., from its First Settlement by Europeans to 1700* (New York, 1881), pp. 226–227; James Riker, Jr., *The Annals of Newtown, in Queens County, New-York* (New York, 1852), pp. 348–350.

of the New Jersey line amidst the horrors of Valley Forge—remained I think in the army after the peace & died a Colonel.*[19]

The family were gigantic in statu[r]e. They tell this story of the Major. He once was su[r]prised with a small party while drinking at a Spring by a detachment of British dragoons.—The Americans fled through a Swamp, & the big powerful Major broke his way forward like a big buck moose—or like that bull in Jefferson's Notes. A little fat poddy drummer was soon left behind, sticking in the mud. The swords of the dragoons were flashing not far in the rear. His terror was mortal & he shouted in phrenzied accents, "Johannus! Johannus! mein Got! will you leave your old school fellow here to die?" The big Major "wore about," swooped down like a condor, caught the little drummer under one arm, & ran faster than ever, while the dangling legs of the little drummer went wiggle to waggle, flippety to flop, sticking out under his arm behind—Read that sentence to Carrington—I am sure it will strike him!) The dragoons were dead beat and distanced!

My wife's grandmother was a *French* woman. Cupid gets up some curious genealogical olla podridas.—I used to think my father in law showed traits of both stocks. He was as steady of purpose and honest as a Dutchman & had a good deal of the mental activity & vivacity of a Frenchman. He was respected and popular, represented in the legislature & held the Sheriffality of his county (one of the strongest counties of the State) and held various other offices. He had been bred to the law, but went into merchandise until he passed the active period of life. He was as true hearted a man as I ever knew.

Another hotch-potch! My wife's father married a spouse who was half English & half Scotch—Colin & Anderson. So my children are Dutch, French, Scotch, & English! I cannot find that a drop of any other blood but surly John Bull's flows in *my* veins. On one side I am from the Cavalier & on the other Side from the Puritan—neither of them types of men I admire.

On both sides, my ancestors were a long race of sea-captains. Thomas Randall, Port Warden of New York in the Revolution, was the founder of that princely charity, the Sailors Snug [blank] (I forget the title)

* Another brother was a commissioned officer in the regular army. He came from the same town as the major and they had been boys together.

[19] Possibly John Polhemus, captain, first battalion, fourth establishment, November 22, 1775; captain, first battalion, second establishment, November 29, 1776; major, first battalion, second establishment; retired September 26, 1780. William S. Stryker, *Official Register of the Officers and Men of New Jersey in the Revolutionary War* (Trenton, N. J.), p. 69.

which is one of the wealthiest foundations in the U. S.*[20] Josiah Randall is one of the ablest lawyers in Pennsylvania.[21] A distinguished family of Randalls belong to Maryland,—several of whom have held high places in the army.[22] Judge Randall of Florida married a daughter of Wm. Wirt.[23]—He was reputed an able man but I never saw him. I suppose all these scattered scions spring from the same root—but I never have enquired into details or made any attempt to ascertain their degree of consanguinety.[24] My paternal grandfather was a farmer, a man of fine appearance as my recollections & his portrait testifies.

My maternal grandfather was a physician, a man of mark in his day, & once of great property.[25] His striking face looks down upon me as I write (his name was Stephens) from the ivory of Dickinson, one of the finest miniature painters of England.[26] My father was bred to the law, but went into merchandise during the war of 1812. He was a man of accomplishment & reading—& was a most finished business man. He was a brigadier General at a time when a military commission was an honor. He is now 71 years old.[27] My mother—a woman of uncommon understanding & energy, is 67 years old.—[28]

* Randalls place in the City & Randall Island in the East River were named after him.

---

[20] Thomas Randall (d. 1797), a prosperous privateer and one of the founders of the New York Chamber of Commerce, established the Marine Society in New York for the relief of indigent and distressed seamen and their widows and orphans. The Sailors' Snug Harbor was founded by his son, Robert Richard Randall (*ca.* 1750–1801).

[21] Josiah Randall, a personal friend and a political adviser of President Buchanan, and the father of Samuel J. Randall (1828–1890), who was in Congress during the reconstruction period.

[22] Randalls of English and Irish stock came to Maryland in the seventeenth century and later gave their name to Randallstown, Maryland.

[23] Thomas Randall received an appointment (*ca.* 1827) to the post of district judge in Florida, and took his bride, Laura Wirt, to Florida, where they established a home on land given them by her father.

[24] One Randall genealogist discovered there were about twenty-five distinct Randall families. See William L. Chaffin, *A Biographical History of Robert Randall and His Descendants 1608–1909* (New York, 1909).

[25] Dr. Josiah Stephens, a native of Wareham, Massachusetts, who removed to Oxford, Chenango County, New York, in 1800, where he was a "physician of eminent abilities and extensive practice." The Reverend Samuel F. Bacon, *Memorial Sermon, occasioned by the Death of Harriet Stephens Randall . . .* (Cortland, N.Y., 1867), p. 11.

[26] Anson Dickinson (1779–1852), portrait painter in miniatures and oils.

[27] Roswell Randall (1786–1871), received a good academic education and studied law but chose to engage in business with his brother, William, with whom he removed to Cortland in 1813 with his wife and two sons, Henry Stephens and William P. Randall, who had been born in Madison County. Henry Stephens Randall's two sisters, Lucy Maria and Harriet Eliza Randall, were born in Cortland. Roswell remained in business after the partnership was dissolved and held the post of postmaster for some years. With his wife, he participated in the growth of Cortland. See Bacon, *Memorial Sermon*, pp. 11–12; [Paul K. Randall], *Genealogy of a Branch of the Randall Family*, pp. 36–37.

[28] Harriet Stephens Randall (1790–1867), daughter of Dr. Josiah and Editha

There is five times over the longest account of my own family I ever wrote, or probably shall ever write again!

With cordial regards from me & mine to yourself, Mrs. Grigsby & Carrington

Yours,
Henry S. Randall

Hugh B. Grigsby E.
[Endorsed by Grigsby]
Henry S. Randall
February 14, 1859

[Grigsby to Randall, February 26, 1859]

Norfolk, February 26, 1859

My dear sir,

I have just read your letter which reached Norfolk during my absence of a week which I spent in Williamsburg about the affairs of the College. I hope the daguerreotypes have reached you in safety by this time. They are sad affairs, and cost us as much as fine ones in New York would have done. I thank you for the interesting details in your letter. The history of families is the truest history of a country.

My visit to William and Mary was a sad but a busy and in the main a delightful one. The old walls stand as firm as they did the day they were put up, and the Board have appointed me a committee with the Faculty to take the matter into consideration. We are doing all that can be done; and when our plan is fully digested I will inform you of its details.[29]

The meeting of the Alumni was full, and President Tyler delivered

---

(Bush) Stephens, was born in Burlington, Vermont. She married Roswell Randall, March 27, 1810, and removed with him to Cortland, New York, where she joined with him in the growth of the community and was known for her kindness to the poor. In 1831 she joined the Presbyterian Church. See Bacon, *Memorial Sermon, passim;* Paul K. Randall, *op. cit.*, p. 36.

[29] The walls of the main building of the College, originally constructed in 1684, were the oldest college walls in the United States and passed through three fires, October 29, 1705, February 8, 1859, and September 9, 1862. "The Walls of the College," *William and Mary Quarterly*, 1st series, XI (January, 1903), 174–179. Despite the severe damage, a plan of restoration was immediately inaugurated. The widow of a former professor wrote: "The citizens have already subscribed $6000 together with the Faculty. The College is insured for $20,000, & it is thought with $50,000 they can put up a handsome building. . . ." Mrs. Cynthia B. T. Washington to Lawrence Washington, Williamsburg, February 9, 1859, in *ibid.*, 1st series, XXIII (April, 1915), 286–289.

before them a fine speech, and St. George Tucker a beautiful poem.[30] But the crowning scene was at the dinner table. More than two hundred of the Alumni sate down at three long tables, and the speaking was most eloquent. Wise delivered the grandest speech in one respect that I think was ever pronounced any where. It united in a supreme degree the highest tragic and the highest comic action. The young alumni, men verging to middle life, spoke with an oratorical power which it was plain to see was native to the institution. In our board Wise and myself had another pitched battle, which resulted in the defeat of his proposition after a fierce debate of three hours. We are on the most friendly and affectionate terms; but our views of business differ materially.

Entre Nous: I am revising Campbell's new edition of his history in Manuscript. My emendations are literal and clerical mainly. As for the form of chronicle which he has adopted, that I could not amend without re-writing the whole work. The advantage of my revisal to him and to me will be that there will be no serious clashing between us when we appear in print. He has changed his views of the Mecklenburg Declaration which were in favor of that instrument in his first edition, and now takes boldly those which we hold.[31]

The loss of the library of William & Mary is too terrible to dwell upon. All was lost.

I much fear that it is not possible to procure a letter of Henry Tazewell. Should I survive Mr. L. W. Tazewell, I will give you a letter of his, and you can tack it in your work. My grand edition or copy of my work on the Convention of 1776, was burned. It was magnificently bound; contained fifteen or twenty steel engravings, and an index to

[30] Henry St. George Tucker (1828–1863), better known as St. George Tucker, author of *Hansford: A Tale of Bacon's Rebellion* (Richmond, 1857), reissued as *The Devoted Bride* (Philadelphia, 1878). A Confederate veteran and an author of fugitive verse, he read one of his poems at the one hundred and sixty-seventh anniversary of the founding of William and Mary College. See Armistead C. Gordon, Jr., *Virginian Writers of Fugitive Verse* (New York, 1923), pp. 96–97; Lyon G. Tyler, *Encyclopaedia of Virginia Biography* (5 vols.; New York, 1915), III, 161.

[31] The early edition of Charles Campbell, *An Introduction to the History of the Colony and Ancient Dominion of Virginia* (Richmond, 1847), pp. 149–150, gives a brief account of the Mecklenburg Declaration and accepts the genuineness of the May 20, 1775, version on the ground that Jefferson used expressions similar to those in the Mecklenburg Declaration. However, in the revised two-volume edition (Philadelphia [1860], II, 615–617), Campbell denies the authenticity of the May 20 version. He gives Grigsby, *The Virginia Convention of 1776*, the chief credit for his change of view. In his Preface (I, xi), Campbell states: "I avail myself of this occasion to express my acknowledgment to Hugh B. Grigsby, Esq. who has contributed so much to the illustration of Virginia history by his own writings, for many valuable suggestions, and for having undergone the trouble of revising a large part of the manuscript of this work." For additional information on Campbell, his history and its revision, see this correspondence and its notes, *passim*.

the plates printed expressly for the vol. I must make up another. Can you help me to an engraving of Peyton Randolph, Wythe, R. H. Lee, or any other of the members of that body?[32] The work called The Signers of the Declaration of Independence by Sanderson[33] contained Wythe and Lee, but all the other plates were destroyed by a fire on Market street some years ago.

By the way, your allusion to my talk with Mr. Tazewell about Lord Botetourt reminds me of an interesting incident that occurred during my visit to Williamsburg. The Faculty were anxious to convince me that the splendid coffin in Sir John Randolph's vault was *certainly* Lord Botetourt's. I had stated that all the *probabilities* were in favor of the fact, but that the fact was not absolutely proved.[34] Accordingly, the Faculty requested me to attend them to the Chapel, and there by the aid of servants who removed the ashes of the late fire, and a bricklayer, the vault was opened, and a servant sent in with six or eight candles which lighted up the vault perfectly. Then a close and critical examination was made, and the result is that the evidence is almost conclusive of the fact that the body was Lord B's. I have made a statement of the facts and arguments under 12 heads, each subsequent one resting on its predecessor, and the proofs seem overwhelming. I handled the large thigh bones of Lord B. The bones of the skull and chest were dissolved, and nearly all indeed except the sacrum and a few vertebrae. The coffin lid was six feet three inches long, and was originally covered with black cloth which was confined by double rows of large gilded tacks in all amounting to near two thousand. No name, which was doubtless put on in tacks, as no plate was found, could be read on the detached pieces of coffin. It was an interesting scene. The vault was immediately bricked up. Next day at dinner with President Tyler and the faculty I was requested to read the items of proof I have just mentioned to the company; when President Tyler dissented and declared that Lord B. was buried in a particular spot in the Chapel which he knew when a boy. After dinner all of us adjourned in a body to the chapel, and having procured entrance we examined every spot and in the vicinage of every

[32] Peyton Randolph, first president of the Continental Congress, see above, Grigsby to Randall, July 25, 1858, n. 74. George Wythe (1726–1806), taught Jefferson law and worked with Jefferson and Edmund Pendleton on revising and codifying Virginia's laws. Wythe is sketched in Grigsby, *The Virginia Convention of 1776*, pp. 119–124, and compared with Pendleton in *ibid.*, pp. 125–130. Richard Henry Lee appears in *ibid.*, pp. 130–144.

[33] John Sanderson (1784–1844) and others, *Biography of the Signers of the Declaration of Independence* (9 vols.; Philadelphia, 1820–1827).

[34] Grigsby's article on "The Dead of the Chapel of William and Mary" appeared in the *Daily Southern Argus*, July 31, 1858.

spot pointed out by President Tyler, and all in vain. So his fruitless effort to point out the spot, and the consequent thorough examination of the ground by the spade, afforded another proof to those I had already formed in the converging series.

The beautiful tablet of Sir John was destroyed. I will save and send you a piece.

All of us are well. Carrington was three years old Sunday week past. He sometimes seats himself at the table with paper and pencil, and when asked what he is doing, answers: "I am writing to Mr Covington" (my overseer in Charlotte). Mrs. G. continues as well as usual at this season—the last winds of the Spring being always unwelcome to her.

With care and kindness to Mrs R and all yours,

I am, very truly,
Yours.
Hugh G. Grigsby

Henry S. Randall Esq.
Cortland Village

[Randall to Grigsby, March 29, 1859]

Cortland Village, N. Y.
March 29

My dear Sir,

Your last very interesting letter reached me in due time, but I do not write at this time to answer it.—I have some news to tell you. Three travellers reached my house (with a box of books) last evening, & I have no doubt they are the persons who you said would visit me from Norfolk.[35] But they won't tell who they are. They are either deaf & dumb, or under a vow. The gentleman resembles you & may be fifty. The lady looks 38 or 40, has a calm, placid, thoughtful face, & is handsome. I have made all sorts of polite speeches to her, but never a word will she speak, nor even smile to show she understands me.—She sits ever & aye with her arm thrown over the shoulder of her child—her eyes intent & seemingly listening—her expression benignant—but she remains as unmoved as a highland loch at the bottom of a deep mountain chasm, which no breeze ever agitates. I will bet she has abundance of calm, undemonstrative fixedness of character—passive resolution. I know I should like her if she would only talk; but I am getting provoked because she will not, & probably shall soon march off in a high dudgeon.—

[35] Daguerreotypes of Grigsby, Mrs. Grigsby, and their son Hugh Carrington.

The little boy is a decidedly fine looking fellow. His eye sparkles with that purpose which will show itself somewhere, one of these days. He looks like both father & mother. The tableau which the silent mother and son constantly form is decidedly graceful. As the little gamins in our streets say, "they will do."

On the whole, odd as it is to entertain people, under such circumstances, I can't help liking my strange guests. They spend most of the time with me in my library—& they are sort of silent company to me.

These are your three Norfolkers, doubtless? Are they really deaf & dumb, or are they under a vow or a spell?

I hope old William & Mary is to rise from its ashes.[36] But if so, some of the ancient glory will be wanting. Helas! what an accident.

My wife & family present their very particular regards to Mrs. Grigsby, yourself, & Master Carrington. They will commit reprisals on you for your politeness, the first time we visit New York. My wife is a little shy about it, however. She thinks (& I assure you *I* think) that Mrs. G. has no right to look both the youngest & h——t, considering that you are older than me!

Cordially yours,
Henry S. Randall

Hugh Blair Grigsby, Esq.
[Endorsed by Grigsby]
Henry S. Randall
March 29, 1859
Daguerreotypes

[Randall to Grigsby, April 25, 1859]

Cortland Village, N. Y.
Apl. 25, 1859.

My dear Sir,

My pleasant Norfolk visitors stay with me, but shew! refusing to speak a word. Even that very fine & very amiable looking woman persists in this contumacy.

[36] The faculty of the College received a report, February 8, 1860, one year after the fire, which stated: "The new College edifice has been completed, and fully furnished.... The chapel has been restored, and the remains of its illustrious dead still lie undisturbed within its walls. The library has been conveniently and handsomely furnished with cases for books, and already contains about six thousand volumes, obtained partly by purchase, and partly by the donations of public-minded individuals. Thus within one year the losses by the fire of February 8th, 1859, have, in every material point of view, been completely restored; and in all the essentials of its building, furniture, apparatus and library, the College is now in a better condition than it was on that day." *Historical Sketch of the College of William and Mary, in Virginia* (Richmond, 1866), p. 21.

I am gradually, when I feel i' the mood, making an abridgement of St. Thomas for popular circulation. I mean to razee my three frigates into one cock boat—make a 12 mo. which can be sold at retail at $1.25. Such are the only books for the million. I have gone through the first vol, & 3 chapters into the 2d.—I rather like the business & find it easier than I expected. The abridgement of a chapter is an easy day's work. I am in no hurry to complete it until near the opening of next winter & then I will have it ready for a rapid publication—if the times seem to encourage it.—

Like the corpse of the Spanish Champion, the dead Jefferson goes on winning fields. Did you observe that the Republicans celebrated his birth day in Boston! All sides now claim him. No tongue now dares assail him any more than Washington.—

By the by, I will tell you what I would *like* to do, if you think it proper, that is, present a set of my works to John Henry. I *love* everything that has a drop of the blood of "old Pat" in it. I have now & then criticized the "forest born Demosthenes"—you know just how much—but it does not seem possible to me that John Henry would take any offence at these criticisms, or feel annoyed to think he had *accepted* the work from the author of them.—You know him intimately—& I know no man whom I would sooner rely on, than you to decide with exact dignity & delicacy on the question I have raised. I would like if you think it entirely proper to have you write him expressing my wish to present him the work—saying that as a personal stranger I did not feel free to address him on the subject myself.

If he accepts, I will write my publishers to direct their agent at Norfolk to supply you a copy for Mr. Henry.

By George! Catch me putting a solitary word into the cockboat edition against "St Patric" (for I am canonizing him too in my feelings) if you can! (And I shall also leave out all discussion with the Lees). Hang it, how queer it looks to see how independently I slashed right and left, when the heat of battle was on me![37]

You'll laugh if I tell you something—& perhaps think I am impudent and egotistical. If I had full materials *I would write a Life of Patrick Henry*. I could do it, perfectly *congusto!* I *do* think—don't frown & shake your head—that Wirt's Henry is the very worst & most smothering & extinguishing biography *to the Subject of it* that was ever written![38] It is all Wirt, Wirt, Wirt,—ornate Wirt—not a bit of native

[37] The one-volume edition was never finished. For a discussion of Randall's treatment of Patrick Henry and Richard Henry Lee, see this correspondence and its notes, *passim*.

[38] Wirt, *Sketches of the Life and Character of Patrick Henry*.

Henry a man of more than 50 times the real genius of his biographer, & who therefore the latter had no right to even inadvertently smother! There now I'm in for a scolding!! Give my kind regards & those of my family to Mrs Grigsby and Carrington, after deducting a pro rata share for yourself

Your friend
H. S. Randall

Dr. Grigsby.
[Endorsed by Grigsby]
Henry S. Randall
April 25, 1859
Answered eo:die

[Grigsby to Randall, April 26, 1859]

Norfolk, April 26, 1859

My dear sir,

Your letter acknowledging the arrival of the daguerreotypes was received in due time, and gave me some relief, as I was fearful that in the course of events they had passed you by.[39] Our friends here thought them hard dealers with the remnants of the good looks of your friends in question; but, as I was fearful that fresh trials would make us look worse rather than better, I determined to settle the hash at once.

Mr Charles Campbell has returned from a visit to New York and Philadelphia, having succeeded in getting Lippincott to publish his work. In New York he saw Bancroft and Lossing,[40] and Hawks. The last named has recently lost a grown son in California—a loss the world can never supply or repair.

Did I tell you that I examined for more than an hour the dust of Lord Botetourt with a view of finding a plate with his name upon it?[41] When we meet, we must talk over this affair.

My wife has not been as well as usual this year; but I hope the warm weather will bring her to. Carrington thrives. I caught him yesterday in the back yard by himself, hunting cats with his terrier Towser. This

[39] See above, Randall to Grigsby, March 29, 1859.

[40] Benson John Lossing (1813–1891), engraver, journalist, and historian. Wrote and illustrated numerous works including *A Pictorial Field Book of the American Revolution* (2 vols.; New York, 1851–1852); *A Pictorial Field Book of the War of 1812* (New York, 1868); *A Pictorial Field Book of the Civil War* (3 vols.; Hartford, Conn., 1866–1868); *A Family History of the United States* (Hartford, 1883); and *Our Countrymen* (2 vols.; New York, 1876–1878).

[41] See above, Grigsby to Randall, February 26, 1859.

looks suspicious and may bespeak a hereditary love of sport. He is *three* years old. Present us kindly to Mrs Randall and your daughter, and believe me very truly Yours,

Hugh B. Grigsby

Henry S. Randall, Esq.
Cortland Village
New York

[Randall to Grigsby, April 30, 1859]

Cortland Village
April 30th, 1859

My dear Sir,

Yours came last night.[42] I have written my publishers this morning to either instruct their Norfolk agent to deliver you a cop. of my work (library i. e. full bound edn.) for Mr. Henry, or to forward you, instanter, a cop. from N. Y. with express charges paid.—I presume therefore you cannot fail to get it in time to carry it to him as you proposed.

I enclose you papers to paste in the vols.

Ha ha! my friend—you set me down a new biographer too quick. I said I would do it *if I had sufficient materials!* So I would. I could do it purely con gusto. I *love* old Pat. I love him in puris naturalibus, & not awkwardly attempting to flaunt in a Roman toga.

But are there *enough new* materials, to find a good excuse for re-writing his life. Mr. Wirt's work has a traditionary reputation. People admire the book because everybody admired the good hearted elegant, & able author. It would not do to write over this ground again, without much *new* & *important* material. I don't like Wirts *manner*. But it would be intolerable presumption in me, on that account merely, to undertake this task.

I would prefer to say nothing to Mr. Henry on that topic. It might even give him an erroneous impression of my motives in presenting him my Life of Mr. Jefferson. I have, however, no objection, that *you* say to him, as of your own knowledge & not as word sent by me to him, that you know I have *some thoughts* of attempting his fathers biography.—In this case, you could tell him, of course, my *"quo animo"* towards his father, & my subject generally. I hope he will write to me on the receipt of the volumes & presume he will.

I am very sorry—we all are—to hear Mrs. Grigsby is not as well as

[42] See above, Grigsby to Randall, April 26, 1859, which does not mention John Henry. It is probable that Randall here replies to a letter not in this collection.

usual. When you get into the country air of Charlotte, she will doubtless recruit. Our united regards to her, Master Carrington, & yourself.

I have scratched this off hastily for the mornings mail.

Yours faithfully
Henry S. Randall

H. B. Grigsby, Esq.
[Endorsed by Grigsby]
Henry S. Randall
Cortland Village, April 30, 1859

[Grigsby to Randall, May 9, 1859]

Norfolk, May 9, 1859

My dear sir,

Your last letter was duly received and the package containing the set of the "life" for my friend John Henry was delivered at my house yesterday, and will be placed in the hands of Mr H. in a few days. I have not opened the package; and will not do so until I deliver the book.

Summer is upon us at last. We are to have a great gathering at the Episcopal Convention which meets here in a few days.[43] Bishop Meade spent an hour with me in my library Saturday. He is delicate at present, but has always some literary topic bearing upon religion on the anvil. His present scheme is a small work tracing the passage of the acts recorded in the old testament through the religious and mythologies of all subsequent time. It is a light production designed for youth.[44]

It would, of course, be politic to look closely into the subject of Henry's life before you came to any conclusion in the premises; but I really think that such a volume as Quincy's life of J. Q. Adams might be safely undertaken.[45] By the way, I was aiding Professor Totten[46] in making collections of books and money for William & Mary College last week; and, as he lodged at one end of the town and I at the other, our morning rendevous was at the Argus office, the editor of which is an alumnus of the College.[47] While there, the compositor came in for matter, and, as the editors had not arrived, was waiting in vain. I grew nervous,

[43] National convention of the Protestant Episcopal Church in Richmond in 1859.

[44] Bishop William Meade, *The Bible and the Classics* (New York, 1861).

[45] Josiah Quincy (1772–1864), lawyer, political leader, president of Harvard (1829–1845), author of *Memoir of John Quincy Adams* (Boston, 1858). Against abolitionists as disunionists, but opposed to slavery.

[46] Silas Totten (1804–1873), a Protestant Episcopal clergyman, professor of belles-lettres at William and Mary (1848–1859), chancellor of the University of Iowa from 1859.

[47] Abram F. Leonard and William Lamb edited the *Daily Southern Argus* from 1856 to 1861.

and told him that I would employ him, and instantly penned the first paragraph of the article I send you. I finished it at once, and set the printer fairly at work, before the editor arrived. I send you the article as showing a hasty estimate of the life of Adams by Quincy.[48]

I leave Tuesday morning for Charlotte. Carrington continues well, and has recently taken a great passion for sewing machines. He watches their operation, and almost breaks his back in his turnings from the wheels to the needle. I hope he may have a turn for mechanics, and carry his passion out in all things save *grist* mills. I have known several planters *broke* by them.

Mrs. G. continues delicate; but I hope much from the warm weather. She joins with me in respects to Mrs. Randall.

I have not written one line in my work since I left Charlotte in December.[49] I cannot write in Norfolk, from sundry interruptions, and from laziness.

In the mean time I have a very poor opinion of lazy people. *You* can hardly conceive of a lazy man. I think my want of health is the cause of my indolence; but I will rouse up in the dog days.

With kind regards,
I am truly yours
Hugh B. Grigsby

Henry S. Randall, Esq.
Cortland Village, New York

[Grigsby to Randall, June 4, 1859]

Norfolk, June 4, 1859

My dear sir,

I did not attend the wedding in Charlotte as I intended; but reached that county on Thursday week last, the day of the general election. While there I could not see the son of Mr. John Henry, but left the parcel[50] with an intimate friend, who would deliver it either to Mr. John Henry himself at Court (next Monday) or to his son William Wirt Henry,[51] a promising lawyer who is a blood relation of Mrs. Grigsby. I wrote a letter to Mr. J. Henry, and I think it probable that you will be the first person to hear from him.

[48] Grigsby's review appeared in the *Daily Southern Argus*, May 5, 1859. He appraised the book as a "tolerable miniature" of Mr. Adams but regretted "that so able a man as Josiah Quincy now approaching his ninetieth year, is as violent in his hostility to the South as he was when thirty-five years ago he received the scathing rebuke of Henry Clay" for his 1808 motion to impeach Jefferson.

[49] Grigsby, *The Virginia Federal Convention of 1788*.

[50] The three volumes of Randall's *Life* sent to John Henry as a gift.

[51] William Wirt Henry (1831–1900), Whig, opponent of Secession, Confederate

What a fine time we had during the session of the Episcopal Convention in Norfolk! It was the largest gathering the Church ever witnessed in Virginia. I saw excellent people from all parts of the State; and had you been present and mingled with the members, they might have concluded that our Saint was not such a wicked man after all.

Summer weather is now upon us; and erelong I will begin to look with my family towards Edgehill. I saw my crop of wheat a few days ago, and it cheered my heart at this time drooping on account of the war in Europe. Fortunate fighting people must eat; and I shall try to feed them.[52]

All of us are well. Carrington is made proud by the present of a fine colt born of my mare Emily three weeks ago, and inquires of all his friends whether they have seen his new horse.

I wish I could give you a true notion of John Henry.[53] But all attempts at description were vain. You must see him, and the grave of the old Thunderer against King George some of these days.

Kind regards to Mrs. Randall from Mrs. G., who flourishes most in hot weather, and from myself, and believe me very truly Yours,

Hugh B. Grigsby

P. S. Have you seen Allibone's Dictionary of Authors? To my surprise I found I had a niche in it.[54] The first volume only has been published, and the letter "R." is not yet reached.[55]

Veteran, commonwealth attorney for Charlotte County, represented Richmond in the state legislature (1877–1880), orator of the Philadelphia Centennial Exposition (1876), president of the American Historical Association (1891), president for many years of the Virginia Historical Society. Published among other books: *Patrick Henry: Life, Correspondence, and Speeches of Patrick Henry* (3 vols.; New York, 1891).

[52] The Franco-Austrian War, April 26, 1859–July 11, 1859.

[53] See above, Grigsby to Randall, September 20, 1857.

[54] Samuel Austin Allibone (1816–1889), lexicographer and bibliographer, *A Critical Dictionary of English Literature and British and American Authors* (3 vols.; Philadelphia, 1858–1871), I, 742. The reference to Grigsby notes *The Virginia Convention of 1776:* "It treats in a clear, concise style, which frequently rises to the level of high oratory, and which is throughout well sustained and deeply attractive, the entire history of the convention in question, embracing admirable biographies of its members. Among the many glimpses which we have had of late months of Revolutionary History—thanks to the patriotism and zeal of our Historical Societies—we can recall none more deserving of commendation than this, as set forth in the volume before us. We commend it with the assurance that every one interested in American history will add it to his library."

[55] Randall's *Life* received an extended notice when Allibone's second volume appeared in 1871. The digest of reviews, reprinted from periodicals, magazines, and newspapers ranged greatly in tone. The publisher's advertisement, attested by favorable reviews from more than ninety daily newspapers, ran counter to the extract from *The London Athenaeum* of June 4, 1859, commenting "It would be less than the truth to say, that, even in spite of his biographer, Jefferson's Life cannot fail to be read with interest." See Allibone, *op. cit.*, II, 1737.

[Randall to Grigsby, September 10, 1859]

Cortland Village
Sept. 10. 1859

My dear Sir,

I have been very little at home for a number of weeks, & when at home have been incessantly occupied with some pressing *business* engagements. Your excellent speech & your letter of Aug. 25th reached me duly.[56] I am very glad to hear that all of you are so well. My family are in good health, & as for myself I have not been so rugged for years. I have been constantly *going*, this summer, & the effect on my health has been most beneficial. It seems as if I had taken out a new lease of life.

I am much flattered by Mr Henry's feelings toward me. I love his father. If there are materials sufficient to justify another biography of him, I could in the leisure of winter put them together & do it con gusto. As you remark, I ought to carefully examine the materials before launching into such an attempt. I have no time at present, nor shall I have for a long period, to go to Virginia & devote the necessary time to an investigation of the papers there: I could be doing it constantly at short intervals, were the papers here. Col. T. J. Randolph[57] of his own accord, put Mr. Jeffersons original private Mss. from which I have quoted in my life of Mr Jefferson into my hands & I carried them home with me.—If Mr Henry felt disposed to take the same course, the papers would be as safe here as in Virginia—& would be returned when the investigation, or the biography, was completed. I would not like to have Mr. Henry pressed to take any such step. Should it meet his views heartily & spontaneously, I will begin my examination as soon as he sends the papers.—If sent they should be placed in a tight wooden box & sent to me by express, or sent to: Derby & Jackson, 119 Nassau St. New York, by express for me.—

With cordial regards to Mrs. Grigsby & Master Carrington & yourself I remain,

Cordially
Your friend
Henry S. Randall

H. B. Grigsby, Esq.

P. S. I don't forget that I owe you & Mrs. G. some daguerreotypes,—but we are both so abominably afraid of being *outshone* that we are not willing "to be *taken*" until we get to the city!! My wife complains that

[56] This letter is not in this collection.

[57] Thomas Jefferson Randolph.

under any circumstances it is not fair to set her up against a young woman!—

If you have not heard from me "for months," I have seen & conversed with you & Mrs G. & Carrington a thousand times within that period!—Mrs. G. often looks at me & C. looks up from his hobby horse at me sideways, *often:* when I sit here writing They & you & Francis Eppes[58] &c are doing "that same" (as the Irish say) at this moment—from the daguerreotype, state. By George! I will lay you a thousand pounds I would go straight up to Mrs Grigsby in a crowd of ten thousand strangers, & claim her as an acquaintance. (You know I am rather observing when ladies are in question!)—

Why on earth have you and Mrs. G not visited Niagara this summer & taken me in the route? Many Southern Gentlemen & ladies have been here this summer.

It seems odd enough to be back in *business.* It is a pleasing change, but I expect I shall tire of it by & by. I have had a little spice of politics too. Our State Convention sits next week, & it will determine the attitude of N. Y. in the Presidential Contest of 1860. I was run for delegate by the national democrats of this Co. & beat my competitor by nearly 2 to 1.—[59]

My blood is coursing through my veins at something like the early rate. How long this will last, who can tell?

Write me a great long *personal* letter. Tell me much about Mrs. Grigsby's little Hugh.—Tell me what you are doing—what you are writing & thinking about—everything.—

I have not heard from Dr Dunglison or any of our Phila. friends this month or two. Majr Brooks U.S.A.[60] (whom I introduced to Dr. D.) wrote me that the Dr. was on the eve of a long western trip, some two

[58] Francis Eppes (1801–1881), son of John Wayles Eppes and Maria Jefferson Eppes, Jefferson's youngest daughter. See Eva T. Clark, *Francis Eppes, His Ancestors and Descendants* (New York, 1942), pp. 260–261, 264–265.

[59] Randall and Grigsby belonged to the now largely forgotten group of men striving to temper extreme sectionalism within their respective states and regions. Randall placed his weight and influence behind the "New York Resolutions" adopted at the Syracuse Convention and was instrumental in securing endorsement of the Cincinnati platform as the true creed of the Democratic party. His view dove-tailed with the attitude of Grigsby and the Richmond *Enquirer,* his political oracle, which took a firm stand for full equality among all the States and "for equal protection for persons and property by each and every department of the Federal Government . . . ," and demanded that all States be "loyal to the cause of States rights and the perpetuity of the Union." Peaceful preservation of the Union depended upon the continuance of the historic Jefferson-Burr alliance which in this instance broadened into a warm personal friendship. See Richmond *Enquirer,* June 10, 1859, and September 19, 1859.

[60] Major William Thomas Harbaugh Brooks (1821–1870), a graduate of West Point in 1841, served in Florida, in Indian fighting, and in the Civil War. He was on sick leave in Philadelphia in 1859.

months since. Renewing my cordial regards and those of my family to all of you, I am your friend.

H. S. Randall

[Endorsed by Grigsby]
Hon. Henry S. Randall
Dated Sept. 10, 1859
Received about the 17th
and answered 23

[Randall to Grigsby, December 14, 1859]

Cortland Village
Dec 14, 1859

My dear Sir,

You of course have my last (explaining my feelings fully in regard to the Henry papers &c.) though I have not your answer.—

Winter is upon us—cold & bitter & intolerable as usual. But the political atmosphere is as hot & livid as that within the crater of a volcano. No this is *not* the fact here, generally. The *body* of *our* people are looking on the John Brown controversy without any particular excitement.[61] But the abolitionists are flaming hot—howling & screeching—undoubtedly anxious to dissolve the Union.—

Judging from the tone of the Richmond Enquirer & of the expressions of meetings published in it—the *body* of the people of Virginia prefer a dissolution of the Union to the Status quo—in other words they wish dissolution unless the Northern States will make positive legislative or executive engagements or assurances to do something which they have hitherto failed to do. Is this so? What do you understand to be the exact & real position of *the body of the people of Va.* in the premises?[62]

One thing I know. Some of your newspapers & public meetings—such of your Congressional speakers as Mr. Iverson[63]—do not understand & do not do justice to the Democracy of the Northern States.—If you join in trampling *them* down, then there is no barrier between you & the wild & furious spirit of Sectionalism, & disunion must come & with it, in all probability, civil war. As long as the Sectionalists understand

[61] John Brown attacked Harper's Ferry on October 16, 1859.

[62] For a sampling of editorial sentiment in the South, see Dwight Lowell Dumond, *Southern Editorials on Secession* (New York, 1931).

[63] Alfred Iverson (1798–1873), United States Senator from Georgia (1855–1861). On January 6, 1859, in the Senate he prophesied early secession, and on July 14, 1859, he demanded full protection of slavery in all the territories. These extreme views caused his defeat for reëlection.

they have to cope with about their own number at home, & with the South besides, they will hesitate. In this great State for example the *national* men outnumber the sectionalists. The portions of the State ticket supported by the different factions of national men succeeded—& the recent election in N. Y. City has shown that nothing like the whole national forces voted in the State election—owing to personal & factional causes.[64]—The same or nearly the same state of things exists in several other States which, without examination, you may be in the habit of setting down as abolitionized.

The National men of the North are willing to defend the Constitution in letter & spirit, & adopt the interpretations of the Supreme Court in deciding what its requirements are. Is this not enough? Is it just, is it expedient for you to join the Sectionalists in destroying us? What will be the consequences?

It is proposed that you pass laws to punish your own citizens who aid or countenance the North. When we—the national party of the north—we with your help reduced to such a situation that the Sectionalists dare do it, they will promptly retaliate your laws of the same class, & impose fines, imprisonments, & confiscations on those here, whom they say give aid & countenance to the South. We shall be reduced to silence & Submission or driven out. And with Abolitionism completely dominant & unchecked at home dissolution is inevitable, & there can be no such thing as a *peacible* dissolution of the Union.

I don't suppose the South *fears* dissolution & Civil war. But does she *desire* them? If the first comes, does she *desire* to render the last inevitable?

But do you say some of the pseudo nationalists of the North are not *sound* nationalists? Concede this. Yet there remain more *voters*, (I think), than dwell south of the Potomac who are undeniably sound. Is these men's aid worth nothing in peace & in war! What is *gained* by this denunciation? Can you tell me a single thing that is gained unless

[64] The New York City election was held on December 6, 1859. The candidates for mayor were William F. Havemeyer, Tammany Hall Democrat; Fernando Wood, Mozart Hall Democrat; and George Updyke, Republican. Wood was elected by a plurality of 3,192 over Havemeyer, and 8,207 over Updyke. The local issue was corruption of the city government by the Tammany Hall Democrats, but national interest was attracted by the slavery issue. Updyke and Havemeyer were antislavery men, inclined to abolitionism. On December 7, 1859, the New York *Herald* stated: "The election of Wood, therefore, may be considered as a vindication of this city against the suspicion of abolitionism, as the success of either of the other candidates would have been the proclamation of its adherence to a policy fraught with ruin to its own commercial interests and the peace and safety of the entire country." For a general discussion of division of opinion in New York on the eve of secession, see Stewart Mitchell, *Horatio Seymour of New York* (Cambridge, Mass., 1938).

the *object* is dissolution & war? I can make great allowances for the feelings of your people, at this moment, when open & strong sympathy is manifested by so many, in north, for that murderous & traitorous & wicked affair at Harpers Ferry—the most inexcusable thing of the kind I ever read of. But oh! take time to consider & do justice to those who do justice to you, & whose final overthrow will open such a flood of woes as the civilized world has never witnessed.

Oh my country! Am I to see thy liberties cloven down—thy strength blasted! Would that I could die to avert such a catastrophe.

I have for a few hours been thinking of writing a series of letters or a pamphlet against the conduct of the sectionalists—to try to show that their hatred of the South is purely a local & political hate—fully based on a wicked desire to dissolve the Union for the purpose of giving more relative importance to parts of the Union (New England for example) & to forward the wicked ambition of individuals to hold office.—

But I don't know that any thing I could write would do any good & I don't know where to publish it.

I had no thought of writing a political letter when I began this—and I have scratched it off hurry scurry without preserving any system in my remarks. Present my warm regards, & those of my family to Mrs. Grigsby & Carrington & accept them for yourself.

Truly yr friend
Henry S. Randall

Dr. Grigsby.
[Endorsed by Grigsby]
H. S. Randall
Dec. 14, 1859

1860

[Randall to Grigsby, January 1, 1860]

Confidential

Cortland Village
Feb 1860

My dear Sir,

I have received several letters from the South asking what were Mr. Jefferson's views on the subjects of the enclosed letter & in substance putting the several questions therein put. Friends have suggested, on hearing from me orally what those views were, that I form a compend of them & publish it for the information of the people—who are taught by abolition lecturers & editors that Jefferson was an abolitionist *in their sense of the term.* It was thought that such information would produce a good effect, especially here in the North, at this alarming epoch.—[1]

To get out all the points in the case correctly it was necessary to put all the enquiries together. This would prevent me, of course, from addressing my whole answer to any one of the real enquirers. Besides if any of those enquirers thought of *publication,* I would be very reluctant to entrust them with it, because they would send the Mss to some careless printer & leave him to convert it into a *botch* of errors.

On preparing within letter partial friends have thought its publication would have an excellent effect in the North.—My own opinion is that *if* so, it will *also* have a good effect in the South, by preventing them from repudiating Jefferson as a standard—because he is so much quoted & praised by Abolitionists.

If it is published at all, I want it *first* published at the South to keep up modesty of appearances! Secondly, I am very anxious that it be published *under your eye,* for I scarcely know anyone so correct, & none such in the South which I am at liberty to ask the services of.—

I want you to read the letter & if you think it *worth* publishing to have it published in one of your Norfolk papers—so you can *yourself see & correct the proofs,* for this my friend I am bold enough to ask you to do! If you observe any little errors in the Mss you will correct them—& please put the punctuation in any shape you see fit for to that I pay no systematic attention.—

[1] This statement on Jefferson and slavery prepared by Randall is not in this collection. But very probably there was little difference between this letter and Randall's well-considered views as given in the *Life,* III, Appendix XXXIV, pp. 667–669.

I have put your name at the top. If there is *any* reason why you don't want it there, put Doct. Balfours in its place, if he is willing—for a letter looks better with a *good name* at the head of it. If Dr. Balfour is unwilling please say, in a short preface, that it was addressed to an "eminent Virginia gentleman" for *that* will be true to the letter!

I clearly see that *my* exposition is of no importance, except so far as it popularizes *truths* now unknown or misunderstood, except in one solitary point of view.—Those who have read my life of Jefferson know that I was an *authorised* biographer, that I had access to all the papers & recollections & opinions of his family.—I ought therefore to understand in relation to this subject not only what rests on previously published authority, but on the unpublished,—& family authority. This last is something besides a *name* in the premises. You will see that it explains the greatest apparent inconsistency of Mr Jefferson's life, his supposed views on Slavery, territorial extension in 1784 & in 1819 & 1820.

I have shown another important thing—that there is nothing to prove directly or by reference that Jefferson believed Congress had the power to restrict Slavery in the *Western* territories. The whole public have mistaken him on this point, & none more so than I did before I wrote my life of him.

I think I show in several *other* important particulars that his views are popularly, if not almost universally, wholly misunderstood. But of all this you will judge after reading my letter.—

If you think the letter worth publishing, please attach a suitable preface to it and give it a "*fair start*." If you don't think it worth publishing or that it is inexpedient to publish it, send it back to me. If published send me, if you please, a dozen copies of the paper containing it. You will understand that if you are willing to stand sponsor for the *questions* I had much rather see *your* name at the top than anybodys else.—Please present the regards of myself & household to Mrs Grigsby & Master Hugh & accept them for yourself.

Your friend
H. S. Randall

Burn this.
[Endorsed by Grigsby]
H. S. Randall
Janry, 1860

[Randall to Grigsby, February 18, 1860]

Cortland Village, N. Y.
Feb. 18, 1860

My dear Sir,

I have just come home and find yours—& if you had any doubts on the subject I am glad you acted as you did—without reference to the accuracy or inaccuracy of my views of our Chief's views.—I have time but to glance through your letter, & I reply at once in a brief note, simply to let you see that your frankness is received as you had a right to expect it would be received.[2]

I am "on the go"—nearly all the time, to get certain business matters off my hands before I set out for the Charleston Convention.[3] With cordial regards to Mrs. Grigsby, Master Carrington, & yourself from me & mine I am

Your friend
H. S. Randall

H. B. Grigsby
[Endorsed by Grigsby]
Henry S. Randall
February 18, 1860

[Randall to Grigsby, May 12, 1860]

Cortland Village, N. Y.
May 12, 1860

My dear Sir,

I have just returned from the city of Charleston—eleven hundred miles from here—& what with the fatigue of travel & what with the

[2] This letter in reply to Randall's proposal of a joint letter stating Jefferson's true beliefs on slavery is not in this collection.

[3] The Democratic party convened in Charleston, South Carolina, April 23, 1860. Randall attended as a member of the regular, or Regency, delegation headed by Dean Richmond, who held control because the delegates were pledged to follow the unit rule. The membership, predominantly "softs" with Free Soil leanings, included a few "hards" generally Southern moderates, among them Randall. As in 1852 and 1856, the anti-Regency faction selected a rival delegation led and controlled by Fernando Wood. After some debate, the Convention seated the Regency delegation. In caucus the New Yorkers expressed their preferences, Douglas receiving 37 votes, Dickinson 20, Guthrie 10, Hunter 2, and Breckinridge 1. Because of the unit vote, Randall's precise attitude during the sessions cannot be documented. He probably threw his support behind a moderate candidate, probably Dickinson, known to be acceptable to Southern extremists, possibly Breckinridge. His ultimate decision is clear, for faced with dissolution of the Union, he endorsed the Breckinridge-Lane ticket, and campaigned actively in its behalf and cast a ballot as a presidential elector. See DeAlva Stanwood Alexander, *A Political History of the State of New York* (3 vols.; New York, 1906), II, 270–280; more valuable is Sidney David Brummer, *Political History of New York during the Civil War* (New York, 1911), pp. 48–61. A compact statement of the disruption of the Democratic Party and its effects is given by Clement Eaton in *A History of the Old South* (New York, 1949), pp. 570–592.

reaction after exertion & excitement, I feel like a man 200 years old. I had my full share of pleasures & annoyances during the trip, but my deepest annoyance arose from my failure to visit you at Norfolk. I had it all arranged. I was to leave the route I had followed in going to Charleston at a town named Weldon (according to my recollection) & go from there directly to Norfolk & then take what I think is termed the "Bay Route."—By a very pro[v]oking Blunder my baggage was checked from Weldon to Richmond instead of Norfolk: & although the conductor civilly allowed me to look for it, it was too deep out of sight to be found. I was begrimed with Carolina sand & had to follow my baggage. So I lost a new & pleasanter route and the pleasure—a great one it would have been—to shake hands with you in your own house & to make the personal acquaintance of Mrs. Grigsby & Master Carrington. I met a number of Virginians who knew you all—one of them a neighbor & a most sensible & pleasant man, John Randolph Bryan Esq[4]

I would have gone down from Richmond to Norfolk, if I could have spared the time.—But I had been absent from home five weeks—considerably longer than I expected—& matters of pressing import called me home. I felt compelled to decline a pleasure trip with some members of Mr. Jefferson's family down the James to Brandon, & did not either in going or returning visit Edgehill urged as I was to do so.

In haste
Cordially your friend
H. S. Randall

Hon. H. B. Grigsby
[Endorsed by Grigsby]
Henry S. Randall
May 12, 1860

[Randall to Grigsby, August 20, 1860]

Cortland Village, N. Y.
Aug. 20, (1860)

My dear Sir,

I had the impression firmly on my mind that I answered your letter of July 14 immediately it was received.[5] But on glancing over the inexorable letter book I find no proof that my impression is well founded,

[4] John Randolph Bryan (1806–1887), namesake of John Randolph of Roanoke, a student at Yale, naval officer for seven years, married Elizabeth Tucker Coalter, goddaughter of St. George Tucker, in 1830, and settled at Eagle Point, Gloucester, Virginia, and later at Carysbrock, Fluvanna County. See George N. Mackenzie and Nelson O. Rhodes, eds., *Colonial Families of the United States* (7 vols.; Baltimore, 1920), VII, 123.

[5] This letter is not in this collection.

& its absence is very certain proof to the contrary. I ought to have written you at once to congratulate you & Mrs. Grigsby on the birth of a daughter.[6] Ah me! As you say—I belong to another generation! Though I bear not the honors of grandfatherhood I have children old enough to have children.—My youngest child is a great strapping lassie of 15. While you, my dear young friend, are playing with young babies and adding to their number I am in the sere and yellow leaf![7] Well, I *can't* help *it*.

Congratulate Mrs. Grigsby for me. Tell her I met an old acquaintance of her family in Va. John Randolph Bryan, who said a good many pleasant things of her.—

If your daughter grows up a nice bonny, sonsie girl,—you don't know the pleasure in store for you.—Don't tell me that Carrington's nose is broken! Show me a mother, if you can, whose pet is not her oldest son.— But nothing warms the heart of a father like a daughter.—I could write poetry about this when I was young & gay, like yourself. I *feel* a transient twinge of it now and then in spite of my gray hairs.

I have nothing to say "by way of offset" to your two great deliverances on the "29th & 9th."[8] I am barren as Sahara.

I am amusing myself with a brush at politics. I was Prest. of our Breckinridge & Lane State Convention[9] on the 7th inst. & they put me

[6] Mary Blair Grigsby married W. W. Galt, paymaster in the United States Navy, a son of W. R. Galt, an educator, and a nephew of Alexander Galt, sculptor.

[7] "That time of year thou mayst in me behold
When yellow leaves, or none, or few, do hang . . ."
W. J. Craig, edition, Shakespeare, *Sonnet* 73, lines 1–2.

[8] The birth of his daughter, in Norfolk, July 9, 1850, and his *Discourse on the Life and Character of the Hon. Littleton Waller Tazewell, before the bar of Norfolk, Virginia, and the Citizens Generally, on the 29th of June, 1860.*

[9] "After the return of the Softs from Baltimore the condition of the Democratic party became a subject of much anxiety. Dean Richmond's persistent use of the unit rule had driven the Hards into open rebellion, and at a great mass meeting, held at Cooper Institute and addressed by Daniel S. Dickinson, it was agreed to hold a Breckinridge and Lane state convention at Syracuse on August 8. At the appointed time three hundred delegates appeared, representing every county, but with the notable exception of the chairman, Henry S. Randall, the biographer of Thomas Jefferson, who had advocated the Wilmot Proviso in 1847, written the Buffalo Platform in 1848, and opposed the fugitive slave law in 1850, practically all of them had steadily opposed the Freesoil influences of their party. To many it seemed strange, if not absolutely ludicrous, to hoist a pro-slavery flag in the Empire State. But the Republicans welcomed the division of their opponents, and the Hards were terrible in earnest. They organized with due formality; spent two days in conference; adopted the pro-slavery platform of the seceders' convention amidst loud cheering; selected candidates for a state and electorial ticket with the care that precedes certain election; angrily denounced the leadership of Dean Richmond at Charleston and Baltimore; appointed a new state committee, and, with the usual assurance of determined men, claimed a large following." Alexander, *A Political History of the State of New York*, II, 324. Nothing in these letters shows Randall's devotion to the Union more than this last, if hopeless, attempt to strengthen southern opinion in his section by keeping the North from adopting a position of irreconcilable hostility.

on the ticket as an elector at large.[10] This makes me a target to some extent,—& keeps me busy in political correspondence. But let us return to our baby. How fortunate you are in family names. Carrington is a royal one; & Mary Blair!—gracious! I would not ask for a more euphonious combination, if I was writing a novel. "Mary Blair"—prettier names or a prettier union of them there is not in English.—

Of course you won't make Mary Blair a poor little hot-house miserability. You'll let—"the winds be free to fan her." You'll let her tear about like a "tomboy,"—till she has all the activity & vigor of limb & all the expansion of chest which nature rendered her capable of.

Present my own & my wife's cordial congratulations to Mrs. Grigsby & believe me Your friend

H. S. Randall

[Endorsed by Grigsby]
Henry S. Randall
Aug. 20, 1860

[10] John Cabell Breckinridge (1821–1875), vice-president under Buchanan, nominated for president by the Southern section of the Democratic party. Joined the Confederate army and became Secretary of War in 1865.

1861

[Grigsby to Randall, March 18, 1861]

Norfolk, March 18, 1861

My dear sir,

Your letter of the 13th ult.[1] refreshed me in spite of the gloomy feelings you exhibit, and which have a sympathetic response in my breast. I would, as you said in one of your letters, willingly lay down my life to preserve the Union on a platform that will endure for a hundred years to come.[2] Virginia will not act hastily; but as yet we cannot say what that action will be.

Thanks for your letter to Dr Okeson.[3] He is laying the foundations of a noble library as respects the worth of its books, the elegance of paper and typography, and the perfection of binding. I had quite a joke about your letter. I called to see him soon after I received it, and inquired for the first volume of the Life of Jefferson, which he handed to me; and when his back was turned, I inserted your note to him in its proper place, and said to him: "Why, what is this? Here is an autograph letter from my friend Mr Randall addressed to *you*. You never showed me this before." Dr. O. took the book in his hands, read the letter twice, and then declared that it was altogether inexplicable to him; that he could not conceive how it happened; and ended by saying: "Now I know how it is. Mr Randall must have been in Philadelphia while this book was in Pawson & Nicholson's bindery and seeing the dress intended for it, was so kind as to send me that letter." I observed that you could hardly have been in Philadelphia recently, or I should have known the fact. He then read the letter again and agreed with me that it was very happily conceived and written. I spoke of the additional value which such a letter would impart to the book hereafter, an opinion with which he fully coincided. It was only when he had long been "in wandering mazes lost," that I told him that true state of the case; and he expressed the warmest thanks to you for your goodness in writing the letter.

I well remember your kind offer to preserve for me some autographs and my declining them on the ground of having no collection of any and of their superior value to others.[4] And I must tell you candidly that

[1] This letter is not in this collection.

[2] See above, Randall to Grigsby, December 14, 1859.

[3] Dr. Nicholas Albertson Okeson (1819–1882), minister of St. Paul's Episcopal Church, Norfolk, Virginia (1856–1882). See *Colonial Churches* (Richmond, 1907), pp. 67–71.

[4] See above, Grigsby to Randall, December 21, 1858.

I begged them in my last letter for my friend Charles G. Barney of Richmond, who has published for private circulation a magnificent edition of Ralph Hamor's Narrative (1619), and who is making up a complete set of the signers of the Declaration for the library of the Historical Society of Virginia.[5] I am sure the character of Mr Barney and his laudable object, if I had candidly told you all, would have had more weight with you than my request. Should any autographs, which would enable him to complete his design, turn up, I know you will help us in the good work before us.

My little Mary Blair has the very hair you describe, and my rhyme of endearment is: Here's Mary Blair with the flaxen hair;"—But I am sorry that five years have touched your colossal strength. Grey hair is no sign of age; rather of some great trial or achievement, or, as in my case, of some terrible catastrophe such as being crushed by an omnibus. I hope you are only preparing me for a youthful face in your daguerreotype when it comes. I am quite gray myself; but remember, as old Jenkins said to a man of 85; "You are a boy to me."

Speaking of likenesses, I will tell a piece of news touching myself. The Faculty of William and Mary resolved to procure my portrait to be suspended by the side of those of the benefactors of the College in the library. I declined the honor on the ground that at such a time I could not consent that the true friends of the College should spend a dollar except directly for its benefit; but I wrote the Faculty that while I highly appreciated the compliment, although unwilling at present it should be carried out, I must not let any body's purse suffer for it at any time, and that I would sit for my portrait at my own expense, and take care that my executor should forward it to the College at my death. I sate for the portrait accordingly, and it was brought home; but my wife and my dear mother who left me for another world on the 31st of December last,[6] could not abide it,—it was so sad. I looked, they said, as if I had lost every friend on earth. The portrait was sent back and

[5] Charles Gorham Barney (1814–1894), M.D., born in Massachusetts, but resided most of his life in the South. In 1850 he married Miss Mary Walker of Richmond and after 1855 lived in that city. During the war he served as a member of the ambulance committee and was able to store many priceless documents in his house, preventing their distruction by military action and fire. He had two hundred gift copies of Ralph Hamor, *A True Discourse of the Present State of Virginia, and the Successe of the Affaires there til the 18 of June 1614. . . .* (London, 1615) printed at Albany in 1860. Extracts from the rare 1615 edition appear in Bishop Meade, *Old Churches, Ministers and Families of Virginia,* II, Appendix XVI, pp. 469–473. For information on Barney, see the *Virginia Magazine of History and Biography,* II, (1895), 335.

[6] Elizabeth McPherson Grigsby, by her first marriage, and widow of Dr. Nathan Colgate Whitehead.

painted anew. Now do you know the secret of that sadness? I sate when the southern troubles were in full blast, when South Carolina had seceded—and when I was sad unto death. Ought I not to have let the portrait remain as it was as a sign of a terrible epoch upon the heart of one who loved his whole country?

Did you ever get a copy of my discourse on Tazewell?[7] I know that the publisher forwarded to you a copy in linen.[8] I am writing this on the bleakest of winter days in our sitting room downstairs, my wife busy at her work, Carrington trying to mend his broken wheelbarrow, and Mary Blair sitting at my feet, playing and crowing over my slipper one moment, and then pulling at my toes; and a dark African girl of 19, a hundred times darker than any negro ever seen in New York, watching and playing with the baby. And here I would rather be day after day than in the proudest office which human voices could bestow upon me.

By the way I received some days ago a letter from Mr Rob. Winthrop,[9] who tells me that he had nominated me the evening before as a corresponding member of the Mass: Hist: Society, and another from President Felton of Harvard,[10] who said he had voted for me and that I was unanimously elected. So remember that *honores mutant mores,* and that I am a corresponding member of the Massachusetts Historical Society.

Do you ever read Greek? I wrote a short note to President Felton the other day, who you know is our greatest Greek scholar, showing that Homer in his famous line describing the priest of Apollo walking in silence by the sea: " Βῆ δ' ἀκέων παρὰ θῖνα πολυφλοίσβοιο θαλάσσης [11] did not design to convey the idea of great *noise* as has been generally thought, but of great beauty; that the epithet πολυφλοίσβοιο meant, not "loud

[7] Grigsby, *Discourse on the Life and Character of the Hon. Littleton Waller Tazewell.*

[8] J. D. Ghiselin, Jr.

[9] Robert Charles Winthrop (1809–1894), member of the United States House of Representatives (1840–1850), and Senate (1850–1851), member of the Massachusetts Historical Society (1839–1894), and its president for thirty-four years. On the occasion of Grigsby's death, Winthrop proposed the following: "*Resolved,* That the Massachusetts Historical Society offer their sincere sympathy to the Historical Society of Virginia on the death of their distinguished and accomplished President, the Hon. Hugh Blair Grigsby, LL.D., whom we had long counted it a privilege to include among our own honorary members, and for whom we entertained the highest regard and respect; and that the Secretary communicate a copy of this resolution to our sister Society of Virginia." Grigsby, *The Virginia Federal Convention of 1788,* I, xxv. *A Catalogue of the Manuscripts in the Collection of the Virginia Historical Society* (Richmond, 1901), notes: "Grigsby correspondence with Robert C. Winthrop, May 20, 1857–November 4, 1881, 1 vol." *Ibid.,* p. 33.

[10] Cornelius Conway Felton (1807–1862), classical scholar and professor of Greek at Harvard (1832–1860), president of Harvard (1860–1862).

[11] He went silently down by the beach of the loud-sounding sea. Homer, *Iliad,* line 34.

sounding," but literally "many crested" or "white crested" sea—a state of the sea inconsistent with great noise which is produced by a long continuous wave; and that, if Homer had intended *noise* as an element in his picture, he never would have made the *silence* of the priest significant under circumstances when, if he had chosen to speak, speaking would have been impossible. But a truce with such things; and with kind regards to Mrs Randall and your family from my wife and myself, I am most truly Your friend & servant,

Hugh B. Grigsby

APPENDIX

LORD MACAULAY ON AMERICAN INSTITUTIONS

On January 18, 1857, Macaulay wrote, "I can not say that he [Jefferson] is one of my heroes; . . . There can, I apprehend, be no doubt that your institutions have during the whole of the nineteenth century been constantly becoming more Jeffersonian and less Washingtonian. It is surely strange that while this process has been going on, Washington should have been exalted into a god, and Jefferson degraded into a demon."

On May 23, 1857, he stated: "You are surprised to learn that I have not a high opinion of Mr. Jefferson, and I am surprised at your surprise. I am certain that I never . . . uttered a word indicating an opinion that the supreme authority in a state ought to be entrusted to a majority of citizens told by the head, in other words, to the poorest and most ignorant part of society. I have long been convinced that institutions purely democratic must, sooner or later, destroy liberty or civilization, or both. . . . I have not the smallest doubt that if we had a purely democratic government here . . . Either the poor would plunder the rich, and civilization would perish; or order and prosperity would be saved by a strong military government, and liberty would perish. . . . Your fate I believe to be certain, though it is deferred by a physical cause. As long as you have a boundless extent of fertile and unoccupied land, your laboring population will be far more at ease than the laboring population of the Old World, and, while that is the case, the Jefferson politics may continue to exist without causing any fatal calamity. But the time will come when New England will be as thickly populated as old England. . . . then your institutions will be fairly brought to the test. . . . I seriously apprehend that you will, in some such season of adversity as I have described, do things that will prevent prosperity from returning. . . . There will be, I fear, spoliation. The spoliation will increase the distress. The distress will produce fresh spoliation. There is nothing to stop you. Your Constitution is all sail and no anchor. . . . Your republic will be as fearfully plundered and laid waste by the barbarians in the twentieth century as the Roman Empire was in the fifth; . . . your Huns and Vandals will have been engendered within your own country by your own institutions. Thinking thus, of course, I can not reckon Jefferson among the benefactors of mankind. . . . "

On October 9, 1858, Macaulay continued: "I am perfectly aware of the immense progress which your country has made, and is making, in population and wealth. I know that the laborer with you has large wages, abundant food, and the means of giving some education to his children. But I see no reason for attributing these things to the policy of Jefferson. I see no reason to believe that your progress would have been less rapid, . . . if your government had been conducted on the principles of Washington and Hamilton. . . . The progress which you are now making is only a continuation of the progress which you have been making ever since the middle of the seventeenth century. . . . enjoyed by your forefathers, who were loyal subjects of the kings of England. . . . I do not admit that the prosperity which your country enjoys arises from those parts of your polity which may be called, in an especial manner, Jeffersonian."

These letters to Randall are taken from Sir George Otto Trevelyan, *The Life and Letters of Lord Macaulay* (2 vols.; New York, 1875), II, 407–412.

INDEX

Abel, Annie, and Frank J. Klingberg, *A Side-Light on Anglo-American Relations, 1839–1858*, 90 n. 2
Abolitionism. *See* Jefferson and slavery; Sectionalism
Adams, Charles Francis, 69, 74; *Works of John Adams and Jefferson,* 69 and n. 93
Adams, John, 12, 13, 14, 43 n. 46, 51, 69 and n. 93, 74, 103, 105, 118
Adams, John Quincy, 50–51 and n. 57, 52
Alexander, Archibald, 112 and n. 54
Allibone, Samuel Austin, 169 and nn. 54, 55
Allston, Robert Francis Withers, 5, 96 and n. 12
Alone, 111
American Archives. See Force, Peter
American institutions: criticized by Thomas B. Macaulay, 96 and n. 13, 185–186; and Jefferson, 1, 13
Ames, Fisher, 118
Anderson, Dice R., 28 n. 25
Anglo-American finanicial relations, 100 and n. 26
Anglo-Saxon heritage. *See* Grigsby, Hugh Blair
Argus. See *Daily Southern Argus*
Atlantic cable, 144, 145
Atlantic Monthly, review of Randall's *Life,* 11–12

Balfour, Dr. E. O., 109, 133, 140, 143, 145, 148, 150, 176
Bancroft, George, 3, 13, 62 and n. 77, 70, 75, 77, 78, 84, 85, 100 and n. 25, 141, 165; and Mecklenburg Declaration, 62 and n. 77, 70 n. 97, 86 n. 131, 127
Barney, Charles Gorham, 182 and n. 5
Barraud, Dr. D. C., 109
Barraud, Otway B., 109
Bassett, John Spencer, 3 n. 3, 62 n. 77
Bayard, James Asheton, 126 and n. 29
Beard, Charles A. 146 n. 113
Becker, Carl, 1 n. 1
Behan, James H., 109
Bland, Richard, 84 and n. 126, 144
Blow, George, 108
Boerum & McLean, 109
Bouldin, W. O., 108
Bowers, Claude G., 16 and n. 27
Botetourt, Baron de Norborne, burial place, 154 and n. 11, 155, 161–162, 165
Boulware, William, 129 and n. 43
Bowden, R. W., 109
Boyd, Julian P., *Papers of Thomas Jefferson,* 1
Bradshaw, John, 78 and n. 116
Breckinridge, John Cabell, 58 n. 70, 64 n. 82, 65, 136 n. 76, 180
Brock, R. A., quoted concerning Grigsby, 133 n. 61, 136 n. 71
Brooks, William Thomas Harbaugh, 171, 171 n. 60
Brougham, Lord Henry Peter, 74 and n. 75
Brown, John, reaction to incident at Harper's Ferry, 172–174
Brown, Mather, portrait of Jefferson, 7 n. 7
Bruce, William Cabell, 6 n. 6
Bryan, John Randolph, 178 and n. 4, 179
Bryant, William C., 113
Buchanan, James, 58 n. 70, 64 n. 82, 65, 177 n. 3
Burke, Edmund, and French Revolution, 8
Burr, Aaron, 130
Byron, Lord George Gordon, and Patrick Henry, 135

Cabell, Joseph Carrington, 101 and n. 29, 144
Cabell, Louisa Elizabeth (Carrington), 138 and n. 85
Cabell, Margaret Read (Venable), 143 and n. 105
Cabell, Nathaniel Francis, 143–144
Cabell, William H., 138 and n. 86
Cabell family, 137 n. 80, 138
Calhoun, John, 7, 16
Callender, James Thompson, and Jefferson, 30 and n. 28
Camp, George W., 109
Campbell, Charles, 83 and n. 124; *History of the Colony and Ancient Dominion of Virgina,* 73 n. 103; and Mecklenburg Declaration, 160; revision of his *History,* 140 and n. 93, 150, 160, 165
Capon, Lester J., 52 n. 60
Cardwell, Wilcher, 108

Cardwell, William, 108
Cardwell, Wyatt, 108
Carlyle, Thomas, 2, 16
Carr, Dabney, 105 and n. 41, 106
Carrington, Clement, 137 and n. 78, 156 and n. 16
Carrington, Edward, 156 and n. 15
Carrington, Henry, 137 and n. 79, 138 and n. 85
Carrington, Paul, 137 and nn. 78, 80, 81, 156
Carrington, Paulina Edmonia, 137 n. 81
Carrington, William Cabell, 138
Carrington family, 137 and n. 80, 138
Carson, Hampton L., quoted concerning Marshall's *Life of Washington*, 25 n. 17
Cavalier-poor-white theme in Southern history, 17 and n. 29. *See also* Anglo-Saxon heritage; Grigsby, Hugh Blair
Chamberlaine, R., 109
Charleston Democratic Convention of 1860, 177 and n. 3
Cincinnati Platform, 58, 171 n. 59
Clark, James, 53, 84
Clarke, Colin, 129 n. 47
Clay, Henry, 16; duel with John Randolph, 132 and n. 56; and Josiah Quincy, 168 n. 48
Cocke, Anne Blaws, 144 and n. 107
Cocke, John Hartwell, 144 and n. 107
Cogswell, Joseph Green, 95–96 and n. 11, 97; quoted concerning Hawks, 95
Coles, Edward, 36 and n. 32, 37, 39, 40, 43 and n. 46, 46, 58, 63, 76, 77, 79, 82, 87, 99, 136, 138, 139; Jefferson's letter on slavery, 59, 60 63, 144
Comfort, David, 108
Commager, Henry Steele, quoted on Jefferson's varied interests, 1
Congregational churches and Jefferson, 9
Constitutional Convention, 142
Coolidge, Ellen Wayles (Randolph), 76–77 and n. 113, 79, 82, 87–88 and n. 140, 134; letters used in Randall's *Life*, 87–88
Coolidge, Joseph, 76 n. 113, 88 n. 140
Cooper, Thomas, 8
Cornich, T. J., 109
Corphew [Corpew], Thomas J., 109
Cortland County, 4
Covington, Mr., 162
Cowdrey, Dr. G. W., 109
Craven, Avery, 17 n. 31
Crump, William W., 129 n. 47
Cultivator, 5
Curtis, Benjamin R., 143 n. 101
Curtis, George Ticknor, *History of the Origin, Formation and Adoption of the Constitution*, 142 and n. 98

Daily Southern Argus, 90 and n. 1, 102, 122, 133, 136, 145, 148, 167
Davie, William Richardson, 22 and n. 7. *See also* Mecklenburg Declaration
Davies, Samuel, 103 n. 36
Declaration of Independence, 116 and n. 68. *See also* Mecklenburg Declaration
Democratic Convention: of 1835, 152–153; of 1860, 177 n. 3
Democratic party, 4, 10, 109 and n. 47, 113, 120, 171 and n. 59, 179
Depression of 1857, 109, 111, 112
Derby & Jackson, publishers of Randall's *Life* 11, 95, 141, 143, 154, 155, 170
Dickinson, Anson, 158 and n. 26
Dickinson, Daniel Stevens, 41 and n. 42
Documentary History of New York. *See* O'Callaghan, Edmund B.
Dorsheimer, William: estimate of Jefferson, 12; review of Randall's *Life*, 11–12
Doyle, John E., 109
Doyle, Walter J., 109
Dundas, Sir Richard Saunders, 88 and n. 137
Dunglison, Dr. Robley, 8, 25 and n. 14, 27, 28, 29, 30, 31, 32, 33, 34, 35, 36, 37, 38, 41, 42, 44, 46, 53, 56, 63, 71, 95, 98–99, 100, 136, 171–172; *Ana* and Jefferson, 30, 31, 32, 33, 34–35 and n. 29, 36 and n. 31, 39
Dunmore, Lord, governor of Virginia, 136
Dunnavant, William W., 115 and n. 64
Dutch on Long Island, and American Revolution, 156 and n. 18

Eaton, Clement, 177 n. 3
Eckenrode, H. J., *The Randolphs* quoted, 73 n. 103, 110 n. 49
Edgehill, 99 and n. 21
Edmunds, John, 108
Edmunds, John F., 108
Edmunds, Nicholas, 108

Election: of 1856, 64, 65; of 1857, 112; of 1860, 171 and n. 59
Elliot, Sir Charles, 88 and n. 138
Emerson, Ralph Waldo, 2
Ellis, Thomas H., 22 and n. 5; quoted, 129 n. 46
Episcopal Church. *See* Protestant Episcopal Church
Eppes, Francis, 171 and n. 58
Eppes, John Wayles, 171 n. 58
Eppes, Maria Jefferson, 141 n. 96, 171 n. 58

Farrand, Max, on James Madison, 142 n. 98, 146 n. 113
Federalist, 142
Federalist biographies and histories, 9, 11, 13, 14, 118 and n. 72, 142–143
Felton, Cornelius Conway, Greek scholar, 183 and n. 10
Ferguson, Finlay, 109
Ferguson, James B., 150 n. 120
Force, Peter, *American Archives* and Mecklenburg Declaration, 55 and n. 61, 66, 67, 75
Francis, John T., 109
Franco-Austrian War, 169
French Revolution and Jefferson, 8

Gaines, R. J., 108
Gaines, R. V., 108
Galt, Alexander, 36 and n. 34, 179 n. 6
Galt, W. R., 179 n. 6
Galt, W.W., 179 n. 6
Garland, Hugh A., *Life of John Randolph*, 110 and n. 50, 112
Ghiselin, John Dyson, 109, 125 and n. 24, 131, 183
Giles, William Branch, 28 and n. 25
Gilpin, Henry Dilworth, 46 and n. 49, 63 n. 80, 99
Graham, George, 53, 84
Graham, William A., 21 n. 3
Gray, Wood, 10 n. 12
Greeley, Horace, 95 and n. 10, 113
Green, William B., 108
Griffith, William P., 109
Grigsby, Elizabeth McPherson, 61 n. 75, 149
Grigsby, Hugh Blair: accident, 125; account of John Randolph's library, 136 and n. 71; on Anglo-Saxon heritage of Virginia, 17 and n. 29, 47 and n. 51, 49, 76, 145 n. 111; aptitude for biography, 6; on autographs, 150, 181–182; biographical sketch of, 5–6; collector of canes, 133 n. 61; College of William and Mary, 6, 128–130, 131, 133, 140, 159–160, 167, 182–183; corresponding member Massachusetts Historical Society, 183 and n. 9; daguerreotypes for Randall, 144, 150, 154, 155, 162, 163, 165, 170; "Dead of the Chapel of William and Mary," 136, 145 and n. 111; *Discourse on Littleton Waller Tazewell*, 179, 179 n. 8, 183; estate, 99, 137; on fireproof repositories, 155 n. 12; indictment of Federalist biographies, 13; on isolation of scholar, 144; key to Virginia circles for Randall, 2; leading Virginian historian, 2; letter to William F. Ritchie on Randall's *Life*, 117–118; library, 5, 136 n. 71; on Madison, 142, 146 and n. 111; member Virginia Constitutional Convention of 1829–1830, 6; notice of George Tucker for *Argus*, 148; owner-editor of Norfolk *American Beacon*, 6; personal information concerning, 23, 52 and n. 60, 56, 60–61 and n. 75, 62, 92, 125, 126, 127, 138, 144, 146, 154, 182; planter, 23, 62, 107, 136–137, 141, 146, 169; political views, 3, 171 n. 59; portrait for William and Mary, 10, 182–183; principal publications, 23 n. 10; Randall's letters to be returned in case of his death, 133, 138–139; refutes lukewarmness of Patrick Henry on independence resolution, 116 and n. 67; relations with historical societies, 6; reviews Josiah Quincy, 167–168; Unionist, 3; *Virginia Convention of 1788*, 48 and n. 52, 102–103; 121, 139, 146, 150–151, 168; *Virginia Convention of 1829–1830*, 112; walker, 130 n. 50. *See also* Grigsby, *Virginia Convention of 1776;* Grigsby, Hugh Carrington; Grigsby, Mary Blair; Grigsby, Mary (Venable) Carrington; Mecklenburg Declaration of Independence; Randall, Henry Stephens, *Life of Thomas Jefferson*
Grigsby, Hugh Blair, *Virginia Convention of 1776*, 1, 21, 23, 27 n. 20, 28, 40, 41–42, 67, 79, 116, 124, 160–161; S. A. Allibone's estimate, 16 n. 54; on William Randolph, 72–73 and n. 103, 76; second edition proposed, 72, 75; sketch of Jefferson, 23, 51, 58 n. 66

Grigsby, Hugh Carrington, Hugh Blair Grigsby's son, 39 n. 40, 48, 51, 62, 77, 91, 94, 100, 107, 112, 122, 127, 128, 130, 132, 133, 140, 141, 148, 151, 154, 162, 163, 165–166, 168, 169, 183
Grigsby, Mary Blair, Hugh Blair Grigsby's daughter, 179–180 and n. 6, 182, 183
Grigsby, Mary (Venable) Carrington, Hugh Blair Grigsby's wife, 6, 23, 39, 52, 77, 82, 88, 91, 99, 112, 122, 125, 127, 133, 136, 138, 143, 150, 154, 162, 163, 165, 168, 171, 183
Grigsby, Reuben, 134 n. 61, 146

Hamilton, Alexander, 3, 12, 13, 14, 139, 140, 142 and n. 98, 143 and n. 101, 186; compared with Jefferson, 67 and n. 92, 70; compared with Madison, 142
Hardy & Brothers, 109
Harland, Marion. *See* Terhune, Mary Virginia
Harrison, William B., 129 n. 47
Havemeyer, William F., 173 n. 64
Hawks, Francis Lister, 165; *Contributions to the Ecclesiastical History of Virginia,* 98 and nn. 16, 17; defense of Mecklenburg Declaration of May 20, 1775, 21 and n. 3, 70 and n. 96, 74, 92–93, 94, 95, 96, 97, 122, 128; hostility toward Jefferson, 7 and n. 7, 21 n. 3, 97–98 n. 16. *See also* Mecklenburg Declaration of Independence
Hazard, Samuel, 48 and n. 53
Hendren, William T., 109
Hening, W. W., *Statutes at Large of Virginia,* 27, 91, 141
Henry, Emma Cabell, 150 and n. 120
Henry, John: son of Patrick Henry, 104, 105, 106, 107, 110, 111–112, 135, 145, 150, 164, 166, 167, 168, 169, 170; described by Grigsby, 103–104 and n. 38; hostility toward Jefferson, 111–112, 145
Henry, Patrick, 103, 104, 106, 107, 110, 112, 135, 164, 165, 166, 169, 170; "forest born Demosthenes," 105 and n. 43, 164; Jefferson's feelings toward, 104–105; Latin instruction, 103 and nn. 36, 37; life of, contemplated by Randall, 164, 166, 170, 172; lukewarmness on independence resolution, 66 n. 88, 115–116 and nn. 65, 67, 121, 122–123, 124, 132, 135 n. 68; relations with John Randolph, 112. *See also* Wirt, William
Henry, William Wirt, 168, 168–169 n. 51
Hidden Path, 111
Hidy, Ralph W., *The House of Baring in American Trade and Finance,* 100 n. 26
Higgins, John, 109
Hildreth, Richard, 3, 13, 90 and n. 2; antislavery works, 90 n. 2; described by Lewis Tappan, 90 n. 2
Homer, *Iliad,* 183–184 and n. 11
Hooper, William, 74 n. 105, quoted, 74
Hunter, Humphrey, witness of Mecklenburg Declaration, 54–55, 66, 70, 74 and n. 106, 85–86. *See also* Mecklenburg Declaration of Independence
Hutchinson, William, 53, 84

Inevitable conflict idea and post-Civil War history, 14
Intelligencer, 70
Irving, Washington, *Life of George Washington,* 5 n. 5, 95 and n. 8
Irwin, Henry, 109
Isham, Henry, 83
Isham, Katherine, 83
Iverson, Alfred, 172 and n. 63

Jackson, Andrew, relations with Jefferson, 135 and n. 69
Jameson, J. Franklin, quoted on early biographies, 25 n. 17
Jay, John, 12, 13, 14, 118
Jefferson, Peter, 99 n. 21
Jefferson, Thomas: act concerning religious freedom, 7 n. 7, 8, 98 and nn. 16, 17; and John Adams, 69 and n. 93, 74; ancestry, 26–27 and n. 20, 99–100 and n. 25; anecdotes concerning, 36, 39–40; apostle of antislavery, 60, 90 and n. 2; attacks on, 7, 120, 130; biographies of, 1; birthday celebrated by Republicans, 164; charged with falsehood by C. F. Adams, 69 and n. 93; common hero of Grigsby and Randall, 7; enemy of English caste society, 7, 8; estimate of William Dorsheimer, 12; experiment of, 37; founder of Democratic party, 13, 113; French Revolution and, 8; governor of Virginia, 113–114, 115; health rules, 48 and n. 54, 99 and n. 23; and Patrick

Jefferson, Thomas (*Continued*)
Henry, 103, 104–105, 111–112; and Richard Hildreth, 90; and Henry Lee, 115, legacy, 1, 2; letters to his daughters, 141–142 and n. 96; and Macaulay, 96–97 and n. 13, 185–186; and Madison, 35 and n. 30, 67 and n. 92, 70, 153; on manumission, 144; Michie papers, 27–28 and n. 24; Missouri Compromise, 59; on nationalism, 7; New England slanders against, 29–30, 69 and n. 93; and North, 12, 60; *Notes on Virginia*, 59 and n. 71, 60; opposed to sectionalism, 59; *Papers of Thomas Jefferson*, 1; and Edmond Pendleton, 124 n. 21; plow, 152–153 and n. 3; political philosophy, 1, 7, 11–12, 17; quoted on posthumous fame, 35; portraits of, 7 n. 7, 36 and n. 33, 43; and Randolph family, 76 and n. 111, 80 and n. 119, 119; regard of Grigsby and Randall, 3, 5, 7, 8, 16, 17; religious beliefs, 7 and n. 7, 8, 9, 50 and n. 56, 53, 61, 98 and nn. 16, 17; and W. C. Rives, 152–153; sketched by Grigsby, 23, 51; on slavery, 8, 58–60, 144, 175–176; statue, 36 and n. 34; universal character, 2; use by abolitionists, 175–176; varied interests, 1, and Daniel Webster, 102–103, 104–105, 134; will, 35 and n. 30. *See also* Randall, Henry Stephen, *Life of Thomas Jefferson*
Jensen, Merrill, 17 n. 31
Jernegan, Marcus W., 146 n. 113
Johns, John, bishop of Protestant Episcopal Church in Virginia, 129 and n. 44, 130
Johnson, Andrew, 16
Johnson, Richard Mentor, 153 and n. 7
Journals of the House of Delegates of Virginia (1776–1790), 146 and n. 113

Kimball, Marie, *Jefferson: The Road to Glory*, estimate of Randall's *Life*, 14–15
King, Rufus, 12
Kingsley, Charles, 99 and n. 24
Knox, Henry, 12
Koch, Adrienne, 17 n. 32, 153 n. 9
Kraus, Michael, 3 n. 3

Lamb, William, 90 n. 1, 136 and n. 76, 167
Lee, Charles, 116 and n. 65, 135 and n. 68
Lee, Henry, 115 and n. 63, 134
Lee, Richard Henry, part in Declaration of Independence, 13, 116 and n. 68, 161
Leigh, Amyas, 99 and n. 24
Leigh, Benjamin Watkins, 120 n. 6
Leigh, William, 120 and n. 5
Leonard, Abram F., 90 and n. 1, 167
Lewis, Andrew, 37 and n. 36
Lewis, George W., 129 n. 47
Lippincott & Company, 11, 98, 165
Livy, 103
Long Island and American Revolution, 156–157
Lossing, Benson John, 165 and n. 40
Lowell, James Russell, 11
Loyall, George, 67 n. 92, 70 and n. 99, 74–75, 108
Lyons, James, 129 and n. 46

Macaulay, Thomas Babington: attack on American institutions, 34, 96 and n. 13, 185–186; correspondence with Randall, 185–186; possible reasons for his attack, 100 and n. 26
McFarland, William Hamilton, 129 and n. 45
McGehee, Capt., 108
McGuire, J. C., 142
MacIntosh, George, 109
Madison, Isaac, 27 n. 20
Madison, John, 27 n. 20
Madison, Mary, 27 n. 20
Madison, James, 35 and n. 30, 36, 39, 40, 71, 94, 105; ancestors, 27 and n. 20; comparison of Jefferson and Hamilton, 67 and n. 92, 70, 153; refuted by Grigsby on state of Virginia under Confederation, 146 and n. 113; role in Constitutional Convention compared with Hamilton's, 16 and n. 30, 142
Mallory, Francis, 109
Malone, Dumas, *Jefferson the Virginian*, estimate of Randall's *Life*, 16 n. 28; quoted, 27 n. 20, 30 n. 28
Marcy, William L., 58 and n. 69
Marshall, Mr., 58
Marshall, H. H., 108
Marshall, Hunter, 120
Marshall, J. P., 108
Marshall, Joel W., 108
Marshall, John, friend of John Randolph of Roanoke, 120 and n. 5

Marshall, John, 12, 14, 25 and n. 17; *Life of George Washington,* 13, 25 n. 17, 97, 114, 127 and n. 34
Marshall, O. F., 58
Martin, Francois-Xavier, 22 and n. 6; *History of North Carolina,* 22 and n. 6, 67 and n. 88, 68, 70 and n. 95, 74, 77, 81 and n. 121. *See also* Mecklenburg Declaration of Independence
Martin, Josiah, colonial governor of North Carolina, 67 n. 91
Massachusetts Historical Society, 6, 27 n. 24, 183 and n. 9
May, David, 129 n. 47
Mayo, Barbara, quoted, 88 n. 140
Meade, William, 98 n. 18, 100, 101, 149, 167; *Bible and the Classics,* 167; *Old Churches, Ministers and Families of Virginia,* 58 n. 66, 98 and n. 18, 136
Mecklenburg Declaration of Independence, 2, 21 and nn. 3, 4, 22 and nn. 6, 7, 8, 25, 51, 53, 55 and n. 61, 57 and n. 65, 62 and n. 77, 63–64 and n. 78, 66–67 and nn. 89, 90, 91, 70, 74–75, 84–86, 92–93 and n. 4, 94, 97, 122; Davie copy, 22, 67 and nn. 89, 90 and n. 95; defended by Hawks, 92–93, 94, 122; depositions of witnesses, 21 and n. 4, 51, 53–55, 66, 74 and n. 106, 75, 81, 84–86; Grigsby's efforts to refute May 20, 1775, version, 21, 26, 53, 63, 66 n. 86, 75, 94, 97, 122, 132; Martin copy, 22, 67 and n. 89, 70, 74; pride of North Carolina, 127; treatment by George Bancroft, 62 and n. 77; treatment by Charles Campbell, 160 and n. 31; treatment by Randall in *Life,* 57, 66–67 and n. 86, 67 nn. 89, 90, 91, 68, 70, 78, 87, 96, 132, 134; treatment by George Tucker, 63 and n. 78
Meikleham, Dr. David Scott, 88 n. 136
Messenger. See *Southern Literary Messenger*
Michie, David, 27 and n. 24, 28, 29; papers concerning Jefferson, 27–28, 29, 30, 41
Middle period of American historiography, 2–3
Millson, John S., 108, 123 and n. 17
Miranda, Francisco de, 127 and n. 30
Missouri Compromise, 59
Mitchell, Stewart, *Horatio Seymour of New York,* 173 n. 64
Monarchical party in the United States, 11, 50–51 and n. 57, 52
Monticello, 1, 15, 122
Moore, J. J., 109
Moore's Rural New Yorker, 5
Morris, Gouverneur, 13
Morton, David, 108
Morton, Jacob, 108
Morton, James D., 108
Morton, William, 108
Moss Side, 111
Motley, John L., *Rise of the Dutch Republic,* 2
Mowatt, Anna Cora (Ogden). *See* Ritchie, Anna Cora
Myers, Myer, 108

Nash, Dr., 109
Nationalism, 7, 10, 14, 172–174; of North late in 1859, 172–174
National Wool Growers' Association, 5
Nelson, Thomas, 116, 124 and n. 22
Newton, Cincinnatus, 109
Newton, Thomas, 109
New York City election of 1859, 173 and n. 64
New York *Commercial Advertiser,* 102
New York *Day Book,* 12
New York Democratic Convention of 1860, 177
New York election of 1857, 109
New York *Evening Post,* 113
New York *Herald,* 93, 113
New York Historical Society, 6, 21 and n. 3, 99–100, 140–141
New York State Agricultural Society, 5
New York State Fair, 5
New York *Tribune,* 113, 115
Nicholas, Robert Carter, 84 and n. 127
Nicholas, Wilson Cary, 28 and n. 26
Northern sentiment toward South late in 1859, 172–174
North American Review, 102
North Carolina. *See* Mecklenburg Declaration of Independence
North Carolina, University of, 126; *Magazine,* quoted, 67 n. 89
Nott, Eliphalet, 4

O'Callaghan, Edmund B., *Documentary History of New York,* 37 and nn. 35, 38, 38, 56, 64
Okeson, Dr. Nicholas Albertson, 181 and n. 3

Osborne, Dr. Nathaniel, 129 n. 47, 130 and n. 49

Paine, Thomas, 8
Palfrey, John Gorham, 3
Pancoast, Dr. Joseph, 27 and n. 22
Panic of 1857, 109, 111, 112
Papers of Thomas Jefferson, 1
Parker, Amasa Junius, 65 and n. 84
Parkman, Francis: *The Oregon Trail*, 2; *The Conspiracy of Pontiac*, 3
Parton, James, biographies of Burr, Greeley, Jackson, and Jefferson, 3
Pawson & Nicholson, 181
Pendleton, Edmund, 116, 124 and n. 21
Pennsylvania election of 1856, 65 and n. 83; financiery, 100 and n. 26
Pennsylvania Historical Society, 6, 97, 99
Pepys, Samuel, *Diary*, 151
Petersburg, Virginia, excitement in 1799, 130
Philips, Josiah, 135 and n. 67
"Pigeon hole slander," 127
Pinckneys, the, 12
Pocahontas, 99
Polhemus, Henry, 156 n. 17, 157
Polhemus, Jane (Anderson), 156 n. 17
Polhemus, Jane Rebecca, 156 n. 17
Polhemus, Johannes Theodorus, 156 and n. 18
Polhemus, John, 156–157 and n. 19
Polhemus family, 156–157
Political history, 1856–1861. *See* Democratic party; Nationalism; Randall, Henry Stephens; Sectionalism
Polk, Col., 54, 85
Polk, James K., 85 n. 130, 122 n. 12
Polk, Thomas, 85 n. 130
Practical Shepherd, 5
Pratt, Julius W., quoted on Madison, 27 n. 20
Prescott, William H., *Reign of Philip the Second*, 2
Priestly, Joseph, 8
Protestant Episcopal Church, Convention of 1859, 167, 169
Princeton University Press, 1
Pryor, Roger Atkinson, 101 and n. 32

Quincy, Josiah, *Memoir of John Quincy Adams*, 167 and n. 45, 168 and n. 48
Quitman, John A., 100 n. 26

Ralph Hamor's Narrative, 182 and n. 5
Ramsdell, Charles W., 17 n. 31
Randall, Harriet Eliza, 158 n. 27
Randall, Harriet Stephens, 149, 158 and n. 28
Randall, Henry Stephens: autographs, 120, 150; biographical sketch of, 4–5; on biography, 9; care of manuscripts, 150; children of, 49–50 and n. 55, 56, 179; correspondence with Thomas B. Macaulay, 96 and n. 13, 185–186; Commissioner of the Land Office, 30; as correspondent, 34, 57–58, 65, 89; Democratic party leader in New York, 4; family history, 156–159; honored by Virginia, 5 n. 5; member of Canal Board, 30; national sentiments, 58; on need for fire proof repositories, 155; personal information concerning, 43, 48, 49, 92, 155, 170, 177–178, 182; pioneer in methodology, 3; as political seer, 64; as politician, 3, 4, 58 and n. 70, 65–65, 152–153, 171 and n. 59, 172–174; 177, 179–180; promoter of public education, 4–5; proposes life of Patrick Henry, 164, 166, 167, 170, 172; proposes pamphlet against sectionalists, 174, 175–176; Secretary of State for New York, 4, 30–31, 58, 64; sentiments on slavery, 58 and n. 70, 89; Superintendent of Common Schools, 4, 30–31, 64; on Tucker's *Jefferson*, 9, 70–72; unionist, 3; wife, 163; work habits, 31–32, 34, 50, 57, 62, 78, 90, 91, 99; works on sheep husbandry, 5, 16, 128, 154, 156. *See also* Randall, Henry Stephens, *Life of Thomas Jefferson*
Randall, Henry Stephens, *Life of Thomas Jefferson*: abridgment started, 165; Allibone's estimate of, 169 n. 55; author's approach, 16, 30, 65–66, 111; circular announcing publication, 102, 106, 111, 115; counterthrust to Federalist histories, 11, 13; critics, 66, 90, 101, 110–111, 113–114, 116, 119, 139, 140; Grigsby's review of Volume I, 12–14, 101–102, 115–116, 117, 119, 120–121, 122–123, 124, 132; Grigsby's review of Volume III, 14, 126–127; interpretative conclusion missing, 132 and n. 59; Jeffersoniana connecting 1850's and 1950's, 2, 5, 14; Jefferson's letters to his daughters, 141–142 and n. 96; materials used by Randall, 15,

Randall, Henry Stephens (*Continued*) 71–72 and n. 101, 78, 87–88, 170; Miranda affair, 127 and n. 30; place in Jefferson historiography, 14–16; preface, 132; publication, 95–96, 101, 109–110, 113; reception by Jefferson's family, 101, 106, 136; reception in New England, 11–12; reception in North, 102, 113, 114, 119, 132–133, 139, 140; reception in Philadelphia, 139; reception in South, 12, 102, 114, 115, 117, 118, 119, 120–121, 122, 123, 124, 131, 132–133, 140; reviewed in *Atlantic Monthly*, 11–12; revision, 65–66; sale, 11; sale in Norfolk, 11, 131, 133, 139; "southern book," 14; treatment of Hamilton, 140 and n. 92; treatment of Patrick Henry, 104–105, 110 and n. 48, 121, 164; treatment of Jefferson as founder of Democratic party, 13, 113; treatment of Jefferson as governor of Virginia, 13, 113–114, 115, 117; treatment of Jefferson's religious beliefs, 8–9, 50, 91; treatment of Jefferson and slavery, 7, 58–60, 61–62, 89, 91, 95, 101; treatment of John Randolph of Roanoke, 110, 131 and n. 54; treatment of Washington, 127; Volume I, 113–114, 115–116, 120–121; Volume II, 125, 126–127; Volume III, 126–127; use of Grigsby, 6–7, 66 and nn. 86, 88, 68, 70, 100–101; use of Tucker's *Jefferson*, 71 and n. 100; writing, 50, 91–92
Randall, James G., 17 n. 31
Randall, Josiah, 158 and n. 21
Randall, Lucy Maria, 158 n. 27
Randall, Paul G., 5 n. 5, 50 n. 55
Randall, Robert Richard, 158 n. 20
Randall, Roswell, 158 and n. 27
Randall, Samuel J., 158 n. 21
Randall, Thomas (d. 1797), 157–158 and n. 20
Randall, Thomas, district judge in Florida about 1827, 158
Randall family, 157–158
Randalls of Maryland, 158
Randolph, Cornelia Jefferson, 88 n. 136
Randolph, Edmund, 116 and nn. 66, 67, 131, 135 n. 67
Randolph, Ellen W., on Pocohontas, 99
Randolph, Ellen Wayles (Randolph). *See* Coolidge, Ellen Wayles
Randolph, George Wythe, 21 and n. 1, 22, 25, 29, 79, 87, 95
Randolph, Sir John: obituary, 83 and n. 125, 84; tomb, 131 and n. 53, 136 and n. 73, 161, 162
Randolph, John (*c.* 1727–1784), 131 and n. 53, 136 n. 75
Randolph, John, of Roanoke, 79 n. 118, 110 and n. 50, 112, 119, 120; duels, 131–132 and n. 54; library, 136 and n. 71; sketched by Grigsby, 112; toast to Martha Jefferson Randolph, 79 and n. 118
Randolph, Martha Jefferson, 79–80 and n. 118, 88 n. 136, 141 n. 96
Randolph, Mary, 83
Randolph, Mary Jefferson, 88 n. 136
Randolph, Peyton, 161; tomb, 131 and n. 53, 136 n. 74
Randolph, Richard, 58 and n. 66, 79, 82
Randolph, Robert, 145, 146 n. 111
Randolph, St. George, 110 and n. 49
Randolph, Sarah N., *The Domestic Life of Thomas Jefferson*, quoted concerning Randall's *Life*, 141 n. 96
Randolph, Septimia Anne Cary, 88 n. 136
Randolph, Thomas Jefferson, 99 n. 21, 152 and n. 4, 153, 170
Randolph Thomas Mann, 79 n. 118, 128
Randolph, Virginia Jefferson, 25 n. 13, 88 n. 136, 142
Randolph, William I: early status discussed, 72–73 and n. 103, 76 and n. 111, 78–80, 81–83, 101, 145 n. 111; tombstone inscription, 77, 78, 82–83
Randolph, William II, 83
Randolph estate, 99 n. 21
Randolph family, 76 and n. 111, 78–79 and n. 115, 82, 145 n. 111
Randolphs and Randall's *Life*, 119
Raumer, Friedrich Ludwig George von, 37 and n. 37
Read, W. W., 108
Read, William Watkins, 137 and n. 81
Read family, 137 and n. 82
Red Hill. *See* Henry, John
Richmond *Enquirer*, 91, 140; Democratic paper, 122 and n. 12; reviews Randall's *Life*, 11–14, 114, 115, 116, 117, 118, 120–121, 122, 123, 124, 128, 131, 132–133; views on eve of Civil War, 171 n. 59, 172, 174
Ritchie, Anna Cora, 120 and n. 7

Ritchie, Thomas, 42 and n. 44, 101 n. 32, 117, 118, 120, 122 n. 12, 140
Ritchie, William Foushee, 117 and n. 69, 119, 120, 121, 122, 123, 124; reviews Randall's *Life*, 12, 117, 119, 120–121
Rives, William Cabell, 125 and n. 25, 127–128, 152–153; Jefferson's plow, 152–153; *Life and Times of James Madison*, 142–143, 146, 153
Robertson, Duncan, 109
Robertson, Harrison, 108
Robinson, Conway, 27 n. 20
Robinson, Robert, 53, 84
Rossingham, Ensign, 100 n. 25

Sailors' Snug Harbor. 157–158
Sanderson, John, *Biography of the Signers of the Declaration of Independence*, 161
Scott, Dr. Edward P., 129 n. 47
Scott, Henry, 108
Scott, James, 108
Scott, William T., 108
Sectionalism, 3, 10, 14, 16, 109, 113, 172–174 and n. 64
Selden, Dr. William, 109
Seward, William H., 16
Seymour, Horatio, 65 n. 85
Shakespeare, William, quoted, 99, 179
Shankland, William H., 4, 58 and n. 67
Sharp, Charles, 109
Sharp, William W., 109
Sherman, Roger, 76 and n. 110
Shield, Charles H., 109
Simms, Gilmore, 113 and n. 59
Slavery. *See* Jefferson, Thomas; Sectionalism
Smith, J. Marsden, 109
Smith, John, 108
Smith, Samuel, 126 and n. 29
Smith, Sydney, 56, 57 n. 63
Smith, William, 108
South Carolina: in American Revolution, 113; secession, 183
Southern Literary Messenger, 135 and nn. 70, 71, 72
Southern sentiment on eve of Civil War, 172–173. *See also* Sectionalism
Southgate, James, 109
Sparks, Jared, 3, 13, 67 and n. 91, 127
Spencer, Alexander, 108
Spencer, John, 108
Stanwix, Fort, Indian treaty of, 37 and n. 36
States rights, 7, 9, 10. *See also* Sectionalism
Stephens, Henry, 4
Stephens, Dr. Josiah, 158 and nn. 25, 28
Stewart, William P., 109
Stokes, Anson Phelps, *Church and State in the United States*, quoted on Jefferson's religious beliefs, 7 n. 7
Stokes, Montfort, 67 n. 90
Stuart, James, 36 and n. 33
Swain, David L., 21 n. 3, 75 and n. 107; described by Grigsby, 126
Syracuse Democratic Convention, 171 n. 59

Tappan, Lewis, quoted on Richard Hildreth, 90 n. 2
Taylor, Edward T., 129 n. 47
Taylor, Robert Barraud, 6, 131–132 and n. 55
Taylor, Tazewell, 108, 129 n. 47
Tazewell, Henry, 89 and n. 142, 160
Tazewell, John N., 108
Tazewell, Littleton Waller, 89 and n. 142, 108, 134, 154, 160, 161
Terhune, Edward Payson, 141 and n. 95
Terhune, Mary Virginia (Marion Harland), 110 n. 49, 111 and n. 51, 141, quoted, 120 n. 5
Thompson, John R., 136 and n. 72
Todd, Mallory W., 109
Toombs, Robert, 16
Totten, Silas, 167 and n. 46
Trexler, Harrison A., 12 n. 21
Trist, Nicholas P., 25 and n. 13, 27, 29, 40, 46 and n. 48, 63 n. 80, 76, 88 n. 139
Tucker, George, 38 and n. 39, 44–45, 56, 63, 68, 70, 71 and n. 100, 94, 99, 101, 147–149; *History of the United States*, 56, 62, 63, 94, 99, 148; *Life of Thomas Jefferson*, 13, 70–72 and n. 100, 75, 147 n. 115; quoted on Mecklenburg Declaration, 63 n. 78; Randall's estimate of his *Life of Jefferson*, 9
Tucker, Henry St. George, 160 and n. 30
Tunstall, Dr., 109
Tunstall, Alexander, 109
Tyler, John, 129 and n. 41, 130, 154, 161–162

Union. *See* Sectionalism
Union College, 4
Updyke, George, 173 n. 64

Van Buren, Martin, 71, 76, 77, 122 n. 12
Venable, Abraham Bedford, 28 and n. 27
Venable, Anne Mayo, 137 n. 81
Virgil, 103
Virginia: in American Revolution, 113–114, 115; during Confederation period, 17 and n. 17; convention of 1776, 77, of 1788, 77, of 1829–1830, 77; Episcopal Church, 9; House of Burgesses, 141; legislature, 122; resolution of independence, 124; settled by Cromwellians, 76; views on eve of Civil War, 10, 181
Virginia, University of, 8, 36
Virginia Convention of 1776. See Grigsby, Hugh Blair, *Virginia Convention of 1776*
Virginia *Historical Register*, 83, 112
Virginia Historical Society, 6, 21, 22, 27, 77, 139, 155 n. 12, 168–169 n. 51, 182

Walker, William, 100 n. 26
Washington, George, 5 n. 5, 14, 118, 164, 185–186; treatment in Randall's *Life*, 127
Watkins, Francis Nathaniel, 27 and n. 23, 28, 29, 34, 41, 42
Watkins, Dr. Joel, 108
Watkins, Thomas, 108
Watkins, William J., 108
Watkins, William M., 107
Webster, Daniel, 7, 16, 41, 102–103, 131 n. 54, 135; *Private Correspondence of Daniel Webster*, 93, 102–103, 104–105 and n. 40, 106
Wertenbaker, Thomas J., 17 n. 31
West, Rev., 149
Whitehead, John B., 61 and n. 75, 108
Whitehead, Dr. Nathan Colgate, 61 and n. 75
Whittle, Conway, 108
Wickham, John, 127 and n. 35
William and Mary, College of, 83 n. 125, 182; alumni meeting of 1859, 159–160; chapel vaults, 84, 131, 136, 145, 154, 155, 161, 162; fire of 1859, 155 and n. 12, 160; meeting of Board of Visitors in June, 1858, 128–130; reconstruction of professorships, 129–131, 133, 140; restoration after 1859 fire, 159 and n. 29, 163 and n. 36, 167; walls, 159 and n. 29. *See also* Grigsby, Hugh Blair
Williams, John, 109
Williamsburg, 84, 130, 131, 159
Williamson, Hugh, 67 n. 90
Wilstack, Paul, 74 n. 104
Wiltsie, Charles, 17 n. 32
Winthrop, Robert, 183 and n. 9
Wirt, Laura, 138, 158 and n. 23
Wirt, William, 105 and n. 41, 158; marriage, 138 and n. 87; *Sketches of the Life and Character of Patrick Henry*, 105 and n. 41, 106, 164–165, 166; work judged by Grigsby, 107, 135
Wise, Henry Alexander: service to College of William and Mary, 129–130 and n. 42, 133, 140, 160; and Jefferson, 130; as orator, 160
Wise, John, 130 and n. 48
Wistar, Caspar, 27 n. 21
Wistar party, 27 and n. 21, 38
Wood, Fernando, 173 n. 64, 177 n. 3
Woodbridge, George, 129 n. 47
Woods, Edgar, quoted, 27 n. 24
Woodward, George Washington, 46 and n. 50, 63 n. 80
Wool Tariff of 1867, 5
Wythe, George, 161 and n. 32